The Protestant Ethic
or the Spirit of Capitalism

The Protestant Ethic
or the Spirit of Capitalism

Christians, Freedom, and Free Markets

Kathryn D. Blanchard

 CASCADE *Books* • Eugene, Oregon

THE PROTESTANT ETHIC OR THE SPIRIT OF CAPITALISM
Christians, Freedom, and Free Markets

Cascade Books
An Imprint of Wipf and Stock Publishers
199 W. 8th Ave., Suite 3
Eugene, OR 97401

www.wipfandstock.com

ISBN 13: 978-1-60608-659-9

Cataloging-in-Publication data:

Blanchard, Kathryn D.

The Protestant ethic or the spirit of capitalism : Christians, freedom, and free markets / Kathryn D. Blanchard.

xxii + 240 p. ; 23 cm. Includes bibliographical references and index.

ISBN 13: 978-1-60608-659-9

1. Capitalism—Religious aspects—Protestant churches. 2. Calvin, Jean, 1509–1564. 3. Smith, Adam, 1723–1790. 4. Knight, Frank Hyneman, 1885–. I. Title.

BR115.E3 B55 2010

Manufactured in the U.S.A.

For Chris

CONTENTS

ACKNOWLEDGMENTS

WHILE NO ONE ELSE should be held responsible for any mistakes found in the pages of this book, countless people must be credited with making it possible for me to sit down and write it. First and foremost, the members of my dissertation committee—Stanley Hauerwas, Allen Verhey, and David Steinmetz from Duke Divinity School, Craufurd Goodwin from Duke University's Department of Economics, and Rebecca Todd Peters from Elon University—were helpful and patient with me as I undertook the long process of learning how to behave like a scholar and complete a major research project. My department chair at Alma College, Brian Stratton, along with the Religious Studies search committee, was kind enough to recommend me for hire as an assistant professor even before the dissertation was done, thereby providing me with the needed incentive to finish it in a timely fashion.

Since then, the Louisville Institute has funded my revisions with a very generous summer research stipend, encouraging me not to waste those precious months in 2007 when I was free of teaching obligations. I then received another generous research grant from the Wabash Center for Teaching and Learning in Theology and Religion, which included a provision for my ethics colleague, Kevin O'Brien of Pacific Lutheran University, to exchange written work with me during the summer of 2008. I cannot overstate the added value that came from writing for a supportive audience of one, whose opinion I respected and whom I trusted to respond constructively.

Members of the American Academy of Religion and the Society of Christian Ethics have allowed me to participate in lively panels alongside a number of economists and theologian-ethicists, as well as to present some of my own papers and receive feedback (however mixed!) on various ideas related to this research. A number of very kind economists and economic historians have also graciously engaged this non-economist in one-on-one conversations, provided needed materials or comments on my work, invited me to serve as a referee or reviewer, or allowed me to participate in their conferences and panels. Among these I especially thank Craufurd Goodwin (again), Paul Oslington, Robert Nelson, Ross Emmett, Deirdre McCloskey, Brad Bateman, and Spencer Banzhaf. In addition, my particularly daring and tolerant colleague at Alma, Feler Bose, ventured so far as to teach a cross-listed "Economics and Religion" course with me for an entire semester. I am deeply grateful for all of these opportunities to strengthen my own understanding of economics, which is still very much a work in progress. I am also grateful to Charlie Collier at Wipf and Stock for being supportive and enthusiastic about publishing yet another book on John Calvin.

My friend Kristi Upson-Saia of Occidental College has spent more than her fair share of time reading my drafts, listening to my whining, and offering comments, suggestions, and (most importantly) moral support. My parents, Gus and Mary Blanchard, have been material providers throughout my academic life, and also—with other members of my family—my most faithful cheerleaders. My uncle, Charles Hibbard, and my research assistant, Dolly Van Fossan, bravely and generously slogged through my proofs in search of errors. Finally, my husband, Chris Moody, not only cleaned up my footnotes and bibliography but has also been the weekday caregiver for our son for the past four years. Such full-time labor does not appear on any balance sheet, but I am ever mindful of it.

INTRODUCTION

After the market crash of 2008, there is no one left who needs persuading that economic freedom is a topic in need of serious attention. The abuse of freedom, after all, is widely agreed to have been the cause of the disaster in which we find ourselves, though accusing fingers are pointed in several different directions. Some think the problem originated with irresponsible individuals who foolishly abused their freedom to take on more debt than they could afford, particularly in the form of mortgages or credit cards. Others think the problem was three decades of government deregulation of banks and businesses, which left greedy executives and traders free to invent financial products, based on others' debts, that made a few people very rich but in the final analysis had no real value (an entirely legal scheme that might make Bernard Madoff blush). The combined results of the individual freedom to run up debt and the corporate freedom to trade worthless products ended up in the lap of the American taxpayer who, for the most part, was not responsible for creating the problem but who was "free" to pay for a multi-trillion dollar bailout, even as much of their personal wealth was vanishing before their eyes.

Economic freedom was an important and complicated issue long before 2008, as any theologian, economist, political philosopher, or historian (not to mention any farmer, business owner, manual laborer, environmentalist, or sales clerk) can tell you. But in the decades following the Cold War it had gotten easier to take economic freedom for granted; communism had "lost" and capitalism had "won," so prudence seemed to demand policies that shifted economic decision-making away from governments and toward individuals (as well as toward corporations, which the law views as individuals). Free markets in the twentieth century generated and distributed unprecedented wealth to unprecedented numbers of people around the globe, and they seemed to be the answer to every problem. What the 2008 crash reminded us was that there were complicated reasons—many of them good ones—that *laissez-faire* capitalism had so long been resisted in many parts of the world. Free markets are not necessarily the predestined final stage in human development but are part of an ongoing, global negotiation of social and material life. Every gain associated with moves toward capitalism has come at a cost to someone or something. Some of these benefits have been well worth the costs, but for a number of individuals and communities (not to mention creation and its non-human inhabitants) those costs have been entirely too high.

One obvious cure for the abuse of freedom is (as anyone who has ever been grounded knows) less freedom. If people abuse their freedom to use a credit card by running up impossible debts, take away their credit cards. If banks abuse the freedom to sell products that are stupid but legal, add regulations to make such products illegal. If corporations abuse their freedom to pollute drinking water, make them pay giant fines (or go to jail) to deter such behavior. But the sharp curtailing of freedom is not always the only solution, or even the most effective one. The teenager who gets grounded, if she does not respect her parents, may simply crawl out the window after they are asleep. The corporation that gets fined for polluting the Mississippi, if it does not respect people's need for clean water, may simply move to Mexico and pollute water there. Economic freedom, like other freedoms, must therefore be viewed as part of a more complicated picture of human interdependence and moral formation. Those of us living in the forgetful period after the 1980s can benefit greatly by looking back to how thoughtful people in the past have attempted to foster greater economic freedom in a humane and sustainable way.

This book is for anyone who thinks it worthwhile to consider what it means for us to be "free" in an economic sense. And it is for Christians in particular, who believe that the God of the Hebrew Bible was incarnate in Jesus of Nazareth, and who therefore believe we are called to a peculiar way of life that is distinguished by loving our neighbors as ourselves. This does not mean that only Christians are capable of neighbor love (indeed, Christians have often been among the least loving people in history); it does mean, however, that whatever Christians believe about economic freedom is subject to the cries of our neighbors—all of them, not just the ones we choose to put at the center of our lives. Neighbor love in an economic sense, moreover, is not simply a matter of individual behaviors (I don't lie, I don't cheat, I don't steal, and the like), though this book focuses largely on individuals. While individual virtue is certainly necessary to a just economy, it is not enough on its own. Communal norms (we don't lie, we don't steal) about the limits of freedom are also necessary in order for markets to operate justly; and the larger the market, the larger the community that must work together to establish norms of fair play. In a globalized marketplace and a global ecosystem, there is virtually no one left on earth that Christians cannot call "neighbor" because no one, however invisible, is truly external to our market transactions.

WHAT IS TRUE "FREEDOM" IN HUMAN ECONOMIC LIFE?

It would be difficult to find an American who does not think freedom is a good thing. Our parents, schools, churches, and media have indoctrinated us since earliest childhood to believe that individual human freedom has been America's defining principle since its very inception by European settlers. Bracketing the question of whether such a narrative is true (as opposed to, for example, narratives told by indigenous Americans, the descendants of African slaves, or those currently incarcerated in Guantanamo Bay), the basic question that frames this book is: What exactly do people mean by "freedom" in the context of their discussions about wealth, economics, and the material conditions of our lives? Although virtually everyone can agree that freedom is better than its opposites (slavery, bondage, servitude, compulsion, oppression, incarceration), it is still necessary to answer some follow-up questions, namely: *Freedom for whom? Freedom from what?* and *Freedom for what?*

There are a number of potential payoffs of spending some time on such questions. Analyzing the writings of a few serious economic thinkers from the past, while paying special attention to the underlying theological narratives about human nature that inform their economics, will shed light on the conversations about economic freedom in which we find ourselves engaged today. It will, moreover, encourage us to view our own ethics with a more critical eye and enable us to begin making constructive changes in both theory and practice, thereby liberating ourselves from the economic mediation of well-funded political parties, self-perpetuating corporate advertisers, and even our own unrealistic desires. Not attending seriously to these issues has its own, potentially grave, repercussions. Without deliberate reflection, people of good will may find themselves either, at one extreme, hindering the freedom humans genuinely need in order to flourish or, at the other extreme, promoting an antinomianism that is ill-suited to the humans they are hoping to benefit.

The study begins with two chapters on John Calvin, whose name has forever been linked with the rise of free market systems in Europe and North America by Max Weber's sociological study, *The Protestant Ethic and the Spirit of Capitalism*. Christians have typically viewed this connection in one of two ways. Critics indict Calvin for opening the church's doors to the evils of usury and capitalism, while supporters frequently appeal to Calvin as a way to justify free-market capitalism against state socialism (which is apparently the only other imaginable option, as current American debates over such things as health care and auto makers demonstrate). Chapter 1 will draw out John Calvin's teachings on freedom and law, paying special attention to how his discussions of human freedom are connected to his theological anthropology (his views about human nature). Chapter 2 will then explore his teachings on freedom as they intersect with his economic teachings. Briefly put, Calvin's vision of economic freedom is paradoxical, in that it is actually *obedience* to the will of God—namely by putting neighbor-love front and center in one's practices of work, consumption, and exchange. Calvin's "obedient freedom" will provide an outline of individual and communal economic behavior that creates the potential for humans to transform economic and material life according to the true nature of human beings. He will then join us as an interlocutor for subsequent chapters.

Adam Smith's theological anthropology will be the subject of chapter 3, particularly as it plays into his thought about economic freedom. Although his name is sometimes used synonymously with greed, I will argue that *homo sympatheticus*—the sympathetic person (not *homo economicus*, the economic person motivated solely by rational self-interest)—is the real protagonist of his narrative. While he does indeed favor freedom for self-interested economic agents to choose their own paths, Smith worked under the assumption that truly free economic agents were those who were most perfectly shaped by sympathy. This sympathy, a natural human trait, is contextualized and shaped by the traditions and virtues of particular communities. Smith's ideal of a free market could therefore flourish only within his ideal community— one guided by honesty, self-limitation, and neighbor love. Though his economics lacks the explicit theological orientation that Calvin's has, Smith—like Calvin—orients his economics around a paradoxical norm of what might be called "sympathetic self-interest," in which the individual and the community depend upon one another in order to flourish. His economics is a subset of his ethics, which means he is not the enemy of people of good will who hope for a just economy, any more than Calvin is; on the contrary, we would be wise to learn whatever Smith might be able to teach us about organizing economic life humanely. This sympathetic understanding of Smith will, with my reading of Calvin, shape my critique of later "non-ethical" economists.

Chapter 4 is a bridge bringing us into the twentieth century, by which time "economics" had become well established as a discrete, scientific, academic discipline. Frank Knight was among the first to be identified with the highly-influential "Chicago school" of economics, and his most important contribution for my purposes was the attempt to do what Smith had not: to break economics apart from its roots in ethics or moral philosophy. Knight rightly judged "freedom" to be an ethical term—a topic related to the criticism of human wants, rather than to their simple form. As such, he argued that freedom was a matter with which economists need not concern themselves. He saw economists as scientists of the form, rather than the content or criticism, of human wants and want-satisfying behaviors; they should study how human wants cause them to behave, rather than making judgments about what they want. And they certainly should not make any pronouncements on how free people should be to seek that which they want. Knight therefore exempted economists from having to consider what freedom meant for *homo economicus*; instead, he insisted that they leave it alone. Because of his view of the division of intellectual labor with regard to human behavior, Knight (to his credit) maintained a certain humility regarding the scope of economic science and its usefulness in the making of public policy. Economists should stick to abstract models and leave policy to ethicists, historians, and politicians.

The next generation of Chicago economists internalized Knight's claim that *homo economicus* was an abstract model, void of any ethical content, but unlike Knight they did not shy away from offering ethical advice about public policy—including the limits of freedom—based upon their scientific conclusions. The fragile wall Knight tried to build between economic theory and "the real world" was easily breached by his less reticent successors, making him a sort of tragic hero who participated in the undoing of his own vision. Chapter 5 deals with three of his students and colleagues: George Stigler, Gary Becker, and Milton Friedman. Friedman, with missionary zeal, *assumed* freedom as the cornerstone of his economic thought, without attempting to offer any description of it or making a persuasive case for its importance. Stigler and Becker, though they shared Friedman's methodology, took a different tack and eliminated the language of freedom altogether, in favor of the term "choice," which they understood to be devoid of any ethical implications. No longer concerned with what is necessary for human dignity (e.g., "slaves should be free"), Stigler and Becker focus on questions about what the rational human being does in isolated incidents when given a limited number of options (e.g., "if given a choice, will a slave choose to work or to suffer a beating?"). In embracing an image of *homo economicus* defined by the power to choose from among options, these economists freed themselves from having to think about the types of choices some people have to make, or what kinds of economic practices might contribute most to human flourishing in any particular situation. Instead they focused on abstract models that could be universally applied, regardless of context. And apply they did; all three of them made extensive policy recommendations based on their narrow understanding of humans as strictly self-interested, utilitarian calculators. Friedman makes explicit what Becker and Stigler attempt to hide, namely that neoliberal economic theory is an *ethical* tradition in addition to being a scientific one—a community of shared understandings about the good and the humane, particularly as they play out in the material world of production, distribution, and consumption.

The book will conclude in chapter 6 by seeking to find common ground between the pro-capitalist and anti-capitalist voices that continue to dominate Christian ethical conversations, beginning with the assumption that freedom is good. Christianity does indeed share a common interest in individual human freedom with a certain thread of free-market ideology, particularly that which connects Adam Smith to contemporary feminist economists such as Deirdre McCloskey and Julie Nelson, as well as to the "social business" model promoted by Muhammad Yunus. But the vision of freedom that arises from the writings of these economists is of a particular, paradoxical sort that—like Calvin's and Smith's—might also be characterized as obedience to a communal set of norms, which is shaped by sympathy as much as individual self-interest. This type of freedom stands in stark contrast to the freedom envisioned by many economists and right-leaning Christians, not because neoliberals are evil or wrong about market principles of supply and demand, but simply because they tend to view the individual's economic choices in isolation from other areas of their lives, as well as in isolation from their neighbors' lives. They ignore both external inputs and outputs in the recitation of their economic narratives, chalking individuals' successes up entirely to their own good choices, while ignoring the material burdens that these individuals' behaviors put on others. The "laws" of supply and demand, scarcity and plenitude, must be located within a larger story about humankind that began in the past and is still unfolding. The economist may choose not to make this story explicit; the ethicist and the Christian must do so.

A note about method: this book about freedom should be read primarily as a work of Christian ethics—an attempt to get a handle on how Christians can and should practice in the marketplace—rather than a historical survey of economic thought. In spite of all appearances, these chapters are about Christians in the twenty-first-century global economy, rather than about uncovering the "real" Calvin or revealing anything definitive about the past. As such, my more historically-minded readers may find themselves jarred by the juxtaposition of the likes of Calvin, Friedman, and Muhammad Yunus. They may notice anachronistic interpretations or imprecise uses of terms like "freedom," "capitalism," and "liberty." Nevertheless I go boldly into this territory, enticed by the hope of possible benefits that an anachronistic probing of past thinkers may provide for thinking constructively about economic ethics in the present and future.

THEOLOGICAL, ETHICAL, AND ECONOMIC SELF-AWARENESS

Marcella Althaus-Reid calls for first-person theology that is "diasporic, self-disclosing, autobiographical and responsible for its own words."[1] If

---

1. Althaus-Reid, *Queer God*, 8.

Christian theology[2] has, like economics, traditionally been written from ostensibly "objective" points of view, and sought truths that are God-given, universally-acceptable, and free of contextual bias, the postmodern era has called this tradition into question. Christians in the twenty-first century cannot, with integrity, claim to present the truth—whether material or metaphysical—for all people in all times and places. We must rather be self-conscious about the "I" involved—an I whose knowledge is ineluctably contextualized by material and social interests and limitations such as age, gender, race, class, education, sexuality, location, nationality, and of course religion. Theology (and for that matter, economics) is always an act of individual confession, whether the theologian admits it or not.

While I do not pretend to have a full handle on my identity, the following is one possible narrative that may be helpful for interested readers to know. I was raised in the suburban American northeast, the firstborn of two girls in a white, Protestant, upwardly-mobile American family shaped significantly by both Jesus and the corporate world. At some point in my adolescence I awakened to the fact that we were conspicuously wealthy, even in relation to friends in my school district. During my years at a liberal arts college—where I first became conscious of "liberals"—this wealth increasingly became a source of guilt and shame for me. In large part, this shame is what propelled me into seminary, a brief career in the philanthropic sector, and a PhD program in Christian theology and ethics where I focused on economic questions. As I near the end of my fourth decade on earth, working in a comfortable position as an assistant professor in a liberal arts college, the sense that I am a spoiled child of untold privileges continues to be a major motivating force behind my thought and practice.

The psychologically attentive reader may discern the "autobiographical" shape of this book in the figures I have chosen to read. John Calvin has been accused of making capitalism virtually synonymous with Protestantism, especially Presbyterianism, with which I have been associated off and on for more than two decades. Adam Smith has been

---

2. Throughout this work I will often use "theology" and "ethics" interchangeably, reflecting the conviction that theory and practice, the metaphysical and material, are wholly intertwined in human experience. There is no theology that does not have ethical repercussions, and there is no ethics that does not co-arise with theological understandings. For this reason, I also resist the convenient idea that economics is "worldly" while Christian theology is "other-worldly" (see, for example, Harper and Gregg, *Christian Theology and Market Economics*, 10).

accused of eliminating all human feeling from the business world, which was the world in which my family's wealth was forged. Though I did not originally set out to rescue these two figures from defamation (in truth, I planned to attack them harshly), the marked contrast I found between their writings and those of later economic thinkers has led me to shift the brunt of my critique. The Chicago school economists I have included are those whose voices most closely resemble the dominant economic voices in my socio-cultural sphere outside of academia (including the George W. Bush administration, during which this project was conceived, written, and defended as a dissertation). These are my familiars, the demons I seek to exorcise, and yet I also find myself unable to turn my back on them entirely. Everything in my life that I experience as "good" has been fostered within a capitalist context. How, then, could I be so ungrateful as to reject all the values and virtues they have given me? My return to Calvin and Smith is an attempt to redeem what is fruitful and humane about the market tradition, to distinguish honorable "dead white men" from the dishonorable, to retain what is compatible with Christianity as I understand it. The feminist economists I have included—white Protestant scholars who build on and critique the teachings of their forefathers— feel to me like sisters in this attempt. Meanwhile, Muhammad Yunus, the "banker to the poor," is a visitor who is nothing at all like me, but who brings good news from afar that renews my hope in the possibility of justice in the *real* world.

My audience should know up front that I am also making some assumptions about you. Since you have picked up this citation-heavy book about Christian economic ethics, I must assume that (unless you are related to me by blood or marriage) you are either a student being asked to read it, or you are some kind of Christian academic, probably a theologian or ethicist, or possibly an economist with religious commitments. I also assume that you have a pre-existing interest in economics (or else in John Calvin) that has drawn you to this particular book. After this my assumptions get a bit more complicated because, although I can assume you have at least some opinions on economic ethics, I cannot be sure what those opinions are. Some of you will fall into one of two clear positions: either you believe that free-market capitalism is exactly what God had in mind for the material life of humankind (at least after Eden), and it is therefore the job of Christian theology to demonstrate why capitalism as we know it is the best of all possible (real) worlds; or you believe that the capitalist narrative (with all its negative concomitants) is a prime example of the fallen nature of humankind that God urges us to crucify, thereby making it the job of Christian theology to offer an alternative model altogether. The rest of you will fall somewhere else on the spectrum; you think perhaps there is some potential for good in market capitalism (after all, you rather like those cheap beach chairs you just bought at Target), and yet you also think human beings are so desperately flawed that *laissez-faire* policy is a recipe for disaster, especially for the poorest and weakest members of God's creation. You hope for a re-imagination of some kind, in which capitalism is either improved or replaced by something better. My hope is that, whoever you are, you find something in this book that stimulates your thinking about your place in the global economy, as well as about the narratives—theological and economic—that have contributed to your own ethical formation.

A FINAL (BEGINNING) WORD

As a quick skim through my bibliography makes obvious, I am far from being a lone voice clamoring in the wilderness about the need for more theology in economics or more economics in theology. Many accomplished scholars have already made a number of good cases for such dialogue. Instead, this study is one particular attempt to connect the dots between Christian notions of freedom and the notions of freedom fostered by modern economics, in this case by drawing from the history of modern economic thought from the Reformation to the twentieth century. Christians (especially Protestants not well versed in the Catholic social tradition) are often given the impression that, when it comes to economics, we are perpetually caught between an other-worldly call to be loving and humane and a worldly need to be practical—between a Protestant ethic and a spirit of capitalism. I will highlight the very real distinctions between Reformed ethics and libertarian economics while also noting certain values that they share, with an eye toward constructing an approach to economics that is *both* humane *and* practical. Economics, like other areas of ethical inquiry, is not a matter that can be viewed in black and white. Rather than giving a blanket critique or stamp of approval to the whole discipline of economics or to all market systems, Christians need to be more deliberate and discerning about how we narrate "capitalism." To be sure, certain parts of today's capitalist systems require disruption and dismantling, but other pieces can and should be fostered. Those who seek to water the seeds of a mindful economy need not abandon market principles altogether but can re-imagine capitalism according to more humane norms, thereby participating in the cultivation of economies of obedient freedom and sympathetic self-interest in which the whole interdependent world may flourish.

Like many others, I believe in the possibility of a more just economic system that can harness the productive power of decentralized markets while also minimizing their destructive tendencies (which some would have us believe are inevitable) toward gross inequality and the exploitation of people and creation. My hope is that those Christians who distrust markets altogether will find something here that causes them to give economic freedom another look; and that those Christians who think individual economic choice must be protected at any cost will reconsider the importance of communal self-limitation in light of human interdependence.

1

CHILDREN, NOT SLAVES

John Calvin on Human Beings, Law, and Freedom

I T MAY SURPRISE SOME readers that this book looks to John Calvin for
hints of what a truly liberating freedom would look like in an economic system. If we have any mental picture of Calvin at all, it is probably of a pale, gaunt, and joyless face framed by an imposing robe and
a funny hat. We may have a vague notion that he ruled Geneva with an
iron fist, imposing strict rules and terrorizing his subjects with the severe
doctrine of predestination. We may have even heard that he was responsible for the burning of an unfortunate heretic who crossed his path.
While there is some truth in this picture, those who take the time to read
and wrestle with his writings, both public and personal, will be rewarded
with a picture of this formidable character that is closer to being three-
dimensional. Most importantly for the topic at hand, Calvin presents
a complicated but keen interest in the subject of human freedom that
includes (but is not limited to) freedom in everyday economic matters of
employment, wealth, and consumption.

Take, for example, the following excerpt in which Calvin muses
empathetically on the material concerns that face his well-intentioned,
middle-class Christian contemporaries. The scrupulous American reader may find it humorous, if not painful, in its accuracy:

> For when consciences once ensnare themselves, they enter a long and inextricable maze, not easy to get out of. If a man begins to doubt whether he may use linen for sheets, shirts, handkerchiefs, and napkins, he will afterward be uncertain also about hemp; finally, doubt will even arise over tow. For he will turn over in his mind whether he can sup without napkins, or go without a handkerchief. If any man should consider daintier food unlawful, in the end he will not be at peace before God, when he eats either black bread or common victuals, while it occurs to him that he could sustain his body on even coarser foods. If he boggles at sweet wine, he will not with clear conscience drink even flat wine, and finally he will not dare touch water if sweeter and cleaner than other water. To sum up, he will come to the point of considering it wrong to step upon a straw across his path, as the saying goes.[1]

One can easily imagine a modern paraphrasing of this dilemma, no doubt involving issues such as whether a Christian can buy regular coffee or must only buy organic coffee; and can she buy the organic coffee at Walmart, or does it have to be purchased at the local co-op, even though it costs twice the price, thus presenting conflicting issues of stewardship; or do Christians living in the northern hemisphere have to forego coffee altogether, because it not only presents economic and political challenges related to issues of fair trade, but also requires the environmental degradation that accompanies the use of fossil fuels to get coffee beans from Colombia or Vietnam or Kenya to Michigan?

Thus Calvin, in spite of being separated from us by more than four centuries, speaks in a voice that still rings true for middle-class American Christians, who are collectively among the richest and most privileged people in the world (recessions notwithstanding). Like us, Calvin lived in a context of expanding markets, new media, increased immigration, and people of varied incomes. Like us, he lived among increased consumer options and faced economic choices that had been inconceivable to the previous generation. Like us, Calvin had to wrestle with the question of how best to live in this new economy, which brought with it not only new products but also, more importantly, new neighbors. In forging a new kind of politics against (what he saw as) oppression by the Roman Catholic Church and other medieval social institutions, he was adamant

---

1. Calvin, *Institutes*, III.xix.7. All further references to the *Institutes* will be cited parenthetically.

that freedom had to remain paramount—but what kind of freedom? And how is this freedom related to the true nature of human beings?

Before we answer those questions, it is worthwhile to turn briefly to a summary of Weber's influential investigation into the historical and sociological connections between Calvinism and capitalism. Even those who have never read Weber may have acquired the vague impression that Calvin paved the way for unfettered markets with his particular brand of innovative theology. I will argue in this chapter that Calvin's theology does indeed hold certain goods in common with classical economic thought—especially individual freedom, even freedom to make consumer choices. But Calvin's understanding of freedom was always paired with his equally important teachings on neighbor-love and self-denial, thus leading him to a markedly different economic vision than a dog-eat-dog world. (Readers already familiar with the Weber thesis may choose to skip the next section and delve right into Calvin's own theological teachings.)

DOES CALVINISM BREED CAPITALISM?

Max Weber's *The Protestant Ethic and the Spirit of Capitalism* (1905) has done more than perhaps any other work to foster the widespread idea that Calvinism and capitalism go hand in hand.[2] While he did not go so far as to say that Protestant religion actually *caused* capitalism, Weber believed the sixteenth- and seventeenth-century phenomenon of greater economic growth in Protestant regions than in Catholic ones demanded some explanation. He concluded that Calvinist doctrines fostered capitalist practices through a unique mix of, on the one hand, a newfound sense of legitimacy about creating private wealth (to aspire to a worldly rather than monastic lifestyle), and on the other hand an increased sense of powerlessness to change one's eternal destiny (predestination). Somewhere between these two movements, what Weber saw as the "spirit" of capitalism was born—the need to work but not to enjoy the fruits of one's labor. It is important to note, however, that

2. Because the Weber thesis has been more than adequately examined by countless authors to whose sociological and historical expertise I defer (see, for example, Tawney, *Religion and the Rise of Capitalism*; Harkness, *Calvin*; Valeri, "Religion, Discipline, and the Economy"; Wolterstorff, *Until Justice and Peace Embrace*; and Lewis, "Christianity and Capitalism"), I will limit my treatment here to what is relevant to my own theological reading of Calvin's economics.

Weber's analysis was predominantly of early Calvin*ists* rather than of Calvin himself.

In the centuries between Jesus and the European Reformations, Christian theologians had exhibited a lasting uneasiness with regard to the "spirit of trade" and its concomitant material gains. A deep suspicion of wealth ("that which by nature is a weight") stemmed from an ancient, even pre-Christian sense of tension between earthly and heavenly pleasures.[3] The Roman Catholic tradition, while generally affirming the necessity and goodness of private property, nevertheless held up priests, monks, and nuns—those who renounced not only sex but also private ownership—as the highest exemplars of Christian living. Thomas Aquinas (1225–1274) taught that usury, or the lending of money at interest, was "unjust in itself, because this is to sell what does not exist, and this evidently leads to inequality which is contrary to justice."[4] Thus in theory, if not always in practice, the church discouraged Christians from any kind of economic behavior that smacked of money-grubbing; those who came by their wealth "naturally" (that is, through the luck of good birth) were relatively safe, but those who came by it through their own bourgeois efforts were to be censured.

But although usury and other proto-capitalist practices were frowned upon by the late medieval and early modern churches, it nevertheless took place, though much penance was required—often followed by gifts of art and architecture to the church. The answer to why development flourished in Protestant areas, Weber argued, lay not with any ecclesiastic, economic, or governmental structures that could be found on the books, but rather with the kind of "spirit" that took root in individual Protestant consciences as a result of their religious formation.[5] "Even the Spanish," he wrote, "knew that 'heresy' (i.e., the Calvinism of the Dutch) 'encouraged the spirit of trade.'"[6] Weber traced the first cracks in traditional (Catholic) economic thought to Martin Luther's innovative teachings on "calling" or vocation. Early in his ministry, Luther began to experience a growing distaste for monastic life. Withdrawal from secular life to pursue quiet and prayer seemed to him a selfish luxury, a temptation for people wishing to shirk responsibility to others; it also

3. Clement of Alexandria, "Who Is the Rich Man," 1.

4. Thomas Aquinas, *Summa*, II–II.78.

5. Weber, *Protestant Ethic*, 260–61.

6. Ibid., 6-7.

encouraged Christians to believe that it was possible to justify oneself before God through saintly living. Perhaps most importantly, Luther thought it was harmful to the larger community (in his case, Germany) to have its holiest Christians depart from it. All of these factors led him to argue that, in contrast to cloistered life, devoting oneself to secular work was the most worthwhile Christian calling of all.[7] As Weber sums up the Lutheran point of view, "labor in a secular calling appears as the outward expression of Christian charity," an important first step toward a bourgeois mindset; but according to Weber, "[t]his view is based in particular on the argument that division of labor forces each individual to work for *others*, an extremely otherwordly argument which is almost grotesquely at variance with Adam Smith's well-known dictum."[8]

This insistence on other-interest, Weber concluded, was an important part of why capitalism did not flourish in Lutheran areas. Although Luther opened a door out of the monastery by sanctifying worldly work, he resisted other economic practices that were essential to capitalism. In particular, because of his traditional suspicion of usury (as well as his German nationalist horror at all things Italian, including trade), "Luther expresses unambiguous views on the nature of capitalism which . . . are, from the capitalist point of view, quite 'backward.'"[9] Moreover, Weber argued, Luther's particular idea of the calling had the flavor of resignation to it; he emphasized the need for Christians to "submit" to God's work assignments more heavily than he emphasized calling as a "divinely appointed task," through which one could serve God.[10] This emphasis corresponded to an attachment to the *status quo* among Luther and Lutherans, and to a reluctance to see radical socio-political changes accompany the upheaval in the churches at the time. The freedom of a Christian to defy the Pope did not extend to rebellion against worldly authorities, before whom submission remained the proper Christian

7. Luther did not attempt to hide his nationalist spirit, nor his concern for a healthy German economy. See, for example, his open letter to wealthy and powerful Germans in which he expresses his mercantilist fears of foreign trade: "[W]e do not need to spend and waste such enormous sums for silk and velvet and golden ornaments and other foreign wares… only let us be thankful, and be satisfied with the goods which God has given us." Luther, "An Open Letter to the Christian Nobility," 26.

8. Weber, *Protestant Ethic*, 29; emphasis added. I believe Weber is wrong in his interpretation of Adam Smith's "well-known dictum," as I will explain in the next chapter.

9. Ibid., 30.

10. Ibid., 32.

posture. Weber argued that Calvin finished what Luther had only started, for "although the Reformation would have been inconceivable without Luther's personal religious development and has always borne the stamp of his personality, his work would never have achieved outward permanence without Calvinism."[11] In Weber's estimation it was Calvinist *ethics*—the way his theological beliefs took shape on the ground—that set it apart from both Lutheranism and Catholicism. While the latter two upheld rather than challenged European political and material life, Calvinism had a uniquely embodied form, an "ascetic morality" that "redirected ethical objectives from traditional social relations to impersonal moral laws, thereby internalizing discipline."[12] Calvinist Christians were not to rely on priests or other authorities to tell them how to live well; they took *sola scriptura* to its natural end and looked to God's law alone, as mediated by their own consciences.

Reliance on their own consciences, however, did not relieve Calvin's late medieval audiences of anxiety about the afterlife. "Without the power of this idea, which towered above all else," Weber argued, "no moral renewal seriously affecting practical life could have been put into effect."[13] The most important and unique doctrine of Calvinism, in Weber's analysis, is the doctrine of election—the belief that an omnipotent God has predestined some humans for heaven and some for hell, with absolutely no possibility for humans to change the plan. Although Calvin did not invent predestination (indeed, he believed he got it from the Bible and Augustine, as Luther also did), his determination to release Christians from the power of the Pope gave it a more prominent place in his preaching. Weber's account is indeed terrifying:

> God was not there for the sake of men, but men were there for the sake of God, and the exclusive purpose of all that happened—thus also the fact (about which Calvin was in no doubt) that only a small proportion of humanity was called to salvation—was to glorify the majesty of God. To apply the yardstick of earthly "justice" to his sovereign decrees was pointless and an affront to his majesty, since he, and he alone, was *free*, that is, subject to no law. . . . For the reprobate, for example, to complain about their fate as undeserved would be like the animals complaining because they

11. Ibid., 33.

12. Ibid., 126.

13. Ibid., 68–69.

were not born as men. For every creature was separated from
God by an unbridgeable gulf and deserved only eternal death
except in so far as he, for the greater glory of his majesty, had
willed differently.[14]

Weber argued that Calvin's teaching inspired terror of never-ending
darkness among his hearers, with unintended but concrete consequences. For Calvin to take away all previous theological possibilities for
earning one's way into heaven (whether through good works, reception
through sacraments, or even buying it from the Pope) was to create a
previously unknown "feeling of tremendous inner *loneliness*" that demanded remedy.[15]

According to Weber's account, the remedy Calvinists found was
work. Baptism and membership in the visible church could no longer
guarantee God's invisible election; and good behavior (not to mention
penance for bad behavior), which Catholics considered necessary to salvation, had also lost the ability to assure Protestants that they could earn
merit in God's eyes. Calvin's followers became unsure of their own status
with regard to justification; lacking proof from the church that they were
among God's elect created an unacceptable psychological state of isolation and fear. Stemming from Calvin's teaching that the world existed to
glorify God and that "the Christian existed to do his part to increase the
praise of God in the world by obeying his commands,"[16] Calvinists began seeking blessed assurance through their vocations. Each person was
given a particular calling, what Calvin called a "sentry post, so that he
may not heedlessly wander about through life" (III.x.6), for the purpose
of glorifying God. If Christians could "make their own callings sure" by
struggling daily through their labors, whether extraordinary or mundane, they might somehow demonstrate to themselves that they were
indeed among God's elect, and so sleep well at night.[17]

As diligent and fruitful work (if not works) became the means by
which Christians could identify themselves as God's chosen people,

14. Ibid., 72–73; emphasis in original.

15. Ibid., 73; emphasis in original.

16. Ibid., 75.

17. Valeri, "Religion, Discipline, and the Economy," 126. This interpretation ob-
scures the fact that, as Weber says, "Calvin described the purpose of one's worldly calling not as the interior sanctification of the individual but as the commonweal." Weber,
Protestant Ethic, 135 (referring to CO 45:569, in which Calvin compares the "life of the
pious" to commerce).

Weber argued, the Calvinist work ethic developed into a new type of inner-worldly asceticism. Denial of self, which persisted as a Christian virtue but was no longer made visible through material signifiers like monastic apparel, came to be demonstrated by long hours of hard work combined with self-restraint in the pursuit of pleasure. The anxiety-inspired emphasis on striving in one's calling was accompanied by a related shunning of leisure and a suspicion against "the *uninhibited enjoyment* of life and of the pleasures it has to offer."[18] According to Weber, Calvin's (and Luther's) emptying of the convents and monasteries flooded the secular workforce with a new breed of laborer, driving "those passionately serious, reflective types of men, who had hitherto provided the finest representatives of monasticism, to pursue ascetic ideals within *secular* occupations."[19] The businessman, street-cleaner, and nursing mother could now be as saintly as any nun or priest, if not more so. Moreover, these hard-working Protestants were spending so much time and energy in their various noble callings that they were increasing their wealth greatly, while spending little of it.

Thus, innerworldly Protestant asceticism succeeded not only in giving fearful sinners something to do with their anxieties but also in making them rich, if inadvertently. The church ceased to discourage the pursuit of lucrative bourgeois occupations previously frowned upon in Catholic tradition. Calvinism had:

> ... the effect of liberating the *acquisition of wealth* from the inhibitions of traditionalist ethics; it breaks the fetters of the striving for gain by not only legalizing it, but ... seeing it as directly willed by God. The fight against the lusts of the flesh and the desire to cling to outward possessions ... is *not* a fight against wealth and profit, but against the temptations associated with them [such as "*ostentatious* forms of luxury" that amount to worship of self rather than God].[20]

In short, Weber argued that Calvinist theology had the overall effect of creating capital by, first, freeing Christians to do virtually any kind of worldly work; second, encouraging them to work hard so as to demonstrate their salvation, thus resulting in profits; and third, compelling

18. Weber, *Protestant Ethic*, 112; emphasis in original.

19. Ibid., 83; emphasis in original.

20. Ibid., 115.

them to save or invest it rather than enjoy it. A new kind of Christian economic life—for both individuals and societies—was born.

Before moving on, it is important to re-emphasize that Weber does not argue that Calvin *himself* encouraged capitalism, or even that later Calvinist cultures (especially Puritans in the United States) were necessarily faithful to Calvin's own theological intentions. R. H. Tawney raised the critique that what Weber called "Calvinism" was something of a hybrid, since social influence is not unidirectional; theology alone does not shape culture, but economic conditions also have an impact on religious thought and behavior.[21] Puritans may have perhaps shaped capitalism with their desire to gain entry into heaven, but they were undoubtedly also *shaped by* the social, political, and economic forces that allowed capitalism to arise in their particular historical context. Which force—theological or social—dominated the other remains forever open to debate. As we delve into Calvin's economic teachings, readers may reflect upon whether the same holds true for Calvin himself. One need not be entirely cynical to acknowledge that economic concerns might have influenced his theology; if every human being is shaped by the language, customs, and culture of the world in which he swims, then Calvin too must have been susceptible to suggestion. (If one supposes, for example, that Luther's repulsion against usury had at least some relation to his desire to protect Germany from Roman influences, we may also suppose that Calvin's awareness of the potential advantages of usury for Geneva had some bearing on his willingness to allow it.) Tawney's corrective to Weber's thesis is one reminder against the temptation to oversimplify when explaining the complicated workings of the human world.

To conclude this section, I wish to return to the question of freedom. As we have seen, Weber's argument is that it was the doctrines of vocation and predestination that, when paired together, were the salient theological features of the rise of capitalist behavior. While vocation gave both Lutherans and Calvinists a new freedom to engage in any number of secular occupations with confidence that they could do so to the glory of God, it was counterbalanced, especially among Calvinists, by anxiety over predestination—which essentially created a feeling of complete and utter *lack* of freedom or power to affect their individual eternal destinies.

---

21. Tawney, *Religion and the Rise of Capitalism*. For an overview of ongoing arguments about the relationship between economics and religion, see Wuthnow and Scott, "Protestants and Economic Behavior," 260–61.

Weber argued that Luther's personal fear of hellfire encouraged him to emphasize grace and dependence on God in his theology, whereas this fear was not one of Calvin's personal demons. Had it been so, and had Calvin demurred from discussing predestination in public, the spirit of capitalism might have had to wait for another religious sponsor. But as it was—whether causatively or coincidentally—Calvin did preach election, and capitalism did flourish among those we now call Calvinists.

I wish to argue for a reading of Calvin's theology that emphasizes freedom, rather than predestination, as the driving force behind his economic thinking. No less than Luther, Calvin saw every aspect of human life as a gracious gift from God; he declared that, having been redeemed through Christ, Christians were free from the need for righteousness under the law. Most economic decisions, therefore, were by and large matters of individual conscience as long as they did not offend God's laws, which included direct commands such as "you shall not steal," as well as the broader commands of Jesus such as "love your neighbor as yourself." Within such boundaries (and within the laws laid down by providentially-supplied local magistrates), the Christian has wide discretion over her particular behaviors. Nevertheless, her freedom is not unlimited but is bounded on all sides by the needs of human beings—both herself and others. We turn now to an exploration of who the human being is in Calvin's thought, as a way to understand the foundations upon which he builds his vision for freedom in human economic life.

HUMAN NATURE: CREATED, CORRUPTED, AND REDEEMED

Calvin's theological anthropology famously provides the starting point for his most significant work, the *Institutes of the Christian Religion*, in which he asserts that understanding the true nature of the human being is the beginning of all knowledge. "Nearly all the wisdom we possess . . . consists of two parts: the knowledge of God and of ourselves. But, while joined by many bonds, which one precedes and brings forth the other is not easy to discern" (I.i.1). Some humans are satisfied to meditate only on themselves and their own nature without reference to God, but Calvin argues that to do so is to miss out on a genuine understanding of the good. True wisdom involves a back-and-forth motion between looking at God's good works and gifts, and then gratefully turning its eye toward the human, whose existence is rightly seen always and only in relationship to God. Thus, for Calvin the answer to "Who is the human being?" is a narrative that includes her creation in God's image, her decision to reject her true nature, and the redemption of her true nature through the gracious work of Christ. The human is therefore a creature full of paradox—both good and corrupt, both wise and ignorant, both free and enslaved, both strong and powerless, and (if elect) both justified and a sinner.

Because the theme of sin comes across more loudly than some of Calvin's modern readers might find edifying, it is important to dwell for a moment on his teachings about human nature's original goodness and the goodness of nature as such. All creation—both nature and human nature—is good and was created by a good God. Calvin claims that God, not unlike trees known by their fruits, is known by God's works (I.v.9). God's intention was "that the frame of the universe should be the school in which we were to learn piety" (II.vi.1); thus, creation exists to draw humans into the "blessed life" that consists in knowing God as good (I.v.1). Moreover, God's self-revelation through nature fosters human happiness, which ultimately is "to be united with God" (I.xv.6). In contrast to Weber's impression of Calvinist avoidance of enjoyment, Calvin explicitly exhorts humans to enjoy the created world in a very deliberate way:

> . . . let us not be ashamed to take pious delight in the works of God open and manifest in this most beautiful theater. For . . . *although it is not the chief evidence for faith, yet it is the first evidence* in the order of nature, *to be mindful* that wherever we cast our eyes, all things they meet are works of God, and at the same time *to ponder with pious meditation* to what end God created them (I.xiv.20).

Nowhere does Calvin declare that the material world is unworthy of human attention or inimical to the life of the soul. On the contrary, the material world is the primary means of God's ongoing reaching out to humankind. Calvin surprisingly goes so far as to say that, when properly viewed, "it can be said reverently . . . that nature is God," though he discourages such language as being too prone to human irreverence and misunderstanding (I.v.5).

Calvin is adamant that God's creating work was not a one-time event that ended with his seventh-day nap; God did not merely create the earth, set its mechanical processes in motion, and then depart. Calvin wants humans to take comfort in the idea that God is not merely a creator but also a sustainer, and God's act of creation is inseparable from ongoing providence. Christian faith acknowledges God as "everlasting Governor and Preserver—not only in that he drives the celestial frame as well as its several parts by a universal motion, but also in that he sustains, nourishes, and cares for, everything he has made, even to the last sparrow" (I.xvi.1). Even a natural process as basic and repetitive as the changes in season must be attributed to the special attention of the ultimate micro-manager (I.xvi.2). The sun would not rise and the rain would not fall, were God not constantly awake and active.

Calvin's faith in providence is especially relevant to our discussion of economics because it relates not only to natural phenomena; God's micro-management also accounts for the ongoing order of society. It is God who makes some crop years fruitful (we might say economically profitable) and others not (I.xvi.5). It is God who decides that some infants at their mother's breasts are fed liberally, while others receive more meager nourishment (I.xvi.3). It is God who supplies human societies with wise and relatively good leadership, in order to keep them running properly (II.iii.4). It is even God who causes the wicked sometimes to prosper, because God mercifully "pursues miserable sinners with unwearied kindness, until he shatters their wickedness by imparting benefits and by recalling them to him with more than fatherly kindness!" (I.v.7). Providence is therefore not only actively in charge of the weather, but is also "the determinative principle for all human plans and works" (I.xviii.2). Nothing in creation—neither gravity nor death, neither love nor greed (though of no uncertain importance for the secondary roles they play)—operates as its own cause (I.xvii.9).

For Calvin, the earth is an excellent place for humans to be, both physically and socially. God created nature—both human and otherwise—good and continues to preserve its ongoing goodness. Perhaps it will surprise some readers that the father of "total depravity" and inner-worldly asceticism should embrace the earthly sphere so wholeheartedly. The obvious pitfalls of embodied life are many—idolatry, the inordinate love of earthly goods like wealth, food, sex, or human admiration—and these obstacles can indeed prevent humans from attaining the union with God for which they were intended. But Calvin does not consider such evils to be an essential part of creation. Following orthodox tradition, Calvin presents evil as having no independent essence; evil is a parasite that borrows its essence from the good and then twists it. True Christian piety, he claims, "does not admit that any evil nature exists in the whole universe. For the depravity and malice both of man and of the devil, or the sins that arise therefrom, do not spring from nature, but rather from the corruption of nature" (I.xiv.3). In thinking about Calvin's vision for economics, we must therefore not dwell only on depravity, not accept that a system based on original sin is the best we can do, but also take into consideration this ongoing movement from goodness to corruption and back again through redemption.

God's creation of all things toward good ends would be plain for all humans to see, were their (originally good) senses and understanding not corrupted by sin. Hints of God's goodness are everywhere shining like "so many burning lamps," and humans are gifted with eyes to see them, but after the fall they perceive these lamps as mere "sparks" (I.vi.14). Human rationality can no longer comprehend the truth unaided. It is not that creation has ceased to be good or ceased to speak of God's goodness, but humans now lack the capacity to see it clearly, willfully choosing distortions over truth. And corruption is not predominantly a matter of the body. Even given perfect information, humans "soon corrupt the seed of the knowledge of nature (thus preventing it from coming to a good and perfect fruit)" (I.vi.15). The human soul—originally designed to animate the body and "arouse it to honor God" (I.xv.6)—has itself ceased to do its job properly; and the human understanding or reason, the "leader and governor of the soul" is also corrupted (I.xv.7).

This corruption, while not a part of humans' original nature and not entirely removing the image of God from them, now pervades all aspects of human life, material, social, and spiritual. Not to know this fact about humankind is, for Calvin, not to know anything at all. The human being, in and of herself, is indeed evidence of God—a beautiful and "rare example of God's power"; "we are God's offspring" endowed with "great excellence" (I.v.3). And yet, to understand one's own greatness is to understand simultaneously that God is infinitely greater. To know one's own strength is to know that God is infinitely stronger. Such a God, were God not to allow us to "taste his fatherly love," would be certain cause for human fear; as it is, however, God graciously draws humans into love and worship (I.v.3–4).

The relationship Calvin envisions between humans and God is one of adoration and mutual delight. It is the loving and joyful relationship between children and parents who recognize something of themselves in the other. The fall into sin, however, represents an essential break in this relationship. Humans—like stubborn teenagers—willfully deny that God is their creator (I.v.4), they substitute nature for God in their minds (I.v.5), and they deny the rightful honor due to their author (I.v.6). This does not change the fact that nature itself bears no flaw. What is "natural" to human nature is uprightness; the human is "the noblest and most remarkable example of [God's] justice, wisdom, and goodness" (I.xv.1). But, as is never far behind this affirmation, Calvin acknowledges that human decision to sin degrades true nature. Human nature is indeed praiseworthy in so far as it conforms to God's image, but the fall means that sin is in some way now also "natural" to humans (II.ii.11). It is a bitter irony that humans' capacity to reject and corrupt the nature they were given by God is itself a sign of their immense gifts; "there was no part of man, not even the body itself, in which some sparks did not glow" (I.xv.3).

Thus, whenever Calvin speaks of the human being it is embedded within a narrative of the human's creation in goodness and voluntary fall into sin. Calvin maintains a willingness to acknowledge that much good still exists in human nature; they retain, for example, an awareness of and attraction to God (I.iii.1) and a desire for the true human happiness that comes from unity with God (though this desire combined with human dullness inevitably results in idolatry [I.v.12]). Humans retain as well the reason and ability to distinguish between good and evil, but because of the flawed understanding that comes from turning away from God, they desire things which are not truly good (I.xv.8). True reason is that which is directed toward "leading a holy and upright life, [that] we may press on to the appointed goal of blessed immortality" (II.i.1), but such reason is hard to come by for post-lapsarians.

On the other hand, though humans are indeed powerless not to sin, Calvin warns them against using this powerlessness as a way to excuse themselves from responsibility for their actions. The good gifts of reason and intellect that God instilled in human nature, as well as the good gifts in nature itself, still enable humans to exercise prudence:

> [H]e who has set the limits to our life has at the same time entrusted to us its care; he has provided means and helps to preserve it; he has also made us able to foresee dangers; that they may not overwhelm us unaware, he has offered precautions and remedies. Now it is very clear what our duty is: thus, if the Lord has com-

mitted to us the protection of our life, our duty is to protect it; if he offers helps, to use them; if he forewarns us of dangers, not to plunge headlong; if he makes remedies available, not to neglect them. (I.xvii.4)

This vote of confidence in human nature is an important counter-balance to excessive self-loathing, willful ignorance, and helpless resignation. As such, I find it especially relevant to questions of economics. Prudence, even for the sinner, is not only possible but required. Nature continues to be good and orderly, and through God's grace humans retain some access to it, through the good and orderly (if undeniably twisted) qualities they still possess. In other words, both individually and socially, humans can— if they so choose—still work with nature in good and orderly ways.

In short, Calvin does not despair about humankind. His contextualizing narrative presents human nature as holy in the same way that God is holy (III.vi.1); it is set apart for righteousness. And yet this holiness is not achieved of humans' own power, for even before sin entered human nature, its goodness came from having God's image engraved upon it. After the fall it simply became more evident that such holiness is wholly borrowed. "[W]hatever good things are in us are the fruits of his grace; and without him our gifts are darkness of mind and perversity of heart" (III.i.3). Through Christ, however, humans are still able to participate in God's holiness. They obtain virtue not simply by "living in accordance with nature," but by being illuminated through Scripture, which "not only enjoins us to refer our life to God, its author, to whom it is bound; but after it has taught that we have degenerated from the true origin and condition of our creation, it also adds that Christ, through whom we return into favor with God, has been set before us as an example, whose pattern we ought to express in our life" (III.vi.3). Ultimately, human nature is determined by its *telos* or end, and for Calvin the true end of human life is integrity—the restoring of the human to the image of God, of which Christ is the perfect pattern. God's elect are constantly being re-formed into that image which was originally "visible in the light of the mind, in the uprightness of the heart, and in the soundness of all the parts. . . . [W]hat was primary in the renewing of God's image also held the highest place in the creation itself" (I.xv.4).

Created in God's image, fallen into sin, and redeemed by Christ into wholeness—this is the human being according to John Calvin. There are obvious tensions in such a narrative, especially for our questions about freedom and economics. Humans who are perfect are in no need of laws or rules, whereas sinners urgently need varying degrees of both incentives and punishments to keep them on track. Calvin holds out Christological hope that sinners can be re-made in the image of God, but Scripture and experience teach that perfection remains out of reach for even the most dedicated persons. It remains to be seen, therefore, what vision of freedom accompanies Calvin's human being and, more specifically, how this freedom plays out in human economic life. To such questions I turn in the next two sections.

FREEDOM AND LAW

Calvin declares that the doctrine of Christian freedom is central to the good news that gave the Reformation its impetus and unrelenting energy—"a thing of prime necessity" and an irreplaceable "appendage of justification" (III.xix.1). This freedom is rooted in the knowledge of God's grace toward sinners and is what allows the Christian to live life with courage and a clear conscience. Without the knowledge of this freedom, without faith that God's love is founded in God rather than in human deserving, a person remains in bondage to fear and can never enjoy the "incomparable benefit" of the gospel. But before addressing the three-fold "Christian freedom" that I believe is the crux of Calvin's economic thought, a word should be said about his view of the created freedom that humanity *originally* enjoyed, as well as about the law that entered human life following its fall into sin.

In their "original nobility," humans possessed the freedom to create, to love, to pursue goodness, to know God fully, and in short, to be fully human (II.i.3). This freedom paralleled the infinite freedom of the God in whose image they were created, but even before the fall it was not without a particular shape that must properly—if paradoxically—be called "obedience." Even in the beginning, Calvin argues, Adam was "denied the tree of the knowledge of good and evil to test his obedience and prove that he was willingly under God's command" (II.i.4). Though humans were the highest point of God's creation, they were not to be confused with their creator. Their willing and free obedience to God demonstrated their acknowledgement of their status as creatures—free creatures, but creatures nonetheless.

At the time, an important facet of human nature was the freedom not to sin. Their nature, being uncorrupted, was fully capable of perfect conformity to Christ's image. It was not to last, however. Humans' pride and ingratitude caused them ambitiously and obstinately to reject their own limitations and seek to take on the role of creator (II.i.4). They took "a nature previously good and pure" and gave it up to sin—the "obliteration" of the original heavenly image in human nature, resulting in a depravity that has been inherited by all humans ever since (II.i.5). This original sin marked the end of genuine human freedom because humans then became slaves to corruption, no longer free to be who they were created to be. Calvin acknowledges that humans do, of course, have the ability to make choices in pursuit of one option or another, but he resists ennobling this paltry capacity of choice—a simple instinct that they share with animals—with a lofty term like "free will" (II.ii.26). Calvin insists that humans consistently choose to follow instinct rather than reason, and thus consistently pursue those things which are not truly goods and which further enslave them. Without God's grace enabling one to choose well, the power to choose remains a kind of obedience to one's corrupted preferences (II.ii.7–8).[22] As we will see, this view will distinguish Calvin's understanding of economic freedom from the simple power to make choices in pursuit of "rational self-interest" through a free market, as celebrated by some economists (and even some theologians). The ability to choose according to one's "desire for well-being" is indeed a natural human trait, but it should not be confused with freedom (II.ii.26). The mark of true freedom for humans is a like-mindedness with God that wholly shapes both their understandings and their appetites, enticing them to behave according to Christ's pattern. Obedience to God is true freedom, while obedience to one's corrupted will is a prison.

As a result of the disobedient use of their original freedom, humans became subject to law, which—far from being a punishment—Calvin understands as a "freely given covenant" from God to Israel and later to the Christian church (I.vii.1). The law is a safety net, a Plan B for sinners, that includes not only the Ten Commandments but the entire religion "handed down by God through Moses." Calvin finds three uses in God's law, the first of which is theological: it reveals to humans their misery. By laying bare the knowledge of perfect righteousness, humans

22. Here he cites Augustine for support; elsewhere (II.ii.4) he also cites Thomas Aquinas.

are convinced of their failure to meet it (II.vii.2). This is especially true when one realizes that God's law includes not only relatively simple commandments and prohibitions, but these "always contain more than is expressed in words"—there is always an implied "shall" contained within an explicit "shall not" (II.viii.8).

Without the law to show humans how far they stray from God's perfection, they would be "blinded and drunk with self-love," prone to using themselves as the measure of all goodness. Take, for example, this excerpt about the human tendency to covet—a trait particularly relevant for discussions about wealth and economics:

> [H]e passes off hypocrisy as righteousness; pleased with this, he is aroused against God's grace by I know not what counterfeit acts of righteousness. . . So deep and tortuous are the recesses in which the evils of covetousness lurk that they easily deceive man's sight. . . . For if by the law covetousness is not dragged from its lair, it destroys wretched man so secretly that he does not even feel its fatal stab. (II.vii.6)

Human beings are so full of pride that they can manage to turn their sins into virtues in their own eyes. Only by comparing themselves against the law God gave them can they see their sins clearly.

Sadly, even when humans do see themselves clearly and are fully aware of what the law commands, they do not have the internal wherewithal to choose consistently to obey it. This gives rise to the law's second use as an externally-imposed order to restrain their harmful impulses. While laws do not entirely purify human souls, they do restrain evil actions by appealing to the natural desire to avoid punishment, and this outward bridle has the beneficial effect of partially re-forming humans inwardly, moving them closer to their original image. "While by the dread of divine vengeance they are restrained at least from outward wantonness, with minds untamed they progress but slightly for the present, yet become partially broken in by bearing the yoke of righteousness" (II. vii.10). The law coerces humans into behaving virtuously, and while behaving virtuously does not create perfection in them, it gradually turns them away from sin such that when God calls them to new life in Christ, they have already been pointed in the right direction.

If Calvin's first use of the law is directed at the self-righteous, and the second use is directed at those in need of external controls (II.vii.11), his third use of the law is especially for the redeemed—those who have been freed from the power of sin. While the original human had an inherent tendency toward godly behavior, those who have been redeemed still dwell in "the prison house of the body" (II.vii.13) and often struggle, both to discern how to act righteously and also to do that which they know is right. In their case the law provides some much-needed inspiration: "Here is the best instrument for them to learn more thoroughly each day the nature of the Lord's will to which they aspire, and to confirm them in the understanding of it. . . . [W]e need not only teaching but also exhortation" to righteousness (II.vii.12). Meditating on God's good law encourages Christians toward the truly good life, and discourages them from giving in to the disordered desires of the flesh that still plague them. This third use of the law is Calvin's pre-emptive response to anyone who thinks that Christ came to abolish the law rather than to fulfill it, or who clings to an antinomian sense of liberty. Lawlessness is not freedom, in Calvin's book; apart from willing obedience to God's laws the human is a slave to sin.

This three-fold view of the law is reflected in Calvin's three-fold description of Christian freedom, which "in the context of the Christian life . . . should be announced to ease problems of doubt, anxiety, and scrupulosity."[23] Christian freedom (as distinct from free will) is the redemption and fulfillment of created human freedom—and in fact is the only remaining form of freedom for post-lapsarian humans. Since the first use of the law is to persuade humans of their sinfulness, the first aspect of Christian freedom is escape from this condemnation. Calvin urges:

> that the consciences of believers, in seeking assurance of their
> justification before God, should rise above and advance beyond
> the law, forgetting all law righteousness. . . . We should, when
> justification is being discussed, embrace God's mercy alone, turn
> our attention from ourselves, and look only to Christ. For there
> the question is not how we may become righteous but how, being unrighteous and unworthy, we may be reckoned righteous. If
> consciences wish to attain any certainty in this matter, they ought
> to give no place to the law. (III.xix.2)

As the law evokes humility and fear before the divine judge, redeemed freedom counteracts this anxiety with the promise of righteousness. Justification before God is not earned through human obedience to the

23. Douglass, "Christian Freedom," 79.

law but is wholly and graciously given by God, who no longer counts humans' righteous or sinful deeds. "The gospel differs from the law," Calvin writes, "in that it does not link righteousness to works but lodges it solely in God's mercy" (III.xi.18).

We recall that Calvin saw the law as, secondly, a type of bridle for those in need of external motivation toward the good. Correspondingly, the second part of Christian freedom is the freedom to obey God's will, but to obey *willingly* rather than under the previous "perpetual dread" of punishment (III.xix.4). In this again, Calvin hastily signals his rejection of any antinomianism that the first part of freedom might inspire. The Mosaic law, he argues, was never a punishment for sin but was originally given to Israel as a good gift, an integral part of God's covenant. It acted on God's people "to hold their minds in readiness until his coming," and to remind them "of that freely given covenant made with their fathers of which they were the heirs" (II.vii.1). While Calvin does not hold Christians responsible for the entire ceremonial religion handed down to the Israelites, he in no way implies that Jewish law was a negative development. As evidenced by his extensive treatment of the Decalogue, he believes the law is both beneficial and necessary to Christian life: "rather than being the antithesis of freedom, [the law] is its foundation and guarantee."[24]

Christian freedom enables a change of heart with regard to this second use of the law, which corresponds to a change in a person's status from fallen to redeemed. Those who labor anxiously under the law like slaves will never be able to obey God with "eager readiness" and will always experience it as a burden. Conversely, those who know themselves to be free in Christ will obey joyfully. He compares these two states of being to the states of "servant" and "son"; servants are those "bound by the yoke of the law" who can never wholly satisfy it, while sons confidently offer to their father "incomplete and half-done and even defective works" trusting that God will find them acceptable (III.xix.5)—an ethical version of refrigerator art. It is worth noting that children and slaves share one and the same law, but they relate to it differently. Calvin urges Christians to take on the narrative and persona of God's children, trusting not in the inherent goodness of their own works but in God's love

---

24. The "law" after Christ is no longer limited to the Ten Commandments, but is a spiritual law based primarily on the teachings of Jesus, in particular his "double love commandment," requiring an inward righteousness as opposed to an outward following of rules. Hesselink, "John Calvin on the Law," 79.

for them; not fearing their own imperfections but offering themselves confidently to God, who overlooks their flaws for the sake of Christ.

In the third aspect of Christian freedom he identifies—freedom in *adiaphora* or "things indifferent"—Calvin's teaching becomes particularly interesting for people struggling with how to live in a consumer-driven culture. Here he addresses those things that are "external," neither explicitly forbidden nor commanded in Scripture, neither good nor evil in themselves, and therefore given to Christians to use (or not) as they choose (III.xix.7). (This includes not only individual actions but communal religious actions as well, such as, for example, whether to worship on Saturdays or Sundays; what a pastor should wear on which days; or whether celibacy or marriage is best [II.viii.32–33].) It is not too much of a stretch to relate this to Calvin's third and most excellent use of the law, exhortation to righteousness, which he insisted benefits Christians first by allowing them to "search out and observe" God's ways in order to be more fully formed by them; and secondly by providing a "whip" to the "idle and balky ass" that is human flesh (II.vii.12). Fretting over *adiaphora*, in Calvin's mind, poisons the Christian's joyful and loving response to God's perfect law. It represents a forsaking of the confidence that comes only from knowing God's grace, in favor of the anxiety that comes of the fleshly desire to earn one's own righteousness through works. Perhaps as a result of his work as a pastor, Calvin seems painfully aware of the countless tiny ethical dilemmas posed to Christians every day of their lives. Christians must make mundane decisions such as what to wear or what to eat, and those whose consciences are still bound by the law will find themselves wound up in a spiraling web of potential pitfalls that leaves them paralyzed (such as the linens, food, or wine in the opening excerpt of this chapter).

Calvin is not satisfied to leave Christians struggling against this sticky web, and he hastens to set Christians free from guilt by assuring them that all outward things are subject to their freedom before God. The savior whose yoke is easy and burden light is not one to lay excessive and useless demands on the shoulders of human beings, whose *telos* is to be joined with God eternally. He observes that religious people (and here we must keep in mind Calvin's suspicion of the Roman Catholic tradition) are especially susceptible to "dreaming up" various rules and ceremonies as means of "contriving some way of acquiring righteousness apart from God's Word" (II.viii.5). They create human precepts to supplement and exercise control over God's already perfect law. They become more concerned with matters of indifference than with matters genuinely addressed under God's law, loving ceremonies and customs more than the true justice that flows forth from genuine piety. While Calvin maintains a concern for righteous living, he insists that "any zeal for good works that wanders outside God's law is an intolerable profanation of divine and true righteousness" (II.viii.5). His teaching about freedom in *adiaphora* is designed to redirect Christians' attention away from the earthly trivialities that bog them down and toward the larger vision of unity with God. It "pinches them awake to their imperfections" (II.vii.14), reminding them that all good works are the result of God's grace, not of their own power.

This three-fold freedom that John Calvin describes—freedom from condemnation, freedom for joyful obedience, and especially freedom in indifferent things—is the center of his ethical and economic teachings. Freedom is not just a theoretical concept for him but is "crucial for all situations the Christian encounters during his life in church and state in this world."[25] Calvin was extremely conscious of life's material conditions—social, political, and economic—and in spite of (or perhaps related to) his repeated references to the human body as a "prison house," he had a surprisingly positive attitude toward worldly comforts because of his firm belief that the proper worship of God arose from an inward posture rather than an outward behavior (again, a correction to what he saw as the Catholic ethical mindset of his time). He boldly rejected ascetic ideals as the true measure of Christian perfection, including the ideal of voluntary poverty embraced by Catholic clergy.[26] He affirmed instead the goodness of earthly blessings and worldly wealth as gifts from God. The concept of "indifference" meant that not material objects themselves but the attitudes and mindsets that humans brought *to* them determined whether such goods were virtuous or vicious. Calvin appreciates good food (something we might expect of a French native) and affirms that the variety of food in creation is proof of God's intention for it to bring "delight and good cheer" and not just bare sustenance (III.x.2). He also

25. Balke, "Calvin's Concept of Freedom," 54.

26. He vehemently opposed the hypocrisy he saw in monasticism: "By shaving off a few hairs the clerics signify that they have cast away abundance of temporal goods, that they contemplate God's glory, that they have mortified the lust of the ears and eyes. But is there no class of men more greedy, stupid and lustful? Why do they not manifest holiness rather than make an outward show of it with false and lying signs?" (VI.xix.25).

allows that clothing is at least partially for "comeliness and decency," not merely for the minimal purpose of covering nakedness. Material goods are, in themselves, external and indifferent, as long as one enjoys them moderately, humbly, and gratefully.

He is especially solicitous of wealthy Christians, who may feel guilty when they see others who have not been so richly blessed as they. But, Calvin argues, Providence covers all things. In this support of private property he stands in mainstream Catholic tradition, in marked contrast to the Anabaptists of his time whose "separation and rigorism" he adamantly opposes.[27] He upholds the freedom of Christians to hold private property—not because he thinks their inherent dignity demands it, but rather because those who would prohibit it grip "consciences more tightly than does the Word of the Lord."[28] Grace-filled freedom is the rule for all things in the Christian's life. But at the same time, Calvin never takes his eye off the potential pitfalls of possessing material goods. He thought that "great wealth was dangerous, and that self-restraint should therefore be exercised in accumulating property."[29] Thus, although he unfailingly affirms the Christian's freedom of conscience and sees the individual human heart as the center of true worship, he never leaves matters wide open to frivolous interpretation. He consciously guards against those inevitable interpreters—especially among those of means—who permit themselves too much license in the name of freedom (III.x.3). One's view of the proper *telos* of wealth, "mutual helpfulness,"[30] must never be lost.

The Christian is meant to participate in everyday life rather than withdraw from it; this includes work, family, sex, and other blessings. But at the same time, as McGrath puts it, "while immersing himself or herself in the affairs and anxieties of the world, [the Christian] must learn to keep it at a critical distance. *Outward investment in and commitment to the world must be accompanied by inward detachment and*

---

27. Hallett, "Calvin: Christian's Conflict with the Word," 128–29. For an example of the kind of economic teaching he rejected, see Riedemann, *Account of Our Religion*.

28. Gilbreath, "Martin Luther and John Calvin on Property," 223–24. Calvin's argument that holding property is a matter of freedom is distinct from the argument others make that holding property is necessary to human dignity. Property for Calvin is neither necessary nor forbidden; it is external and indifferent, and merely there for the human's good use.

29. Ibid., 225.

30. Verhey, "Calvin and the 'Stewardship of Love,'" 160.

the fostering of a critical attitude towards the secular."[31] Calvin knows he is walking a theoretical–practical tightrope here. His insistence on freedom is central to his entire theological system; if justification before God rests in absolutely no part on human action, then all human action is to some extent irrelevant to salvation. Good behavior is an addendum, a fruit, a byproduct of prior assurance of one's salvation. But if Christians were to take this gospel of grace too much to heart, the Church might be ruined by a lack of concrete, bodily acts of Christian charity. To wit,

> as soon as Christian freedom is mentioned, either passions boil or wild tumults rise unless these wanton spirits are opposed in time, who otherwise most wickedly corrupt the best things. Some, on the pretext of this freedom, shake off all obedience toward God and break out into unbridled license. (III.xix.1)

As a counter-measure to this danger, he appeals to hope of the future life in order to foster an inward detachment from this world, so as to prevent luxury and excess without giving rise to an un-Christian de-valuing of earthly life. Calvin seeks a middle way; "Let believers get used to a contempt of the present life that gives rise to no hatred of it, or ingratitude towards God" (III.xi.3).

As with all attempts at middle ways, Calvin's teaching on *adiaphora* is accompanied by unavoidable dangers. The target of his attacks is the works-oriented Catholic culture in which he was raised, while the target of his good news seems to be those of both means and an anxious spirit, perhaps those who believe life in the world is to be merely tolerated rather than enjoyed, who desperately need deliverance from the law and relief from guilt. Freedom is his message to them. But Calvin (like his critics) sees that in unscrupulous and immoderate hands, "freedom" becomes a mockery of the liberation from sin for which Christ died. Nevertheless, Calvin believes it is worth the risks and refuses to "say good-by" to Christian freedom, without which "neither Christ nor gospel truth, nor inner peace of soul, can be rightly known" (III.xix.1). He does want Christians to obey the law of God (which he considers the only way to live a truly and fully human life), no less than they would if they faced eternal damnation. Yet he wants them to do so freely rather than by coercion. God's people must never again become slaves; children—in the best-case scenario—operate from a sense of love and fidelity to their parents rather than as if they had no other choice.

31. McGrath, *Life of John Calvin*, 220.

FREEDOM'S LIMITS: SELF-DENIAL AND OTHER-INTEREST

Yet children, as we know, do not always feel as free as they might like. Until they have learned and internalized the rules laid out for them by their guardians, even if they are good rules, children may complain of feeling like slaves. Freedom, according to the parent–child metaphor, is therefore an ongoing negotiation; one becomes free as one matures and is molded by contextual limitations. To the young child, being forced to brush one's teeth may feel like a terrible burden, but to an adult who has come to appreciate the joy of clean teeth, going even one day without brushing is virtually unthinkable. Or the teenager learning to drive may feel humiliated by having to have an adult in the car to enforce the rules of the road, but once she has internalized the rules of the road to her community's satisfaction, she can set out on her own.

Likewise, the freedom that is central to Calvin's vision of human life is a lifelong learning process. His previous chapter on self-denial, what he calls the "sum of the Christian life" (III.vii.1), is the context for his discussion of Christian freedom.[32] Self-denial involves the voluntary limitation of one's desires, in favor of presenting one's body as a living sacrifice to God.[33] Calvin sees an inordinate desire to serve one's own interests as the heart of all human sinfulness; moreover, as we know from watching children, unlimited self-interest can cause harm to self and others. Disordered self-interest must be rooted out through the "renewal of the mind" enabled through the imitation of Christ:

> For, as consulting our self-interest is the pestilence that most ef-
> fectively leads to our destruction, so the sole haven of salvation is
> to be wise in nothing and to will nothing through ourselves but to
> follow the leading of the Lord alone. . . . They set up *reason alone*
> as the ruling principle in man, and think that it alone should be
> listened to; to it alone, in short, they entrust the conduct of life.
> But the Christian philosophy bids reason give way to, submit and
> subject itself to, the Holy Spirit so that the man himself may no
> longer live but hear Christ living and reigning within him.[34]

32. "Calvin's doctrine of the Christian life incorporates the significant and control-ling principle of self-denial. Along with the principle, two corollaries are included: cross-bearing and meditation on the future life. . . . Christ is the motive and pattern that the Christian must imitate. For this reason Calvin may be said to be following the principle of 'Imitatio Christi.'" Greve, *Freedom and Discipline*, 125.

33. Rom 12:1.

34. III.vii.1: emphasis added. His distrust of human reason becomes more interest-ing in the context of the economic literature we will see in subsequent chapters.

While Calvin affirms the natural traits of reason and self-interest as good gifts of God, his belief that human sin has corrupted both of these faculties means that he cannot rely on them to create good results, either in individual lives or in human societies. Without the Holy Spirit's presence to limit freedom by picking up where the law leaves off, reason and self-interest are the very least productive motivating forces in human life.[35] True humanity, in Christian terms, is not about autonomy; it is instead about being ruled by Christ.

This is possession of a most joyful kind. Christ removes the obstacles of ungodliness and worldly desires that hinder Christians on their path to the well-ordered life (III.vii.3), and frees them from the "blindness with which we all rush into self-love," thinking ourselves somehow better or more important than our neighbors (III.vii.4). The resulting humility allows Christians to renounce themselves, becoming loving and helpful toward their neighbors, until the godly person "provides for himself in no way other than to have his mind intent upon the common upbuilding of the church" (III.vii.5). Although she is free to enjoy the gifts of the earth, the Christian who is in proper relation to God and others does not first seek her own good but sees herself as a steward of God's good gifts and tests her behavior solely by the rule of love.

This has obvious importance for questions regarding personal wealth. "To begin with," Calvin writes,

> in seeking either the convenience or the tranquility of the present life, Scripture calls us to resign ourselves and all our possessions to the Lord's will, and to yield to him the desires of our hearts to be tamed and subjugated. To covet wealth and honors, to strive for authority, to heap up riches, to gather together all those follies which seem to make for magnificence and pomp, our lust is mad, our desire boundless. On the other hand, wonderful is our fear, wonderful our hatred, of poverty, lowly birth, and humble condition! And we are spurred to rid ourselves of them by every means. (III.vii.8)

He argues that devotion to God is the only antidote to the double anxiety of greedily striving after wealth and worldly honors, while dreading poverty almost more than death. This requires the sense that one's existence is wholly dependent upon God, a knowledge that is sometimes best cultivated through material adversity. What more than money can hinder a

35. Self-denial for Calvin is a mortification of the "flesh" that includes not only the body but the soul as well. See Hallett, "Calvin: Christian's Conflict with the Flesh," 203.

person's sense of dependence on God? Humans, he thinks, always seek their own comfort, and naturally become arrogant when things are going well; so to help humans learn self-denial, God "afflicts us either with disgrace or poverty, or bereavement, or disease, or other calamities. . . . Thus humbled, we learn to call on his power, which alone makes us stand fast under the weight of afflictions" (III.viii.2).[36] This is not to say that the cross is God's way of "beating the believer into submission," but it is rather a way to train her to depend upon God for everything.[37]

This proper posture of dependence on God—which Calvin sees exemplified in the appeal to God for daily bread (III.xx.44)—is the beginning of true piety, and a necessity to Christian freedom. Without it, humans are doomed to rely on their own power and the accumulation of concrete goods; they take matters into their own hands and resist placing themselves in God's care. Likewise, it is the awareness of their true indebtedness to God that allows Christians to withstand the hardships of poverty: "if things do not go according to our wish and hope, we will still be restrained from impatience and loathing of our condition, whatever it may be. For we shall know that this is to murmur against God, by whose will riches and poverty, contempt and honor are dispensed" (III. vii.9). One who has truly mastered self-denial accepts everything that comes as being from God's hand, including afflictions, which allow her to share in Christ's sufferings.[38]

It is important to note that Calvin's vision of self-denial is not merely a private, spiritual matter; it is also political in that it enables love of one's neighbor by awakening one's mind to their true identity. The neighbor "is worthy of your giving yourself and all your possessions" simply because she, like you, bears the living image of God. This goes

36. Elsewhere he (perhaps foolishly) asserts that the poor find it easier to pray, while the rich forget to do so: "the more harshly troubles, discomforts, fears, and trials of other sorts press us, the freer is our access to him, as if God were summoning us to himself" (III.xx.7).

37. Greve, *Freedom and Discipline*, 131.

38. As I mentioned in this chapter's introduction, such a teaching would have been important for those who enjoyed relative financial security but was perhaps less helpful to those hearers living in dire poverty. He believed the teaching of self-denial (and freedom) is beneficial to all Christians, regardless of their situations, because all Christians benefit from the knowledge that they are in God's care (that is, knowledge of their true condition). However, it is not difficult to see how such a teaching could be easily twisted into the kind of "opiate" that Marx accused religion of being, against which Christians must remain on guard.

for all neighbors, not just those who are "worthy" or "deserving," but even the neighbor who has committed unjust acts (III.vii.6). This bears repeating because it runs so contrary to conventional American wisdom: charity and social justice are demanded not only for those people who are virtuous or who are expected to use it responsibly. Instead, the Christian gives to the neighbor *simply because she is the neighbor* and was made in God's image. The ability to love one's neighbor as oneself comes directly from a sense of equality with her, and this sense of equality can come only from limiting oneself, seeing oneself and the neighbor in light of God. The fact that Christians pray to "our Father" means that all are siblings, co-receivers of God's grace and therefore co-debtors (III. xx.45). Neighbor love is especially important with regard to people in physical and material need, who are particularly vulnerable to hardship and oppression, and it is itself a gracious gift from the Holy Spirit. "Love calls us to be liberal in helping the poor," Haas paraphrases Calvin; "Christ set an example for us. By pouring Himself out for those who needed his help, He incites us 'to beneficence so that we should not spare ourselves when our brethren require our help.'"[39] Thus, the individual with wealth[40] is constantly called to share what she has with anyone who needs it, recognizing that her wealth has come to her through no work of her own, and to show compassion on her fellow human beings even if it means giving up everything.[41]

Economically-minded readers of Calvin find, based on his understanding of who humans are called to be, an economic norm that may cause some of us (as well as the economists we will look at in the following chapters) to cringe at its impracticality:

> [O]ur life shall best conform to God's will and the prescription of the law when it is in every respect most fruitful for our brethren. In the entire law we do not read one syllable that lays a rule upon man as regards those things which he may or may not do, for the advantage of his own flesh. And obviously, since men were born in such a state that they are all too much inclined to

39. Haas, *Concept of Equity in Calvin's Ethics*, 60.

40. The church itself is also called to such generosity (IV.iv.8; IV.v.19).

41. Valeri writes, "Calvin chastised Protestant merchants who gave money to the indigent with the expectation of remuneration or on the condition that the gift be used prudently. He also derided Catholic almsgiving as misdirected to impersonal objects: ceremonies, cathedrals, and monastic houses, when 'the poor are destitute and forgotten.'" Valeri, "Religion, Discipline, and Economy," 136.

self-love—and however much they deviate from truth, they still keep self-love—there was no need of a law that would increase or rather enkindle this already excessive love. Hence it is very clear that we keep the commandments not by loving ourselves but by loving God and neighbor; that *he lives the best and holiest life who lives and strives for himself as little as he can, and that no one lives in a worse or more evil manner than he who lives and strives for himself alone, and thinks about and seeks only his own advantage.* (II.viii.54; emphasis added)

Economic life, no less than any other aspect of Christian life, must be guided not by self-interest but by love of God and neighbor. To some extent this involves a disagreement with economists over what "self-interest" means; as economists will argue, Calvin's preference for care of others is still a preference, and still serves his own sense of utility. But from an ethical point of view not all preferences are equally good, and the Christian must be wary of the malformation of people who are immersed in a culture in which self-interest is praised and congratulated as the most "beneficial" kind of behavior for self and society.[42]

CONCLUSION: THE PARADOX OF CHRISTIAN FREEDOM

Readers may detect a bit of a split personality emanating from Calvin's writings. At times, he can be incredibly inflexible, insisting on his own interpretation and calling names at any who would dare to disagree with him; while at other times, his attitude is surprisingly easy-going, often couched in nearly poetic language about the beauty and goodness of God.[43] The term "paradox" comes up quite frequently with regard to Calvin's theology and ethics,[44] and it is appropriate here with regard

---

42. Gordon Menzies plays with this idea of identity formation by putting the imaginary "economic man" and "theological man" in conversation with each other. Menzies, "Economics as Identity," 95.

43. Balke, "Calvin's Concept of Freedom," may go too far when he writes, "in [Calvin] there is neither a lack of humour nor the narrowmindedness of the fanatic . . . for Calvin and the whole reformation freedom is exactly the end of all narrowmindedness, the end of all fear for life and man. All the pedantry of the schoolmaster is far from Calvin" (45). But the point is well taken that freedom is a genuine and central concern of Calvin's.

44. For example, Wendel, *Calvin*, 358; Hallett, "Calvin: Christian's Conflict with the Word," 126; Stevenson, *Sovereign Grace*, 8; and Gustafson, *Ethics from a Theocentric Perspective*, 32.

to his description of Christian freedom, in that freedom is a form of willing obedience that takes the forms of self-denial and loving one's neighbor as oneself. With regard to *adiaphora*, externals are indifferent and subject to individual freedom, *except* as they relate to a person's posture toward God and the neighbor. While Calvin affirms that "the freedom of believers in external matters is not to be restricted to a fixed formula, yet it is surely subject to this law: to indulge oneself as little as possible" (III.x.4). Every freedom assumes obedience to some law; for Calvin this law is love.

This leaves Calvin in a position of being in the world but not of it—a both/and rather than an either/or position. The Christian must possess an inward asceticism even amidst the enjoyment (or suffering) of God-given worldly circumstances.[45] Moreover, this inward posture is manifested outwardly whenever one interacts with others. Against anyone who might use Calvin's teaching as an excuse to accumulate wealth without regard for either their own souls or the needs of others, Calvin offers a resounding no: "Throughout its course, the life of the godly indeed ought to be tempered with frugality and sobriety, *so that as far as possible it bears some resemblance to a fast*" (IV.xii.18; emphasis added). His advice to the Christian contains an ever-present tension between freedom and self-denial—a tension that is the inevitable condition of sinful humans who have been redeemed through Christ but who continue to live in the prison house of the body. One should be like Abraham, who "preferred to leave the land and raise his heart on high rather than look for the means to acquire wealth and inheritance. So he passed through this world in such a way that he did not amuse himself" with its goods.[46] Christians are indeed free to have wealth, but regardless of how much worldly wealth they might have, all humans are equally poor and in need of Christ's generous alms (IV.xvii.42).

As always, Calvin's economic teachings are rooted in the anthropological narrative he tells of humans as created, fallen, and redeemed by God in Christ. In Calvin's mindset, none are "worthy" or "deserving" of the material goods that have been entrusted to them. God graciously

---

45. Greve, *Freedom and Discipline*, puts it thus: "The believer's present responsibility was to avoid the double dangers of 'mistaken strictness' or legalism and 'mistaken laxity' or antinomianism. Calvin sought to avoid both extremes" (135).

46. McKee, *John Calvin*, 140, from Calvin's sermon on Gen 21:33—22:2 (OC 23:741–57).

gives each person some wealth so as to enable them to serve the neighbor more freely. Although God is the giver of goods, humans need not give goods to God in return but should instead "pay forward" the benefits they have received. "[T]he Lord well knows," Calvin writes, "and also attests through his prophets, that no benefit can come from us to him"; God therefore "does not confine our duties to himself but he exercises us 'in good works toward our neighbor'" (II.viii.53). Calvin is quite clear that proof of Christian piety is in works of love done to others, a teaching that (as Weber might say) "is almost grotesquely at variance" with Weber's own thesis that Calvinists' only proof of piety was to be found in earned wealth. These works of love, which are the true evidence of God's grace and the whole point of earthly wealth, are made possible by seeing oneself and others in the context of living before God.

2

"WE ARE NOT OUR OWN"

Christian Freedom in Calvin's Humane Economy

HAVING EXPLORED SOME OF Calvin's teachings on human nature and freedom, it is time to see how these come together to shape his vision for an economy (and an economics) that does justice to a true description of the human person. While Calvin is far from offering a scientific theory or model that holds for all places and times, he is nevertheless clear that the *telos* of all humankind is regeneration, i.e., "that Christ should reform us to God's image" (I.xv.4). For Calvin, human economic life is not subject to unique laws but is an aspect of human life generally; we can therefore infer that *the goal of economics is the same as the goal of all theological ethics*. A vision for a distinctively Christian economy can be effectively summed up in the following well-loved and well-worn passage from Calvin's *Institutes*:

> We are not our own: let not our reason nor our will, therefore, sway our plans and deeds. We are not our own: let us therefore not set it as our goal to seek what is expedient for us according to the flesh. We are not our own: in so far as we can, let us therefore forget ourselves and all that is ours.
>
> Conversely, we are God's: let us therefore live for him and die for him. We are God's: let his wisdom and will therefore rule all our actions. We are God's: let all the parts of our life accordingly

32

strive toward him as our only lawful goal. *O, how much has that man profited who, having been taught that he is not his own, has taken away dominion and rules from his own reason that he may yield it to God!* (III.vii.1; emphasis added)

Here is the clearest possible rejection of any ethics or economics in which rational self-interest is the determinative principle. It is true that Calvin does indeed allow for a modicum of self-interest in the redeemed human life, since grace-directed self-interest is not evil but is a providential gift: "whenever we are prompted to choose something [truly] to our advantage, whenever the will inclines to this, or conversely whenever our mind and heart shun anything that would otherwise be harmful—this is of the Lord's special grace" (II.iv.6). Nevertheless, after the fall into sin, natural human self-interest is hopelessly corrupt and cannot be allowed to provide the blueprint for any Christian economic model. Calvin urges Christians toward a more difficult and worthy task in economic life: loving one's neighbor as oneself.

ON THEFT

In Calvin's framework, the fact that worldly wealth is given by God offers the Christian no excuse to try to increase that wealth at all costs; nor does it guarantee the Christian any unconditional right to private property. The Christian understands herself as one of God's adopted children, and as such she is the undeserving recipient of any and all good things she possesses. Because she knows it is not truly hers, she does not consider wealth something to be grasped but rather something that must be held with a gratefully open hand toward her neighbors in need. Christian freedom does not set her free from observance of God's law—on the contrary, one's own interests and innermost thoughts are always subject to God's judgment (II.viii.49)—but freedom allows her to obey God more fully by going to the core of the law of neighbor love. Calvin's teaching on theft, which Allen Verhey explores in an excellent article on the eighth commandment, offers us one window into his economic approach. God's command not to steal must be read within the context of "the mercies of God" who is "the fountain of every good" (I.ii.1). The prohibition against theft is more precisely a prohibition against judging the workings of Providence—that is, taking away what God has willed to give another person. But far from being a license for those with possessions to hoard and increase them and thus fortify the status quo (as Verhey notes has unfortunately been the common practice among wealthy Calvinists in need of justification for their prosperity[1]), real gratitude moves Christians to become "living sacrifices" to God. In this way, Christians freely do even *more* than human law requires, since human laws often reflect more closely the frailties of fallen humans than the laws of God's creation. Christians always conduct themselves as if God were watching.

Calvin's claim that wealth is given by God is hardly surprising, given his doctrine of Providence and concomitant rejection of any belief in fortune or fate (II.viii.45). Sometimes the wicked prosper because God wills for them to be turned away from sin and toward God's mercy and goodness—a lesson that is difficult to learn when one is destitute. At the same time, God's elect sometimes suffer because God wills to teach them deeper humility and total dependence on God—lessons that are difficult to learn with a full belly, a warm coat, and a comfortable bed. The call to all Christians is the same, regardless of situation in life:

> [H]e who is ashamed of mean clothing will boast of costly cloth-ing; he who, not content with a slender meal, is troubled by the desire for a more elegant one, will also intemperately abuse those elegances if they fall to his lot. He who will bear reluctantly, and with a troubled mind, his deprivation and humble condition if he be advanced to honors will by no means abstain from arrogance. To this end, then, let all those for whom the pursuit of piety is not a pretense strive to learn . . . how to be filled and to hunger, to abound and to suffer want (Phil. 4:12). (III.x.5)

It is not for humans to judge God's mysterious actions, since human reason is too flawed to understand them. True faith (or piety) consists of knowing God as good, even when material evidence apparently speaks otherwise. Thus, to steal is to seek to override God's generosity, which is loaned to elect and reprobate alike. All earthly things "were so given to us by the kindness of God, and so destined for our benefit, that they are, as it were, entrusted to us, and we must one day render account of them" (III.x.5).

1. He writes, "Let's be honest. . . . Calvinists have accommodated themselves to an economic culture that insists that more is better, that equates wealth with virtue and poverty with vice, that delights in conspicuous consumption, and that anxiously strives to secure its future by its possessions." Verhey, "Calvin and the 'Stewardship of Love,'" 157–58.

But "stealing" is not only that kind of unlawful taking that is recognized and punished by earthly authorities. Because many in his audience might be quick to think themselves innocent of stealing, Calvin quickly glosses over the most obvious kinds of theft—robbery, embezzlement, and the like—and spends his time on those types of stealing which are less clear-cut to fallen human reason (and are therefore much more prevalent). He writes,

> Let us remember that all those arts whereby we acquire the possessions and money of our neighbors . . . are to be considered as thefts. Although such possessions may be acquired in a court action, yet God does not judge otherwise. For he sees the intricate deceptions . . . the hard and inhuman laws with which the more powerful oppresses and crushes the weaker person. (II.viii.45)

The weight of this warning is not laid upon those who might resort to stealing bread for their hungry children, or even for themselves.[2] Instead, Calvin writes to those who are especially gifted at acquiring worldly goods through "inhuman" (though technically lawful) means, or who might be tempted by greed to increase their already great possessions.[3] He also criticizes those with a less-than-sufficient Protestant work ethic, who might feel justified in receiving payment for services they have not actually rendered.

The eighth commandment, in short, illustrates the kind of freedom Christians can enjoy within an economic community: freedom to work, freedom to live honestly and justly, freedom to possess that which is not sought for selfish gain or taken from one's neighbors unlovingly and unjustly. Calvin summarizes the criteria for authentic economic obedience as:

> if, content with our lot, we are zealous to make only honest and lawful gain; if we do not seek to become wealthy through injustice, nor attempt to deprive our neighbor of his goods to increase

2. Thomas Aquinas defended such taking: "In cases of need all things are common property, so that there would seem to be no sin in taking another's property, for need has made it common. . . . It is not theft, properly speaking, to take secretly and use another's property in a case of extreme need: because that which he takes for the support of his life becomes his own property by reason of that need." Thomas Aquinas, *Summa*, II-II, Q.66.7.

3. Valeri writes, "Part of the viciousness of usury was its multiplicity of forms"; it morphs easily into theft, especially when legalized. Valeri, "Religion, Discipline, and Economy," 130.

our own; if we do not strive to heap up riches cruelly wrung from the blood of others; if we do not madly scrape together from everywhere, by fair means or foul, whatever will feed our avarice or satisfy our prodigality. (II.viii.46)

Although he certainly does not theorize any kind of class warfare (since all are equal bearers of God's image), Calvin anticipates Marx's critique of the workings of the market in which the benefits of productivity can—and, because of sin, most likely will—be "cruelly wrung" and unjustly redistributed away from those who actually produce goods, or who can least afford to lose wealth. Calvin's rhetoric reflects a privileged socio-economic status in that he mainly writes not for those on the margins, but to those with wealth and money (among them King Francis), to discourage them from abusing their power. Nevertheless, the beginnings of solidarity with the poor are visible in Calvin's teaching on theft, as in his broader theology, particularly in his constant recall of the knowledge of God that makes equal siblings out of all humankind.

ON USURY

Calvin's vision for a theft-free economy is not original; as one might expect, it put him squarely in the mainstream of Christian tradition up till his time. But Weber, as we recall, argued that Calvin took center stage in the development of early capitalism, in part because of his notable break from Christian tradition with regard to usury.[4] Luther did not make this move; although he made an important theological shift with regard to vocation, his medieval sensibilities (and German hatred of Italian bankers) made him ultimately unwilling to follow his theology of liberty to its inevitable economic conclusions.[5] Calvin, on the other hand, took a bold step into the modern era, removing usury's scarlet letter and bringing it out into the theological mainstream, thus making him what one author exuberantly, if exaggeratedly, calls "the founder of Western-style

---

4. See Calvin, *De Usuris*, a reply to Sachinus's letter of inquiry. See also "De Usuris Responsum."

5. Regarding Luther's hatred of bankers, Forell, *Faith Active in Love*, 29, writes, "It is worthy of note that the Pope who clashed with Luther was a Medici banker and that the indulgence salesmen were always accompanied by a representative of the Fugger banking house." For more about the medieval character of Luther's economic sensibilities, see Langholm, "Martin Luther's Doctrine on Trade and Price."

capitalism."[6] (This can be an illustration of either his triumph or his failure, depending on one's point of view.)

Despite scholastic prejudice and the interdict of canon law, the lending of money at interest had been part of the economic and social mainstream of medieval and early modern Europe, long before Calvin's time; but in spite of its widespread use the Catholic Church continued to condemn it publicly.[7] What this means is that Calvin's unique contribution was not the legalization of usury, but rather a serious and yet common-sense theological treatment of it. On this topic, Calvin sought to walk the now-familiar tightrope between Christian freedom and unrestricted license. In a letter responding to an acquaintance's inquiry, he wrote:

> I have learned by the example of others with how great danger this matter is attended. For if all usury is condemned, tighter fetters are imposed on the conscience than the Lord himself would wish. Or if you yield in the least, with that pretext very many will at once seize upon unlicensed freedom, which can then be restrained by no moderation or restriction.[8]

Calvin's concern, as always, was to allow for Christians to make use of their liberty without deteriorating into the excesses so commonly found among free people.

At issue was a Scripture passage in which Jesus says, "If you lend to those from whom you hope to receive, what credit is that to you?"[9] and which had traditionally been interpreted by Christians to mean that lending was forbidden outright. Also at issue were certain Old Testament prohibitions against usury. Calvin, however, was not a biblical literalist; he recognized that economic context was relevant to the interpretation of Scripture, since political orders are merely provisional or external, and as such are subject to change as concrete situations change.[10] While the Mosaic prohibitions may have made sense in the context of ancient

---

6. Tiemstra, "Financial Globalization and Crony Capitalism," 30. He goes on to say that Calvin's main contribution was the idea that, "in economic life, everyone should be treated equally"; Christians, unlike the ancient Hebrews, did not create separate rules for their internal and external economic dealings.

7. According to historian Herbert Lüthy, the bishop of Geneva had made money-lending legal there two centuries before Calvin. Lüthy, *From Calvin to Rousseau*, 41–42.

8. Calvin, "De Usuris Responsum," 32.

9. Luke 6:34.

10. Sauer, *Faithful Ethics According to John Calvin*, 205.

Israel, Calvin (as one biographer puts it) "refuses to let certain injunctions relating to a primitive Jewish agrarian society have binding force upon a progressive modern urban society, such as sixteenth-century Geneva."[11] Calvin maintained that nowhere in scripture does Jesus explicitly *ban* the taking of interest, thus leaving the question open for free Christian consciences to discern. He believed that the economic relations in Geneva in his time, which depended on the free circulation of money for the purpose of maintaining good standards of living, allowed for some morally permissible changes to the teaching.[12]

He ultimately identified usury as a matter of indifference, in that it was an external practice that had evolved as European economies were evolving from rural to urban. Of particular interest to Calvin was Geneva's economy, which was experiencing a boom in the mid-1550s due in part to unrest elsewhere. Valeri writes that the "influx of foreign merchants with ties across Europe, professionals such as lawyers and notaries, textile manufacturers, printers, and nonagricultural laborers accelerated the rate of Geneva's commercialization."[13] Calvin understood that money in this new atmosphere had become a kind of capital, just as if it were land or livestock, the borrowing of which presented a legitimate claim on some payment for use that had been foregone for a time. Thus, he decided, even as God frees rural Christians from laws regarding which crops they can grow in their fields, so urban Christians are also free to invest their money as stewards of that which God has entrusted to them.

But at the same time, Calvin also sees usury's great potential for deterioration into sins like exploitation, cruelty, and violence toward neighbors, and thus guards carefully against these. Valeri notes that Calvin saw the dealings of the marketplace as a great threat to Christian truthfulness, in that it promoted lies in the "economic" sphere that inevitably bled into the life of the community and the church.[14] His was not an unqualified approval. "I do not consider that usury is wholly forbidden among us," he wrote, "except it be repugnant to justice and charity."[15] Seeking to cut to the heart of the matter, Calvin focused on what he believed to be the

11. McGrath, *Life of John Calvin*, 231.

12. Haas, *Concept of Equity in Calvin's Ethics*, 120.

13. Valeri, "Religion, Discipline, and Economy," 130.

14. Ibid., 132–33.

15. Harkness, *John Calvin*, 206 (from *De Usuris*, OC xii 210).

normative *intention* of the original biblical prohibition, namely love and equity among God's people. He argued that the main reason usury was usually so harmful was that, because it was illegal, undisciplined usurers connived to practice it by stealth.[16] He believed that if the underlying principle of neighbor love were applied to the modern practice of charging interest, it could be redeemed and made constructive for the community. In this, Calvin exhibits a conviction that (as Sauer explains), "right action is a matter of the heart rather than the mind."[17] Usury, when executed with right intentions, was a potentially righteous thing for Christians to engage in. While laws governing external conduct generally prove easier to enforce than freedom of inward souls, Calvin does not shy away from defending human freedom even when it puts him in the difficult position of having to offer a slippery definition of what determines loving and just conduct for Christians.

At the same time, Calvin was well aware that humans tend toward greed and need the guidance of good laws, and moreover that it was normally society's most vulnerable members who suffered from the unscrupulous practice of lending at interest.[18] As Hans Esser summarizes, the question is particularly difficult: "[O]n the one hand a total ban on interest would mean to bind people's conscience, which is not done by God. But on the other hand even the smallest concession could lead to a lack of restraint which needs restrictions."[19] So although Calvin interprets away the necessity of this commandment for Christians, it is important to note that he also lays down principles to limit usury according to the law of love, which he sees as the true measure of freedom. Among the regulations he attaches to the charging of interest are a prohibition against Christians doing so professionally; the requirement not to take interest from the poor; the need for agreements to adhere to the golden rule of Christ; and the recognition that *God's* word—not human law—is the final criterion for establishing the interest rate.[20] Christian freedom

16. Valeri, "Religion, Discipline, and Economy," 138 (from OC 24:681–83; 31:147–48).

17. Sauer, *Faithful Ethics According to John Calvin*, 72. He goes on to acknowledge the difficult position Calvin puts himself in by refusing to succumb to literalism or legalism: "But once this move [toward rightness of the heart] is made, Calvin is faced with the problem of grounding a fundamental confidence for knowing what actions may or may not be good."

18. See Keesecker, "Law in John Calvin's Ethics," 36.

19. Esser, "Contemporary Relevance of Calvin's Social Ethics," 170.

20. Ibid., 171.

from legalism never includes freedom from living in the sight of God. This means Christians are expected to go above and beyond the minimal justice of political and economic policies and must consider God's will in each case of *adiaphora*.

Not one to leave things to chance, Calvin instituted a communal insurance policy against those who might forget they were living in God's sight. He made use of both the pulpit and the government for this purpose, insisting that "vices must not be permitted in a people who make a Christian confession," and explicitly forbidding anyone in Geneva to keep silent when observing an economic sin in one of her neighbors.[21] In his survey of Genevan Consistory hearings in 1557, Mark Valeri demonstrates the importance the authorities placed on commercial practices in the community, where one in twenty criminal cases had something to do with "fraud, usury, price gouging, or hoarding."[22] The church governors' boldness in intruding on individual money matters represents a major cultural discrepancy between sixteenth-century Genevans and twenty-first-century American Christians, who tend to consider money matters (other than outright theft) "private." In Calvin's Geneva, there was virtually no economic privacy. Instead, Calvin "insisted that Genevans identify themselves as members of the body social"—the paradigm which, Valeri argues, informed Calvin's economic policy.[23] Christian freedom is never without form—not even in a free market—but is distinctively shaped and bounded by the shared body of which each person is but one of many gratefully grafted-in limbs.

ON LUXURY

If cynical readers could easily enough interpret Calvin's teaching on theft as a time-tested way of protecting the property of the wealthy, or interpret his teaching on usury as a way of boosting the economic power of Geneva, an unpublished "forgotten fragment of Calvin" reiterates his interest in economic justice and care for the poor. One of Calvin's only overtly negative statements about Christians and wealth, *De luxu* (On

---

21. McKee, *John Calvin*, 263. See also Battles, "Against Luxury and License in Geneva," 186: ". . . certain persons of good life . . . if they see any vice worthy of note to find fault with in any person, that they communicate about it with some of the ministers . . . "

22. Valeri, "Religion, Discipline, and Economy," 128.

23. Ibid., 123.

luxury), demonstrates his constant concern for even the freest person to seek moderation and temperance in the enjoyment of earthly life.[24] In this fragment, Calvin emphasizes the need for self-denial more heavily than Christian freedom, an emphasis that seems to arise in response to the particular audience he has in mind. If the quotation in the introduction to chapter 1 seems to be written to those Christians whose consciences are constantly worrying that they are too comfortable, *De luxu* is written for wealthy people with no such scruples, whose consumption of worldly goods Calvin deems an abuse of Christian freedom. He condemns those Christians who "rest their case [for excessive luxury] on Joseph's many-colored cloak and Rebecca's earrings and bracelets," making biblical excuses for themselves to own sumptuous garments and jewelry.[25] Such are the signs of people who have not yet internalized the gospel of Christ. "They fancy such diaphanous garb as no passerby can overlook," he writes; "We are worse than children delighted with cheap necklaces; we go in for expensive absurdities."[26] Forgetting to pursue the regeneration of their souls, they squander their attention on fleeting comforts of the body in a manner incompatible with their true humanity. "Be ashamed," he writes, "when you lavish great care on your comeliness—of being surpassed by dumb animals, lest your dress be marked by a mere show of thrift."[27]

Talk of Christian freedom is notably lacking in this fragment, and he scoffs at those who argue that their consumption is simply in accordance with local custom, an external matter of indifference. Calvin exhibits no patience or sympathy for the fashionable people he derides. His concern here is not so much the frivolity of a few people privately harming their own souls with their possessions, but the damage he sees them doing to others and the greater community through their self-love. He observes that those who spend money on themselves often do so to the detriment of others; they "treat all men stingily to keep something

---

24. Battles, "On Luxury and License in Geneva," 182–202. He dates the fragment around 1546–1547. His thought here may partially be traced to the classical Stoic influences in Calvin's thought, though he was always careful to critique their resignation to fate (I.xvi.8).

25. Ibid., 192.

26. Ibid., 193.

27. Ibid.

to be liberal with—or rather, prodigal—toward themselves."[28] This, he fears, creates a vicious cycle, an entire culture in which each person must become ever stingier toward others in order to keep up with the latest luxuries. Genevan Christians "push one another into vices," he complained, "and though we are the cause of one another's wicked ways, we put forward as an excuse custom and the example of the crowd."[29] Even funerals, in Calvin's mind, had become vain and pompous ceremonies—the ultimate occasion for what Thorstein Veblen dubbed "conspicuous consumption"—in which riches are showered upon the deceased who cannot even appreciate them, all for reasons of "invidious distinction."[30]

This type of invidious distinction was to have no place in Calvin's city on a hill. "[O]n the contrary," he recommended in the *Institutes*, Christians "with unflagging effort of mind . . . [must] insist upon cutting off all show of superfluous wealth . . . and diligently . . . guard against turning [those gifts which God intended as] helps into hindrances" (III.x.4). Thus, in spite of being a champion of human freedom, Calvin still feels compelled to make it extremely clear that not all economic behaviors—however culturally normal—are simple matters of indifference. He strongly condemns the extravagant balls, excessive feasts, and showy adornment of wealthy Genevans, because of his awareness that "the vices of individuals breed public error" just as "public error breeds the vices of individuals."[31] Moreover, such expenditures constituted a very real version of theft, in that they robbed others of the basic things they needed to live humanely. "Let no one say: I dress harmlessly, &c. All men bear the blood of the poor . . . I will say your whole body has become infected because it is decked in such clothing."[32] In a bizarre twist at the end, he even links Geneva's love of luxury to a hatred of children (a connection that, interestingly enough, anticipates the economic thought of Gary Becker that we will encounter in chapter 4).[33]

28. Ibid.

29. Ibid.

30. Veblen, *Theory of the Leisure Class*, 26 (invidious distinction), 68 (conspicuous consumption).

31. Battles, "On Luxury and License in Geneva," 194.

32. Ibid.

33. "Our native land's hatred of offspring is to be censured." Ibid., 195. While a declining birth rate was a relatively new feature in the sixteenth century, in the twenty-first century it seems almost laughable *not* to connect love of luxury with lessened desire for children, since this "economic way of looking at behavior" is fairly commonplace; we

It is perhaps not so surprising that these fragments remained unpublished. His anti-luxury impulse seems to have met with a competing impulse of protecting Christian freedom, including freedom in economic matters. In spite of his youthful horror at the frivolous love of earthly goods he sees in his society, Calvin's commitment to Christian freedom with regard to money perhaps caused him to censor the overwhelmingly guilt-inducing and anti-wealth tone of the document. (Here one might pause to reflect back on Tawney's ultimately unanswerable question as to whether Calvin's theology was influencing his economics or vice versa.) On the other hand, Calvin still understood that freedom required a well-designed infrastructure, and he thought it "quite proper for the government and the church to intervene into labor disputes" and other economic matters.[34]

Calvin never forgot the "fallen" part of his theological anthropology, and human sinfulness—particularly the excess of self-interest—always needed to be factored in. In his *Institutes* he offers a more moderate version of the message in *De luxu*:

> There is almost no one whose resources permit him to be extravagant who does not delight in lavish and ostentatious banquets, bodily apparel, and domestic architecture; who does not wish to outstrip his neighbors in all sorts of elegance; who does not wonderfully flatter himself in his opulence. And all these things are defended under the pretext of Christian freedom. They say that these are things indifferent. I admit it, provided they are used indifferently. But when they are coveted too greedily, when they are proudly boasted of, when they are lavishly squandered, things that were of themselves otherwise lawful are certainly defiled by these vices. (III.xix.9)

Calvin nowhere condemns the actual *possession* of wealth or earthly goods, but reserves his condemnation for those who practice conspicuous consumption, immoderately and with pride drawing attention to themselves and their wealth; who seek more than their share of comfort, take more than they need, and deny others what is duly theirs; and who ignore their interconnection with the poor, who bear the image of God and by whose blood he says their luxuries are purchased. He displays

---

will address this again in chapter 5 with regard to Gary Becker. See also Blanchard, "Gift of Contraception."

34. Valeri, "Religion, Discipline, and Economy," 140.

in this text the glimmerings of a liberationist consciousness of how the wealth of the rich is often implicated in the poverty of the poor. Rather than accepting the divide between rich and poor as a fact of modern Christian life, he prescribed the withholding of the Lord's Supper as discipline for economic crimes that offended Christ's body.[35]

We must conclude that Calvin's actual writings reveal little of the "Protestant ethic" that Weber so memorably connected to the capitalist spirit. Weber's emphasis on Calvinists' hard work and the acquisition of wealth as a means of attaining assurance of election is at best an interpretive departure from Calvin's own teaching, and at worst entirely contrary to it.[36] As an alternative to Weber's interpretation of events, McGrath proposes that Calvinism did not so much *create* the atmosphere for capitalism as it did *appeal* to the same sensibilities that also attracted the rising middle classes to capitalism. Those already disposed toward capitalism may have embraced the Reformation as a way of achieving their own political and economic ends.[37] Calvin himself was aware that Geneva's viability as an independent city relied on its economic independence, and though he did not set out to create radical economic reforms he did nothing to hinder the economic forces already at work there.[38] He was, according to McGrath, "perfectly aware of the financial realities at Geneva, and their implications. Although he does not develop an 'economic theory' in any sense of the term, he appears to have been fully cognizant of the basic principles of capital. The productive nature of both capital and human work is fully recognized."[39] He was not a whole-hearted free marketeer (Valeri notes, for example, that "the innovations of commerce irked Calvin because they portended the individual cut loose" from the community); but he was willing to make some compromises to accommodate the material realities of his context.[40]

In sum, a Calvinist economy is based on freedom, but a freedom that is defined by true human nature, the *telos* of which is to love God

35. Ibid., 141.

36. See Harkness, *John Calvin,* 183, and Wendel, *Calvin,* 277, for more on the question of how "Calvinist" Calvin actually was.

37. McGrath, *Life of John Calvin,* 225.

38. Ibid., 227.

39. Ibid., 231.

40. Valeri notes that Geneva was flooded with refugees (to the tune of a nearly 75 percent population increase during Calvin's time there), which demanded radical changes to the small city's economy. Valeri, "Religion, Discipline, and Economy," 127.

and love one's neighbors as oneself. This means theft is prohibited, of course, but Calvin expands his definition of theft to include other practices that are lawful in the world's eyes—such as lending money to the poor at high rates of interest, conspicuous consumption, unjust wages and prices, unjust laws, and the infinite escalation of desire for luxury. Though these practices may be legal or customary, they are not mere matters of indifference; they affect negatively one's own soul and the souls of others. While Calvin affirms the goodness of the body and the material world, he hastens to add that the love of earthly beauty must always be tempered by a greater love of God and the image of God that one finds in one's neighbors.

Moreover, Calvin was not afraid to back these teachings up with the force of punishment, executed by both earthly and heavenly authorities (in the forms of the Consistory and the church, respectively). A freedom-based economy must be framed by laws that fulfill their threefold function of exposing wrongdoing, restraining evil actions, and exhorting Christians to righteousness. Calvin's economic vision calls Christians to seek true happiness, "the happiness promised us in Christ [which] does not consist in outward advantages—such as leading a joyous and peaceful life, having rich possessions, being safe from all harm, and abounding with delights such as the flesh commonly longs after. No, our happiness belongs to the heavenly life!" (II.xv.4).

CRITIQUE OF CALVIN

One of Calvin's major failings (or limitations) is, to a certain extent, also a failing (or limitation) of this book. That is to say, he wrote from the point of view of what Americans might call "deciders"—people with options, like himself and many in his audience. His theology does not "adopt the perspective of the poor and powerless as its starting point when formulating its theology."[41] While he is clearly aware that there are low-level workers in his community (he even held early-morning Lord's Suppers so that servants could receive the elements before work), he primarily treats the economic issues that face middle-class persons. He seems to write for the rising bourgeoisie, non-aristocrats who have suddenly found themselves possessing a growing amount of worldly wealth and are in need of advice on how best to manage it. In his desire to set his

41. Rosario, "Calvin or Calvinism," 149.

theology apart from the Catholic mentality of his day, Calvin strives to help such people understand that they do not need to feel guilty for earning wealth through labor; but though they need not embrace a strict asceticism, they do need to keep their love for worldly goods in check. In order to motivate moderation in his listeners, he urges them to remember the people with fewer options than they, who might be victimized by the rapid economic changes in Geneva. He remembers the poor, certainly, but this is different than really involving the poor as interlocutors in his theology.

While we cannot (without gross anachronism) call Calvin a capitalist, it is reasonable to think that his teachings on personal piety may have contributed at least somewhat to his later association with modern capitalism. To begin with, he—like Luther, but unlike both Catholics and Radical Reformers such as the Hutterites—did not consider the renunciation of private wealth a requirement for Christian perfection. "Surely ivory and gold and riches," he taught, "are good creations of God, permitted, indeed appointed, for men's use by God's providence" (III. xix.9). Such assurances undoubtedly went far to ease the consciences of those Christians who had managed to accumulate wealth and its accoutrements, and may have also discouraged certain pious people from seeking the perfection of monastic life. Moreover, it may have inspired others to seek, again without guilt, the acquisition of such material goods, thus (from a positive point of view) "invigorating life and adding to its zest and drive."[42] At the same time such teaching, combined with his warning that all wealth was distributed according to God's justice, must also have served to create stability in the community by persuading the poorer members not to resent (or at least not to steal) the possessions of the wealthier.

In this vein, Calvin's teachings on Providence also reveal a bias toward the status quo (at least as the status quo was found in Protestant Geneva, if not in Florence or Munich). He was perfectly aware of and often bemoaned the fact that there were powerful people in his community who chose to steal from the poor (if in legally-sanctioned ways); he also instituted certain public and ecclesial disciplinary measures against such people wherever possible. Nevertheless, he avoided any radical measures of redistribution to right these wrongs, precisely because of his commitment to the freedom of individual consciences. His admonition

---

42. Leith, *Introduction to the Reformed Tradition*, 218.

to the poor to accept their lot as God's will, rather than seek restitution from (or worse yet, retribution against) the rich and powerful, betrays a point of view that seems to prioritize social and economic stability over social and economic justice.

With regard to vocation, the teachings that Calvin shared with Luther emphasized, in a manner that was new to Christian ears, that hard work even in secular situations was a spiritual activity and a way for believers to worship God concretely. He offered them "a singular consolation: that no task will be so sordid and base, provided you obey your calling in it, that it will not shine and be reckoned very precious in God's sight" (III.x.6). It was no longer only those with family money who could become rich. This new affirmation of worldly work allowed—even required—all Christians to engage in business or manual labor with their whole hearts. Harkness agrees with Weber that,

> With Luther and Calvin, *Beruf*, or vocation, came to have a religio-economic significance that it did not formerly possess, and it was a stimulus to economic progress when the distinction between the cloister and the market place, as spheres of God-serving activity, was broken down. In part, Calvin was an unwitting contributor to the undoing of that for which he labored.[43]

Meanwhile, his call for temperance and moderation with regard to the acquisition and enjoyment of worldly pleasures led to the accumulation of unspent wealth (and perhaps wealth from added interest) that left Protestants quite well off financially. Calvin's middle way thus fosters a church of hard-working, frugal, and prudent Christians who eventually, and inevitably, become wealthy. It is clear to most Calvin scholars, however, that this was an unintended side-effect of the Calvinist "work ethic," which was originally intended as a means to creating justice, sobriety, moderation, and true worship of God among believers.[44]

Calvin's teaching on wealth bears the mark of paradox, and it seems largely connected to the way he perceives his audience.[45] While he—in order to comfort those with scrupulous and guilty consciences (and to

---

43. Harkness, *Calvin*, 191.

44. McGrath, *Life of John Calvin*, 234.

45. Calvin's instructions for "The visiting of the sick," for example, demonstrate his keen attention to the mindset of his hearer, even upon her deathbed. One who is contrite receives a message of comfort; while one not sufficiently mournful over her sins receives a reminder of God's justice. McKee, *John Calvin*, 292–93.

scold the monks)—insists that wealth and its accompanying benefits are from God and therefore can be "very good," he also stresses the dangers and temptations for the wealthy person who does not gratefully keep her eyes ever on God. As with most religious teachings, the farther Calvinist theology moved from its source the more it became distorted. "It would be a mistake," writes George Thomas,

> to speak of Calvin or his early followers as defenders of economic individualism in the modern sense. Calvin attempted to prevent Genevan merchants from securing monopolies on essential products and selling them at unjust prices. In the same spirit . . . other Puritan writers attacked excessive interest on loans, insisted upon just prices, and stressed the principle of stewardship in the use of wealth.[46]

But while Calvin himself may have had an appreciation for the delicate balance between wealth and self-limitation, some Calvinists were not so balanced. Over time, the self-interested motivations behind certain theological interpretations and economic practices came to be seen as deserving of free rein in the marketplace. Interest rates once seen as "excessive" evolved over time into normal and just; prices once viewed in the public eye as extortionate become a fact of life.

Calvin is not entirely to blame for the ways in which Calvinism evolved alongside capitalism. He could not have predicted the Industrial Revolution or the rise of the United States as an economic and military superpower; had he done so his teachings would likely have looked different. But if Calvinists had actually heeded Calvin's words against exploitation and greed, argues one writer:

> Calvinism might have been a deterrent, rather than a promoter, of the capitalistic spirit. His injunctions to industry, frugality and docility were heeded; his warnings against avarice were forgotten. The explanation lies in the almost irresistible power of economic forces and in the tendencies of human nature. Competition, acquisitiveness, and social conservatism reinforced the one set of teachings, nullified the other.[47]

46. Thomas, *Christian Ethics*, 309. Stephen Berry explores in depth one example of Calvin's monopoly-busting: he insisted on spreading around the printing of his many writings among the various presses in Geneva, so as to assure that all had enough work to do. Berry, "Jean Cauvin."

47. Neill, *Makers of the Modern Mind*, 43.

But by the same token, it was the lack of consciousness about the first-person nature of his theology that allowed such ready distortion of his teachings. Again, Calvin could not have predicted post-modernism, but his ethics suffer from the fact that he assumed he could understand all things theological from his own limited point of view (as a Christian with some wealth in a city of rising economic prominence). His insistence on the goodness of work and wealth, put in the hands of those who ignored his exhortations to self-limitation, sobriety, and love, may have ironically given reign to the very tendencies in human nature that he was trying to root out. As he himself argued, though "men may with a clear conscience cleanly use God's gifts" when desire is controlled, it is also to be expected that, "should this moderation be lacking, even base and common pleasures are too much" (III.xix.9).

Calvin's interest in freedom does not automatically make him an early liberation theologian. Calvin himself never experienced economic oppression (though he knew something of the life of persecution and exile), and his theological interest in freedom did not lead him to a political interest in freeing economically oppressed people from systemic evils. While he encouraged a certain amount of *ecclesiastical* disobedience, the extent of his *social* critique seems to be to shame the rich when they live too luxuriously while encouraging the poor to be patient. Nevertheless, I see John Calvin as an important conversation partner for Americans seeking a just economy. This is in part because Americans—shaped as we have been by Puritan forebears—can scarcely understand our own history without understanding something of Calvinist thought. Moreover many of us (including, I would guess, most readers of this book) are, like Calvin, in positions of at least some degree of choice. Compared to the rest of the world's population, we are extremely privileged.

I also believe it is possible, as some have already done, to push Calvinist thought into a more critical, world-transforming social stance.[48] (And in fact, as one author has persuasively argued, "transformation" may ultimately be a more fruitful theological model for economic justice in the twenty-first century than "liberation," in that transformation includes everyone as an active participant, rather than some as victims who wait passively for rescue.[49]) Calvin's view that all people are made in

48. See especially Bieler, *La Pensée Économique Et Sociale De Calvin*; Verhey, "Calvin and the 'Stewardship of Love'"; and Waterman, "Economics as Theology."

49. Heslam, "Role of Business," 166. I also see Muhammad Yunus's "social business"

one image and therefore share equal footing means that the poor have a legitimate claim on the wealth of the rich, whose goods are merely on loan from the one true owner of all things. It is not that all have equal "rights" or are equally deserving of earthly wealth; it is rather that all are equally *undeserving*, equally indebted to God's grace. An economic system based solely on notions of worthiness or just deserts tells only a partial truth, neglecting the entire narrative of human history to the detriment of all. Americans, for the most part, have at least some power to make choices about how and where we will live, work, and consume. In each of the decisions we make, Calvin calls us to be mindful of our underlying choices to acknowledge or ignore our true identities, and to act in greater or lesser accord with human nature—both our own and our neighbors'.

CONCLUSION: THE PARADOX OF CHRISTIAN ECONOMIC FREEDOM

The primary goal of this chapter has been to connect Calvin's teachings on human nature and Christian freedom with his teachings on wealth, ownership, work, and poverty. While this cannot properly be called "economics," the fact that he shares modern economists' interest in human liberty as it intersects earthly, political matters invites comparison with the economists we will approach in later chapters, most of whom also associate sound economics with freedom (mainly from what they see as governmental meddling). As a pre-modern theologian—not to mention a political leader who sought to re-shape the world according to Christian norms—Calvin did not consider economic matters as somehow lying outside of his purview.[50] He was bold, for example, both to affirm usury in moderation and to insist that immoderate usury be punished. This was because he did not see usury as an economic abstraction or a simple matter of market forces, but as part of a larger narrative in which God creates good things, distributes them according to justice

---

model as an act of transformation rather than liberation, in that the poor of Bangladesh are actively transforming their own lives through business; Grameen Bank, which makes loans to the poor, is not a charity but a self-sustaining business.

50. Calvin "and his colleagues continued to exercise their prerogative of religious intervention into the economy while they demanded that the government do likewise. The Consistory often discovered that economic concerns could not be separated from other spheres of moral activity." Valeri, "Religion, Discipline, and Economy," 131.

and grace, and calls all people to distribute them further according to the laws of love. In Calvin's imagination, one does not first participate in the impersonal "worldly" market and then later give "other-worldly" alms; rather one's behavior in the market is itself a heavenly vocation, an expression of grateful service to God.

Calvin offers a description of freedom that, to a certain extent, is common sense: freedom from guilt, freedom from sin, freedom from deterministic fate. But other aspects of Calvin's freedom are highly paradoxical: freedom to obey God, freedom to serve one's neighbors, freedom to love, and strangely enough, freedom from the horrors of unchecked self-interest. This notion entails an underlying theological anthropology that sees humans as God's children—created good, fallen into sin, and living in various stages of redemption. Although modern Americans might agree with Calvin that freedom is a non-negotiable characteristic of redeemed human life, it must be said that his ideas were of a most unmodern, un-economic, and un-American flavor. He was not speaking of a freedom based on resignation to human sin (i.e., humans are selfish, this can't be changed, so the competitive market is the best we can do). He was also not speaking of a merely spiritual or inward freedom that bears no outward signs in a person's life. He was speaking of a concrete, bodily, and earthly freedom, entirely and peculiarly shaped by the fundamental acknowledgement that all good things come from God. Any human freedom that did not bear this particular shape would not be freedom at all; it would be slavery of a most deceptive kind, particularly seductive to corrupted human reason.

Knowing oneself as a free child of God also relativizes any concept of "personal" vocation or "private" property; such terms may be useful for the sake of order, but must be understood as merely provisional. One's vocation is not a simple matter of personal preference but is about using the gifts God has given in such a way as to be helpful to one's neighbors, all of whom share the image of God.[51] Not all vocations are created equal—the burden of proof is on the usurer (for example) to demonstrate that her calling is actually aiding, rather than exploiting, the neediest in

---

51. In a similar vein, Meeks writes that economy is about the "public household," not just the market. "Economy should serve democratic community, which in turn serves the creation of conditions of human beings finding their calling." While he adds democracy as a mediator, the ultimate goal he sees for humane economics is for humans to be free to answer God's call. Meeks, *God the Economist*, 181.

her community. And the wealth one earns through her labors—whether as a usurer, farmer, or pin factory worker—is not, properly understood, one's *own* wealth (nor even truly "earned") but rather God's, given on loan to humans in order to allow them to help their neighbors. Human "ownership" is better understood as stewardship. One is indeed free to use external gifts such as money "indifferently," but its use ceases to be indifferent when one begins to believe it is rightfully hers. For this reason, Calvin reminds us, true freedom is intertwined with self-denial and love of neighbors (all of them), without which a person is not free but rather still enslaved by the illusion of autonomy and control.

The differences in the way theologians and economists talk about human beings is not merely semantic or abstract, and a Calvinist vision of freedom has genuine repercussions. The decision to aspire to a community of mutual helpfulness, rather than to a symbiotic collection of viciously self-interested individuals, cannot help but have normative and concrete consequences. As we will see in the next chapter, Adam Smith shared Calvin's understanding that, in order to be fruitful, the economic freedom to make decisions must take place within a community established on the rule of neighbor-love. But later economists would choose to untie freedom from its moorings in fellow-feeling, making the power of individual choice the one and only rule of human life. Calvin's teachings on freedom and economics act as a direct critique on the assumptions of rational-choice-based theories, casting radical doubt on its lack of (explicit) normative goods. Moreover, Calvin's theology requires us to re-think what we mean when we speak of a "Protestant work ethic." At least according to Calvin, this does not involve a workaholic lifestyle of earning and hoarding, motivated by the fear of hellfire. Nor does it involve a typically American conviction that everyone must pull herself up by her bootstraps (and a corresponding sense of self-satisfaction for those who believe themselves to have done so). Rather, a truly Protestant ethic is one of liberation and transformation, built on a freely-chosen commitment to serve one's neighbors through one's vocation, motivated by both gratitude toward God and the recognition of God's image in the neighbor. A Christian is one who has been "freed" by Christ—not only to *enjoy* the good gifts of creation, but also to *share* them with others.

The approach I have highlighted so far might be called Calvin's "microeconomics"—that is, it deals with economics at the level of individual actors and small communities, rather than at a national or international level. I have argued that a humane economy, according to a Protestant ethic, is one that gives individuals freedom from externally-imposed authority, but that this freedom is limited by the commands to love God and neighbor—laws which, over time, become so internalized that one obeys them freely. It is a paradoxical principle of obedient freedom, or free obedience. If capitalism is seen as a system demanding freedom for the self-serving economic individual who must exploit her neighbors and the earth as far as her power allows, the Protestant ethic would have little truck with such a model. I now want to show, however, that this rigid model of individualistic capitalism is not the only option, simply because a few self-appointed spokespersons act as if it is. The possibility of more fruitful theological treatments of capitalism comes from looking beyond these to the vast number of voices in economics that—even while they allow for self-interested decision-making—locate themselves within a more moderate, mindful, and humane tradition.

3

LOVE YOURSELF AS YOUR
NEIGHBOR LOVES YOU

Adam Smith and Freedom for Sympathy

Systematic theologians like John Calvin usually take pains to make their theological anthropology fairly obvious; indeed, Calvin dedicated the entire first quarter of his *Institutes* to questions about who the human being is. And as we have seen, once we understand his beliefs about human nature, it becomes quite easy to find the connections between these and his understanding of human freedom in an economic sense. But it is not only theologians who make conceptual connections between anthropology and freedom. Economists do it too, although they are not necessarily as explicit about it as Calvin was. Adam Smith, however, is one economic thinker who deliberately spent time trying to understand the nature of human individuals and human communities, and his thought therefore lends itself well to our exegesis. Moreover, because he is generally (though not unanimously) considered the father of economic science, reading Smith carefully will help us to better understand the anthropological assumptions behind the views of later economists who see themselves as part of Smith's tradition.

In this chapter we will explore who the human being is that underlies Adam Smith's economic inquiry, what kind of freedom is necessary for this human being to fulfill her calling as a human, and what kind of economic system most successfully builds upon this human being and her freedom. Like Calvin, Smith gave freedom a central place in his economics; and like Calvin, Smith often plays the role of villain in Christian economic ethics. But Smith's view of human freedom, while not explicitly theological, was deeply and deliberately moral.[1]

Economics, at least in its beginnings, was not an attempt to leave ethics behind in favor of utilitarian calculus and was far from being antithetical to a Christian vision for a humane society.[2] Smith's descriptions of human nature and freedom, and consequently his vision for a humane economy, are much closer to Calvin's descriptions and vision than we might expect. This is not a coincidence because, like Calvin, Smith had an interest in liberating human beings from oppressive forces so that they (or at least more of them) could lead fully human lives. He did indeed see self-interest as a constructive force in human society, particularly with regard to the organization of economic life, but *only* in so far as there is a just moral and institutional framework that prevents abuses. For this reason, as others have rightly noted, Smith may have more in common with theological ethicists than with modern economic scientists.[3]

THE "ADAM SMITH PROBLEM": *WEALTH OF NATIONS* VIS À VIS *THEORY OF MORAL SENTIMENTS*

As Max Weber observed, the habit of life cultivated by certain Calvinists —working hard at their worldly vocations, combined with not living extravagantly—led some to accumulate great wealth. While Calvin did not defend rich people's property on the basis of any virtue of their own, he taught that those who were wealthy could be free from guilt and scrupulosity regarding their possessions—to a point. As long as wealthy Christians saw their lives as an active and grateful response to God's call to serve others, especially the poor in their midst, their wealth was not necessarily a burden. It was a blessing of sorts—not a *reward* for being good, but an undeserved *gift* of concrete goods (all of which really belonged to God) that enabled them to serve their neighbors gratefully and freely in concrete ways. Nevertheless, Christians whose wealth came

1. Hill, "Hidden Theology," 293, argues that the logic of *Wealth of Nations* (WN) makes no sense without the invisible hand of (a) god.

2. See Waterman, "Beginning of 'Boundaries,'" for an argument about how Malthus, not Smith, was the original source of tension between Christianity and economics.

3. Milbank, *Theology and Social Theory*, 321.

from the exploitation of their neighbors, and even those who hoarded wealth in the face of their neighbors' need, were subject not only to God's judgment but also to ecclesiastical scrutiny.

It was within an atmosphere of an eighteenth-century "Protestant ethic" that Adam Smith spent much of his life, and it is fair to say that Calvinism left its mark on him. As a professor of moral philosophy at the University of Glasgow, he "publicly ascribed his assent to the Calvinist Confession of Faith before the Presbytery of Glasgow"; and while he was careful to keep Christian language out of his scientific writing, Smith was openly in favor of Presbyterian polity over against both "superstition" (Catholicism) and "enthusiasm" (Methodism).[4] Our primary concern here is not with any outward manifestations of his Calvinist influences; instead, we are interested in unpacking his thinking on the interrelated topics of human nature, freedom, and just economic organization. Yet we cannot remain entirely blind to Smith's historical significance. Among twenty-first-century Americans, there are both "liberals" and "conservatives" who look to Smith to support their economic positions (in much the same way as liberal and conservative Christians both look to the Jesus of the Gospels, or even to John Calvin). Who, then, is the "real" Adam Smith?

The trouble here, sometimes known as the "Adam Smith Problem," arises from the fact that Smith's two major works seem so disparate in subject and tone. Should his second and more famous book about economics, *An Inquiry into the Nature and Causes of the Wealth of Nations* (1776), be read as a continuation of his earlier book of moral philosophy, *The Theory of Moral Sentiments* (1759)? Or should *Wealth of Nations* be seen as an entirely new and separate manifesto, perhaps even a correction of his earlier thinking?[5] If the latter reading is correct, then Smith can be seen as promoting a *laissez-faire*[6] stance toward the economy that

---

4. Polanyi, *Great Transformation*, 333. Evensky also cites Polanyi, who wrote that Adam Smith "marked the close of an age which opened with the inventors of the state, Thomas More and Machievelli, Luther and Calvin." Evensky, *Adam Smith's Moral Philosophy*, 111.

5. Hill, "Hidden Theology," 21. She succinctly writes that the Adam Smith Problem "posits a fundamental moral (and hence theological) shift in outlook between the TMS and the WN." See also Polanyi, *Great Transformation*, 295.

6. The French term *laissez-faire* (literally, a command to "leave [it] to do/make") expresses the idea that leaving people and markets alone to follow their own natural inclinations is more efficient than trying to orchestrate things deliberately. The term is associated with a school of economic thinkers known as Physiocrats (including François

ostensibly does not concern itself with ethical questions about justice or virtue. But if the former is a better reading and Smith's economic teachings actually *assume* his earlier teachings about moral sentiments, then Smith can be seen as promoting an economic model that is based on socially sanctioned ethical norms supported by appropriate and just social institutions.

I tend to agree with those who present Smith as a life-long moral philosopher, who never cast aside his earlier concerns about human morality in his later pursuit of economic truths. For example, A.M.C. Waterman goes so far as to call Smith a "natural theologian" in that he sought out ecumenically accessible truths from the "Book of Nature" for both of his major works.[7] Waterman argues that Smith uses the terms "God" and "Nature" interchangeably in his writings, and behind these terms he has a particular being in mind who works to orchestrate human happiness. Smith's creator "does not merely wind up 'the great machine' and leave it ticking, as the Deists were held to have believed. She continues to act in various ways, but always wisely and well, so as to make creative use of human folly and wickedness in ways that bring good out of evil."[8] Lisa Hill also regards Smith as a theologian, one specifically interested in questions of theodicy (an attempt to explain the mysterious workings of God to humankind). She writes:

> Smith's apparently cold, utilitarian equations are deceptive; although he initially strikes us as a secular mind, his realism is better understood as a function of his sincere belief that world order is underwritten by the beneficent and guiding hand of God. In

---

Quesnay [1694–1774]) who argued (over against mercantilist thinkers like Thomas Mun [1571–1641] who sought to ensure that their nations' exports outweighed their imports) that nature was the best rule for the production and distribution of goods. But as Karl Polanyi argues, the term has undergone significant evolution since its first use: "To antedate the policy of laissez-faire . . . to the time when this catchword was first used in France in the middle of the eighteenth century would be entirely unhistorical. . . . Only by the 1820's did it stand for the three classical tenets: that labor should find its price on the market; that the creation of money should be subject to an automatic mechanism; that goods should be free to flow from country to country without hindrance or preference; in short, for a labor market, the gold standard, and free trade. . . . Not until the 1830's did economic liberalism burst forth as a crusading passion, and laissez-faire become a militant creed." Polanyi, *Great Transformation*, 135–37.

7. Waterman, "Economics as Theology," 332.

8. Ibid., 358.

this regard we might think of Smith's "invisible hand" elaboration as his particular contribution to eighteenth-century theodicy.[9]

It is thus entirely reasonable to engage Smith as if he were *primarily* a moral theologian, whose particular interest was in how understanding and morality played out in human *economic* life. As I argued in the introduction, everyone is already a theologian (even if a secular one), an ethicist (even if a bad one), and an economist (even if an ignorant one). Adam Smith is no exception.

THE HUMAN BEING IN SMITH'S MORAL PHILOSOPHY: SELFISHNESS AND SYMPATHY

"How selfish soever man may be supposed, there are evidently some principles in his nature, which interest him in the fortune of others, and render their happiness necessary to him, though he derives nothing from it except the pleasure of seeing it."[10] Smith begins his first book, *The Theory of Moral Sentiments*, with the deceptively simple idea that the human being is first and foremost a social creature whose happiness depends, at least in large part, on the happiness of others. This has everything to do with the human being's power of imagination.[11] While living in contact with other people who experience a wide variety of their own joys and sorrows, humans cannot help but put themselves in others' shoes. "As we have no immediate experience of what other men feel," he writes, "we can form no idea of the manner in which they are affected, but by conceiving what we ourselves should feel in the like situation."[12]

This ineluctable human ability to imagine changing places with our neighbors is the source of all human "sympathy" or "fellow-feeling" and genuine concern for the fates of others. On one level, Smith understands sympathy as an emotion. When a person is grieving over the death of a child, or rejoicing over winning a race, these passions are contagious; seeing someone experiencing such emotions naturally gives rise to

9. Hill, "Hidden Theology," 333.

10. Smith, *Theory of Moral Sentiments* (TMS), 9 (I.i.1.1).

11. "Imagination" is a term McCloskey appropriately emphasizes in her reading of Smith; McCloskey, "Avarice, Prudence, and the Bourgeois Virtues," 6, 35. (Smith uses it himself; see for example TMS, 317 [VII.iii.1.4].)

12. Smith, TMS, 9 (I.i.1.2).

"analogous" feelings "in the breast of every attentive spectator."[13] Humans imagine how they would feel had they lost a child or won a race, and then they emote and behave accordingly. Because humans experience both pleasure and pain through sympathizing and being sympathized with, it is a dynamic that can both draw people together and alienate them from one another. Humans are attracted to joy but repulsed by sorrow; they would rather sympathize with the happy person than with the sorrowful. Thus the joyful person always has company while the sad person is often alone.

Though he does see sympathy as an emotional capacity, on a more basic level Smith finds that sympathy is simultaneously rooted in human rationality or understanding. In an echo of Calvin's teaching that the human appetite and will follow the understanding, not *vice versa*, Smith argues that one's ability to sympathize with another's emotions comes less from any instinctual response than from one's *opinion* of the events that have brought those emotions about. "Sympathy, therefore, does not arise so much from the view of the passion, as from that of the situation which excites it."[14] It is a matter of approval or disapproval, of whether one intellectually regards another's emotions as appropriate (in both character and intensity) to the situation at hand. Is a person too happy over something we see as rather small? Is a person excessively despairing over a circumstance that seems to us to be of little or no consequence? If so, our sympathetic joy and despair will diminish accordingly. Sympathy is ultimately about approbation rather than feeling. "To approve of another man's opinions is to adopt those opinions, and to adopt them is to approve of them."[15] Not to approve of another person's feelings or opinions is not only not to adopt them for oneself, but also to withhold the precious sympathy that every human craves, being social by nature.

Because humans are not merely flies on the walls of other people's experiences, imagination and sympathy go both ways. "Nothing pleases us more than to observe in other men a fellow-feeling with all the emotions of our own breast,"[16] but there is no fate worse for a social being than a "consciousness that his misery is felt by himself only,"[17] particularly

13. Ibid., 10 (I.i.1.4).
14. Ibid., 12 (I.i.1.10).
15. Ibid., 17 (I.i.3.2).
16. Ibid., 13-14 (I.i.2.1).
17. Ibid., 60-61 (I.iii.2.10).

when one is experiencing something disagreeable. Obtaining sympathy for oneself is conditional upon others' ability to imagine one's situation and agree with one's feelings, so it is important for the person who is experiencing a joy or a sorrow to exercise her own rational imagination as well. One who desires sympathy cannot be carried away by her own emotional experience and demand that others do so as well; she must rather consider the feelings and understandings of others in order to cultivate a *mutual* sympathy. She must be able to imagine how an outside spectator of her situation would view it, and to be respectful of the human limitations of that spectator's sympathy.[18]

The cultivation of reciprocal sympathy is not merely for the purpose of preserving one's social acceptability, but has the added benefits of individual healing and wholeness. One who is bereaved, for example, in seeking to express her emotions in such a way as to enable the outside spectator to understand and agree with her, is required to view herself with a degree of equanimity, much as she would view a stranger in a similar situation. A willingness to meet the limits of others' sympathetic imaginations is a necessity if one hopes to be understood, agreed with, and approved of. Such an exercise is helpful rather than repressive; she knows that the other can never fully feel what she is feeling, so she lowers her "passion to that pitch, in which the spectators are capable of going along with" her.[19] But this dynamic of fellow-feeling, of putting oneself in another's shoes, even while asking her to put herself in one's own, actually changes the character of the bereaved's own experience. In presenting her passions to another, the person concerned actually begins to see herself as (she imagines) others see her, to view herself as a spectator would, which thereby "abates the violence" of what she was originally feeling and helps her feel calmer and more composed. Her experience of unspeakable (and, Smith notes, potentially indelicate or even indecent) grief is transformed by the encounter with others into a more comfortable "majestic sorrow" that is not only easier for others to respect, but is easier for herself to handle as well.[20]

This refining dynamic of mutual sympathy provides the foundation upon which productive social interactions are built. The "unsocial passions" (hatred, anger, and resentment) are curtailed, the "social passions"

18. Ibid., 21 (I.i.4.6).
19. Ibid., 22 (I.i.4.7).
20. Ibid., 24 (I.i.5.2).

(generosity, kindness, and love) are encouraged, and the "selfish passions" (grief and joy "conceived upon account of our own private good or bad fortune") are put into greater perspective.[21] All of these passions, though springing naturally within each human individual, are at the same time formed and shaped in particular ways by the society in which one finds oneself. Society helps humans to judge their emotions intellectually, in light of the situations that give rise to them, and in so doing society also shapes individuals' actual *experiences* of those emotions. For example, love, a social passion, generally calls forth greater sympathy than anger, an unsocial one, for the obvious reason that one tends to be constructive, the other destructive of human society. Nature dictates that one is to be encouraged through peer pressure, the other discouraged.

Thus, as Calvin puts the individual in perspective by making all humans equal under God, Smith presents a secular version of how the human animal may put herself into a more global perspective in which she decreases and others increase. She would not, for example, sacrifice all of China for the sake of sparing her own little finger.[22] Smith offers a "dual process model" in which the individual is a battle ground between "doer" and "planner," between appetite and understanding, passion and sympathy-informed reason.[23] The person who would master herself must become her own impartial spectator, shaping her experiences in ways that translate readily to those in her society and, presumably, in ways that also allow her to approve intellectually of herself. To do so is not to repress one's true emotions; it is to become a better and more mature version of oneself, a self with integrity and authenticity, albeit a self that is importantly formed by the particularities of the society and values of those around her. Put another way, it is to acknowledge that one's emotions and one's description of those emotions arise together and shape each other; thus one may express her feelings in terms that operate constructively rather than destructively, increasing rather than diminishing happiness both for herself and for others in her vicinity.[24]

21. Ibid., 34–41 (I.ii.3-4). Following this he writes, "[H]e always appears, in some measure, mean and despicable, who is sunk in sorrow and dejection upon account of any calamity of his own." Ibid., 49 (I.iii.1.15).

22. Ibid., 136 (III.3.4).

23. Ashraf et al., "Adam Smith, Behavioral Economist," 132.

24. Hill, "Hidden Theology," 302, writes, "Smith perceives in the miraculous order of Nature a divine purpose. The human constitution and the entire human environment is designed with a hedonistic goal in view: our happiness, prosperity, perpetuation and

Theologically speaking, we might say that she learns to express her emotions and passions in such a way as to train herself in the knowledge of her true humanity, thus cultivating an understanding that brings her closer to real happiness and unity with God.

These "moral sentiments" are what constitute not just the good human life, but human life as such. The ability to become one's own impartial spectator and imaginatively to put oneself in another's shoes is, in Smith's mind, what sets humans apart from brute animals; it sets adults apart from children and the respectable apart from those worthy of disdain. Sympathy is the universal human vocation. He writes:

> [H]ence it is, that to feel much for others and little for ourselves, that to restrain our selfish, and to indulge our benevolent affections, constitutes the perfection of human nature; and can alone produce among mankind that harmony of sentiment and passions in which consists their whole grace and propriety. As to love our neighbor as we love ourselves is the great law of Christianity, so it is the great precept of nature to love ourselves only as we love our neighbour, or what comes to the same thing, as our neighbour is capable of loving us.[25]

This description of human flourishing may astound some readers who have been led to believe that Smith's "invisible hand"[26] can loosely be translated "greed is good."[27] It therefore bears emphasizing that Smith describes the human being as most *perfectly* human when she is feeling and acting out of sympathy and other-interest. Indeed, she strays furthest from her humanity when she denies her social nature and acts out of an unsympathetic self-interest or indulges selfish passions at the expense of another. The argument that an individual should love herself only as much as she imagines her neighbor is able to love her would

---

material comfort. The system of Nature is demonstrably moral because it promotes human happiness."

25. Smith, TMS, 25 (I.i.5.5).

26. For Smith, the invisible hand is a force that makes human individuals, motivated by self-love, work together cooperatively (and competitively) to produce and distribute goods; that is, it is what makes the market work. I will return to this concept in greater detail later in this chapter.

27. This saying—sometimes unfairly associated with Smith—is attributed to the character Gordon Gekko (played by Michael Douglas) of Oliver Stone's 1987 film *Wall Street*. Generally interpreted, it means that when individuals act out of greed they work together to maximize production and create the most wealth, which in turn (though it is accidental) results in the greatest good for the greatest number.

seem to put to rest any accusations against Smith for promoting greed as a norm. No less than Calvin, he points the human community toward greater mutual identification and solidarity.

Where, then, does the idea come from that Smith promotes a view of humans as essentially greedy, and that this is a good thing? To begin with, Smith does not altogether condemn self-love or desire for material goods. He sees the human "propensity to truck, barter, and exchange one thing for another" as a basic and natural survival instinct, a tool or means to an end, which can serve humans well.[28] In fact, Smith claims it was Providence who created humans with self-interest and a desire for material goods in the first place. As Hill puts it, "Our 'natural' esteem of trinkets is a deliberate 'deception' engineered by God but one which is the most important source of human progress. . . . Without it our species would be stalled at a stage of indigent barbarism."[29] In this he does not differ much from the Christian theology of John Calvin. While Calvin would never attribute deception to God, he might concede that trivial desires are one of God's ways of teaching humans to desire better things; and that even greed—a twisted version of God's good gifts of self-love and worldly wealth—can nevertheless be used by God for the larger end of human reformation.

Moreover, Smith sees individual human desires as playing an important role in the healthy functioning of a harmonious society shaped by sympathy. A famous early passage in *Wealth of Nations* makes clear the value of self-interest. Smith argues that the human (in contrast to most other animals who, once grown, fend for themselves):

> . . . has almost constant occasion for the help of his brethren, and it is in vain for him to expect it of their benevolence *only*. He will be more likely to succeed if he can interest their self-love in his favor, and shew [sic] them that it is for their own advantage to do for him what he requires from them. Give me that which I want, and you shall have this which you want. . . . It is not from the benevolence of the butcher, the brewer, or the baker, that we expect our dinner, but from their regard to their own interest. We address ourselves, not to their *humanity* but to their self-love, and never talk to them of our own necessities but of their advantages.[30]

28. Smith, WN, 21 (I.ii).

29. Hill, "Hidden Theology," 311.

30. Smith, WN, 22 (I.ii), emphasis added. It is the claim expressed in this passage that one reader of Smith labels as his fateful "mistake"; see Lux, *Adam Smith's Mistake,*

While this passage may seem self-explanatory, it is crucial for us to pay close attention to what it does *not* say. It does not say that one's neighbors have one single human motivation (self-interest) to the exclusion of all others (such as benevolence); only that—in sympathetic regard for the neighbors' own needs—one does best to convince them that one's own interest is also theirs. It does not say that the entire *humanity* of the butcher, the brewer, or the baker can be summed up in the self-interested search for utility; only that sympathy and respect for others' interests requires that a person not demand a one-way gift. [31] According to this understanding, Smith's *Wealth of Nations* is decidedly not "a stupendous palace erected upon the granite of self-interest."[32] On the contrary, one is able, as Smith says, to love others as one loves oneself, and to pay others the same respect one wants for oneself. In this, sympathetic self-interest can best be seen as an instrument of humane justice because it has a God-given *telos* of drawing humans toward the good. Such a gift can of course be twisted toward evil, but this does not change its original purpose.

Thus, self-love is a given part of human nature and serves a vital purpose; it is "the spring for action in a human being. It . . . motivates in each of us 'the hope of bettering his condition.'"[33] It is only natural for humans to want good things for themselves (even in addition to the bare necessities of life), and as long as one's understanding is well-trained through sympathy, pursuing these goods need not be incompatible with proper and humane social behavior. But though self-interest is not immoral in itself, this is not to say that Smith sees all self-love as equally virtuous and praiseworthy; there are varying degrees of propriety and

---

10, 86. Lux's mind might have been put to rest had he read Evensky, McCloskey, Hill, and/or Waterman; but although his critique of Smith may be overstated, it holds true for certain of Smith's readers.

31. Smith's non-emphasis on utility can be seen more clearly when contrasted with his contemporary, Jeremy Bentham, who does indeed think all human life is a matter of the search for pleasure (and avoidance of pain) and any attempt to guard a sphere for "humanity" or "benevolence" that is about more than pleasure and pain is mere sentimentality. See Bentham, *Principles*, I.i.xiv.

32. See McCloskey, "Avarice, Prudence, and the Bourgeois Virtues," 315 (quoting "the Nobel laureate and leading misreader of Smith, the Chicago economist George Stigler," from Samuel Fleischacker's "Talking to My Butcher: Self-Interest, Exchange, and Freedom in the Wealth of Nations," unpublished paper [Chicago: Department of Philosophy, University of Illinois, Chicago, 1999] 1).

33. Evensky, *Adam Smith's Moral Philosophy*, 35 (citing WN, I.viii.)

impropriety. Smith insists that true virtue, that is true humanity, goes above and beyond the instinctual:

> Virtue is excellence, something uncommonly great and beautiful, which rises far above what is vulgar and ordinary. The amiable virtues [including gentleness toward others] consist in that degree of sensibility which surprises by its exquisite and unexpected delicacy and tenderness. The awful and respectable [namely self-control], in that degree of self-command which astonishes by its amazing superiority over the most ungovernable passions of human nature.[34]

Smith here shows that the truly humane individual is one who rises above herself and her basest instincts, not an animal wholly subject to the "two sovereign masters" of pain and pleasure.[35] He does not claim that self-interest is the primary or even the most basic impulse of human nature. In Smith's view, humans have sympathy-formed reason with which they may aspire toward virtue; they consider rightness or wrongness first—that is, whether or not they approve and sympathize—and utility comes only as an afterthought.[36] Thus, a buyer approves of the baker's human need to sell bread at a particular price; and though the buyer appeals to the baker's self-interest out of respect for the baker's humanity, the baker sells bread primarily based on her approval and sympathy with the buyer's very human need for food. (The baker presumably chooses not to sell pornography, although it might have a higher profit margin than bread, because she does not sympathize with or approve of those who desire it.)

In short, *The Theory of Moral Sentiments* presents *not* self-interest but intellectual approbation and natural sympathy as the primary characteristics of human beings, and as the motivators that keep the social world running smoothly. In Smith's moral schema, sympathy and other-interest are the most humane of motivations, whereas self-interest must be kept in check. At bottom it is sympathy people want, not material pleasures. They pursue wealth because they want the approbation of their

---

34. Smith, TMS, 25 (I.i.5.5).

35. Bentham, *Principles*, I.i. It is of course not difficult to give a Benthamite, utilitarian reading of Smith by removing such "sentimental" terms as "right and wrong" or "sympathy" and replacing them with "preferences" and "incentives," but to do so would be to miss out on the description of humans that Smith apparently intended.

36. Smith, TMS, 20 (I.i.4.4), 52 (I.iii.2.3).

fellow humans, along with the positive mind states that accompany this approbation. (The reverse is not true—they do not seek human approval so as to increase their stores of wealth.) Smith offers a reason for Calvin's observation that, "To covet wealth and honors . . . our lust is mad, our desire boundless. On the other hand, wonderful is our fear, wonderful our hatred, of poverty, lowly birth, and humble condition!" (III.vii.8). In poverty is invisibility, which brings with it a lack of sympathy that represents humanity's most wretched state. Wealth, on the other hand, buys fame, which buys sympathy and love, and love is what makes a person happy. All self-interested behavior is thus directed at the happiness that comes from fellow-feeling, and nature has orchestrated it so that the human desire to receive sympathy both fosters and is fostered by one's own skills at giving it.

Where does Smith get this remarkable (and rather un-economic) idea that to love others is a higher calling than to love oneself? Why does he believe that "the chief part of human happiness comes from being beloved" rather than from having a large quantity of material goods?[37] Extrapolating from his teachings, we may surmise that he gets these ideas about human nature and virtue from his societal formation—in particular, his understanding bears distinct traces of Christianity. Although Smith is decidedly not a theologian, and he does not *deliberately* venture to theologize the human being in light of God, the mark of Protestant theology is undeniably and indelibly upon him. As Evensky puzzlingly puts it, "the logic of Smith's moral philosophy does not require a deity," but he "did have faith in a deity" and it had an important impact on his thinking.[38] That deity placed human passions in the custody of each individual's impartial spectator—best characterized as sympathy-formed understanding. Smith's version of the human being is not governed by only her own pleasure and pain, but also by her capacity to imagine others' pleasures and pains. The benevolent feelings that arise from her sympathetic imagination are every bit as natural as self-interest. The

37. Smith, TMS, 41 (I.ii.5.2).

38. Evensky, *Adam Smith's Moral Philosophy*, 23. In this assertion Evensky differs from Hill and Waterman, who, as I have noted earlier, insist that Smith's logic *does* require a deity. The fact that Evensky believes Smith's internal logic does not require a deity, but that religious thinking was still important to the formation of Smith's moral philosophy, seems to bolster the argument that, at the very least, Smith's thinking is thoroughly steeped in ethics and does not pretend to stand outside the moral community in which he finds himself.

human being in Smith's work cannot sufficiently be categorized as *homo economicus*—the individualized "economic man" who makes decisions about costs and benefits based upon bare self-interest. A more accurate (and more fruitful for purposes of economics) shorthand for Smith's human being might be *homo sympatheticus*[39]—the sympathetic person, who is a reflection of the norms, desires, and understanding of the society to which she is most deeply connected.

Because humans are by nature social creatures, it is sympathy, not greed or desire for material goods, that is the dominant force in human motivation. The impartial spectator, whom human individuals internalize and call upon to help them understand their emotions, is entirely a product of collective human sympathy. It is informed by the human social imagination, by putting oneself in another's place, loving one's neighbor as one wishes to be loved, and loving oneself only as much as one can expect the neighbor to love her. In loving and being loved—not in being rich—is human happiness. Through mutual sympathy, human individuals and societies both perpetuate and critique themselves. While in practice this seems to favor the status quo (in that those who suffer are required not to expect others to suffer with them too deeply), change is always a theoretical possibility. If enough victims, for example, express disapproval of offenders in a way with which impartial observers can agree, offending parties may be required to adjust their behavior. (On the other hand, if the victims are unable to speak for themselves, or if the "impartial observers" are themselves implicated in the offense—as for example male oppression of women, or white oppression of non-whites—change can be extremely slow in coming.)

To be sure, it is possible to interpret Smith's anthropology through a utilitarian lens; Bentham and his heirs can easily say that what Smith calls a desire for love is in fact a simple matter of pleasure and pain, albeit with a romanticized, sentimental, or religious flourish. But it must be acknowledged that Smith's own narrative does not follow this path. More importantly, his narrative, as we will see in a later section, does not lend itself to a vision of the economy as an all-encompassing system of unchecked humans chasing naked self-interest. Critics (Christian or otherwise) of today's global economy sometimes make a sport of demonizing

---

39. I have been able to find this term used in theology (namely by Abraham Heschel and, later, Jürgen Moltmann), over against *homo apatheticus*; but as far as I can tell, it has not been used with regard to Smith's vision of humankind.

Smith with utilitarian readings of *Wealth of Nations*, but a more careful look at Smith shows that he was seeking to make sense of economic matters *within* an assumed context of already existing social and individual human sympathies. "Smith's world is not inhabited by dispassionate rational purely self-interested agents, but rather by multidimensional and realistic human beings."[40] With regard to human flourishing, it is not the impersonal "market" but human imagination that makes the critical difference.

FREEDOM FOR SYMPATHY

What constitutes a truly humane freedom in Smith's worldview? As we have seen, the term "freedom" is not a neutral, universal, or self-explanatory concept, but is always embedded within a narrative about who the human being is. If, as Smith suggests, the human person is primarily motivated by a mutual exchange of fellow-feeling, it follows that the shape of freedom that is most appropriate to that person is *that which allows the human most fully to experience sympathy—both for and from others.* This freedom results not necessarily from any hands-off approach by government or by one's elders or superiors, but rather from the individual's development into a willing and integral player in the society in which she finds herself. The human being, as she grows up in a context of human community, learns which kinds of behaviors and emotions are virtuous (that is, which ones her community understands to be acceptable and praiseworthy) and which are not. Such learning comes not primarily through legislation (though this may indeed be a factor), but largely through forces closer to home such as parental guidance, social and religious norms, or peer pressure. Her desire for sympathy and love encourages her to accommodate the limits of her neighbors' sympathy toward her; at the same time she learns to have sympathy for others whose behaviors she understands to be worthy of intellectual approval (as well as to withhold sympathy from those behaving viciously). True

---

40. Ashraf et al., "Adam Smith, Behavioral Economist," 142. I note, however, that humans in this particular article are frequently likened to Capuchin monkeys, the study of whom presumably produces conclusions that are easily translated to human behavior. In doing so, the authors may undercut somewhat the complicated anthropology they are trying to foster.

freedom is therefore shaped through the process of individual hearts learning to "adopt the principles" of their nearest and dearest.[41]

A human is thus in a lifelong process of becoming free. It is a difficult process at first—it begins in earliest childhood when one's experiences of sympathy are yet unformed by culture, and when unchecked self-interest is a necessary condition for survival. The community approves a high degree of self-interest in an infant, but grows less and less sympathetic as a child grows up. At first a five-year-old may be shocked by the disapproval of her (previously tolerated) self-interested behaviors, but as she grows into an adolescent her mutual sympathy is shaped by those around her, and behaving according to sympathetic norms (not to say peer pressure) slowly becomes second nature. All humans act according to their own understanding; when her emotions and understanding finally match those of her society she will act freely, as a fish swims in water.[42] It therefore takes time and history to create a truly free human being: she is one whose reason and passions have come into sync; she has mastered herself, freely experiencing only those emotions that she and others approve. At the same time, she freely gives sympathy to others, particularly to those whose behaviors demonstrate a sentiment with which she can freely agree and offer her approval—agreement and disagreement being based not on an emotion itself but on the end toward which it is directed.[43] She has learned to love her neighbor as herself—that is, sympathetically, as her neighbor can love her—and does so freely, not through any coercion. To be completely governed in our sentiments and behaviors by sympathetic reason and reasoned sympathy is to be most truly human and thus, most perfectly free.

Freedom for Smith parallels virtue; there is no freedom without it. The free person is the one who does the right thing at the right time for the right reason. She is that uncommon person "confirmed in wisdom and real philosophy,"[44] whose propriety is praiseworthy because it arises spontaneously from genuine goodness and sympathy, not merely from

41. Smith, TMS, 73 (I.i.4.1).

42. Smith might have been fascinated by interesting work on "authenticity" currently being done in the realms of sociology and psychology. See for example Franzese, "An Exploration of Authenticity," which explores the influence of social context on an individual's sense of whether or not she is being her "authentic self."

43. Smith, TMS, 67 (II.i.2).

44. Ibid., 57 (I.iii.2.8).

an instrumental desire for the pleasure of others' approval. When addressing matters of economics, it is especially necessary to specify *which* virtues make a person truly human. In common economic parlance where human action is summed up as rational choice based on self-interest, prudence—the ability to make rational choices regarding the most efficient means to given ends—becomes the prime human virtue, if not the only one. The prudence-only approach is certainly far from any Calvinist norm, but it is also an inaccurate portrayal of Smith's own perspective. Smith was aware that prudence governed by self-interest is but one aspect of human virtue, and a vision of *laissez-faire* freedom that gives credence only to this aspect is bound to reflect, at best, a caricature of humankind. As Deirdre McCloskey writes, "We want to have people around us who are prudent, who can take care of themselves—every parent knows that," but "we also want our children or friends to be courageous, temperate, just, loving, faithful, and hopeful."[45]

Smith is careful as well to distinguish freedom from license. For example, he notes that being famous or prominent actually results in sacrifices of some liberties that many hold up as defining the good life—such as freedom to express unrestrained sentiments or freedom of "leisure . . . ease . . . and careless security"; but this loss, he surmises, is well worth the dramatic increase in sympathy that accompanies it.[46] (Indeed, people often sympathize with the wealthy and prominent even when it is not in their best interest to do so.[47]) It is not license to behave individualistically and self-interestedly that brings happiness, but the enjoyment of mutual sympathy that comes from well-ordered human relationships. Moreover, an incomplete or overly simplified vision of freedom is harmful in that it leads people to settle for partial freedom instead of pursuing full and true freedom, which is to say, becoming fully

45. McCloskey, "Avarice, Prudence, and the Bourgeois Virtues," 318.

46. Smith, TMS, 51 (I.iii.2.1).

47. Ibid., 52 (I.iii.2.3). It is pertinent to note the outpouring of support that Bill Clinton enjoyed during his highly-publicized sex scandal with a White House intern, and subsequent impeachment in 1998; or the sympathy that multi-millionaire Martha Stewart received from her many non-millionaire fans when she was tried for insider trading in 2003. Thomas Frank's *What's the Matter with Kansas?* explores the related phenomenon of how working-class Kansans have given unwavering support, based on social sympathies, to a political party of wealthy elites who fail to represent the economic interests of working-class Americans, which speaks to the idea that issues other than simple economic welfare are at play in human societies.

and truly human. Being fully human may in fact demand the willing *loss* of certain liberties, in order to enable a fuller experience of sympathy and love.[48] According to Smith's vision, a person who lived by pure self-interest would in reality be the most miserable of all humans because, although she might be able to calculate her way to great wealth, she would do so at the unbearable expense of becoming (in Frank Knight's words) "repugnant" to her neighbors for being the "selfish, ruthless object of moral condemnation."[49] She would end up captive to a self-inflicted prison, behind bars of social disapproval. In reality, no one lives this way; everyone (apart from a few notable exceptions) is guided by her understanding, which in turn is guided by the sympathies she has imbibed since infancy.

Thus genuine human freedom, in the imagination of Smith, is the freedom experienced by the human being who is wholly governed by her own sympathies, which arise naturally in her and are formed over time through the natural course of social contact. It is freedom *from* the unbearable human experience of loneliness and lack of sympathy; and freedom *for* the happiness that comes from flourishing human social relationships arising from mutual sympathy. Smith's vision of humane freedom can best be summed up as integrity—the wholeness that comes from aligning one's passions with one's intellectual opinions about what is good and appropriate. Put in another way, it comes from self-awareness—from *knowing* that one's passions arise from one's understandings, and that these understandings can be transformed at any time through the practice of sympathetic imagination. The freely sympathetic person is the happy person, because she is able to receive the kind of love from others that equally matches her need for it (and she does not need more than she can get).

---

48. Frank Knight argues, for example, with regard to "sex-feeling" that, far from wanting license for unlimited sex, humans almost always opt for order and decency. "[S]ocial existence and well-being in the abstract are more potent than sex attraction in any crude interpretation. With sex experience as with food, it is not the thing as such which dominates the civilized individual. . . . when the biological form of the motive conflicts with the cultural, aesthetic, or moral part of it . . . it is the former which gives way. Sex debauchery is, of course, common enough, but this also rather obviously involves about as much cultural sophistication as does romantic or conjugal love, though of a different kind." Knight, "Ethics and the Economic Interpretation," 27.

49. Ibid., 38.

It is worthy of note that Smith's vision of freedom is decidedly not *laissez-faire*, at least not for everyone. While those whose self-interest is fully shaped by sympathy can theoretically be trusted to rely on their own understanding, Smith still assumes that a certain amount of coercion will be practically necessary in any harmonious society. This coercion will certainly include a government that provides and enforces sympathy-shaped laws; but it also includes more grass-roots institutions such as families, congregations, and neighborhoods. Moreover, these forms of coercion are imposed largely on those whose sympathies are not fully developed—such as children, criminals, or other adults whose self-interest ventures beyond the limits sanctioned by mutual social sympathies. The person fully shaped by sympathy will not experience these limitations as an offense to her freedom. But though all humans are innately endowed with the capacity for sympathy, the free human being does not look the same everywhere or at all times. Because different cultures and societies come to different understandings based on their distinct experiences of mutual sympathy, freedom will inevitably take a wide variety of concrete forms even while it shares certain characteristics. Of particular interest to us is how Smith sees "freedom" and "sympathy" coming into play in humanity's concrete economic practices, which will be the subject of the next section.

SMITH'S VISION FOR A HUMANE ECONOMY

If *Theory of Moral Sentiments* is an inquiry into human nature and its telos, happiness, *Wealth of Nations* might be seen as Smith's innovative attempt to discover the "effectual means" to achieving this happiness. By "acting on the dictates of our *moral faculties,*" Smith claims, "we necessarily pursue the most effectual means for promoting the happiness of mankind, and may therefore be said, in some sense, to co-operate with the Deity."[50] Smith's inadvertent invention of (what would become) the discipline of economics was largely his attempt to discover the best way to "co-operate with the Deity" to promote human happiness through the ordering of economic life. As Polanyi writes:

> Adam Smith, it was true, treated material wealth as a separate field of study; to have done so with a great sense of realism made him the founder of a new science, economics. For all that, wealth

50. Smith, TMS, 166 (III.5.7); emphasis added.

was to him merely an aspect of the life of the community, to the purposes of which it remained subordinate; it was an appurtenance of the nations struggling for survival in history and could not be dissociated from them.[51]

Smith's innovations grew out of his disturbance at the current economic trends of his day, which he feared were being dictated by businessmen, who self-interestedly sought to protect the profits they made by maximizing British exports while keeping imports to a minimum, all the while arguing that it would be better for the nation as a whole. In his mind, this created wealth for a few mercantilists but decreased the community's well-being. He thus wrote *Wealth of Nations* "to expose the sophistry of a system that served no one but those who advocated it, and to appeal to current and future leaders to be models of civic virtue . . . to govern for the good of society as a whole," not for the powerful few who could afford lobbyists.[52]

If a humane economy should be shaped with respect for the true character of human nature and "the good life,"[53] an understanding of Smith's economic vision must take into consideration his remarkable description of human happiness, which is particularly interesting with regard to material (or what we typically consider "economic") concerns:

> What can be added to the man who is in health, who is out of debt, and has a clear conscience? To one in this situation, all accessions of fortune may properly be said to be superfluous; and if he is much elevated upon account of them, it must be the effect of the most frivolous levity. This situation, however, may very well be called the natural and ordinary state of mankind. Notwithstanding the present misery and depravity of the world, so justly lamented, this really is the state of the greater part of men. The greater part of men, therefore, cannot find any great difficulty in elevating themselves to all the joy which any accession to this

51. Polanyi, *Great Transformation*, 111.

52. Evensky, *Adam Smith's Moral Philosophy*, 25. Prior to the mercantilist system, feudalism had ruled, which Smith considered equally undesirable.

53. Frank Knight surmises that "A large proportion of civilized mankind would certainly commit suicide rather than accept life on such terms [subsistence, or the satisfaction of mere physical needs], the prospect for improvement being excluded." Humans do not want life, they want a *good* life. Knight, "Ethics and the Economic Interpretation," 18. Rebecca Todd Peters' *In Search of the Good Life* explores the work that four different visions of "the good life" have historically done in the course of globalization. Peters, *In Search of the Good Life*, 26.

> situation can well excite in their companions. . . . But though little
> can be added to this state, much may be taken from it. Though
> between this condition and the highest pitch of human prosper-
> ity, the interval is but a trifle; between it and the lowest depth
> of misery the distance is immense and prodigious. Adversity . . .
> necessarily depresses the mind of the sufferer much more below
> its natural state, than prosperity can elevate him above it.[54]

This description contains a stripped-down narrative of creation, fall, and redemption. Human nature is originally happy, with or without great material prosperity. Happiness is the benevolent purpose for which God (or "the Author of nature") created humanity; it is therefore relatively easy to come by because all of nature appears to be geared toward this anthropocentric purpose.[55] And although worldly misery can do great harm to natural happiness, it is yet a hope (even a reality) for anyone with the understanding to recognize it. Those who feel they cannot be happy because they do not have enough wealth, friends, or honors, are deceived. Adversity can bring an individual low, but a human being (like the lilies of the field) does not need much more than the bare necessities in order to be happy.

Sympathy is the unspoken but overarching element in this descrip-tion. It is mutual sympathy that discerns what the "necessities" for hap-piness are in any given context. Only sympathy-informed understanding can complete the happiness that comes from the basic state of being free of illness, free of debt, and free of guilt. It is likewise fellow-feeling that provides the answer to why adversity creates such terrible depth of human suffering; the "natural and ordinary state" of equilibrium is not remarkable in itself but brings happiness in so far as it allows for the mu-tual enjoyment of human sympathy. Meanwhile, adversity of any kind repulses external spectators and adds the horror of being ignored (or even despised) to the adversity itself, thus exponentially increasing the pain of a sufferer's situation. So while humans are responsible for their own happiness up to a point, their happiness is never complete without observation and approval from others whom they respect.

Given Smith's interest in the happiness of humankind, it is then to be expected that his economic "discoveries" would be geared toward achieving this most worthy goal. The economic system he decided was

54. Smith, TMS, 45 (I.iii.1.7).
55. Ibid., 166 (III.v.7).

most compatible with human nature and most conducive to human flourishing was a system of liberty, what is commonly (though usually without further qualifications) called a "free market." Crudely put, he believed people—both alone and in groups—should be left free to do as they pleased, and this would result in the greatest possible happiness for individuals, communities, and nations. This is where Smith's (in) famous "invisible hand" comes into play.[56] He saw the overall success of this apparent human free-for-all as being achieved not necessarily through the merits of anyone in the system; rather it is God (or Nature, or the Deity) who mysteriously directs individuals' works (even the selfishly motivated ones) toward the greater end of human happiness. This is not to say that Smith encouraged bad behavior, but merely that he, like Calvin, saw broad human flourishing as being largely outside the realm of human control.

On a microeconomic level, Smith wanted individuals to have "the natural liberty of exercising what species of industry they please,"[57] and he therefore proposed that laws should enable individuals to pursue any occupation they desired. One's labor is the "original foundation of all other property" (in which he differs markedly from a Calvinist idea that the foundation of property—including even one's ability to work—is God's grace); thus, "to hinder (anyone) from employing this strength and dexterity in what manner he thinks proper without injury to his neighbor, is a plain violation of this most sacred property."[58] Where Smith particularly saw this kind of hindrance happening in his own context was with regard to corporate guilds and apprenticeships. Such institutions were protected by European policies that, "by not leaving things at perfect liberty," artificially kept certain prices and wages artificially high.[59] Examples included the requirements that certain urban professionals (blacksmiths, weavers, and the like) begin their careers in long apprenticeships with low or no pay. Not only did he see this as reflective of an unjust preference among the ruling elite for city jobs over country jobs,[60] but he also believed it developed a work force with poor habits, since being uncompensated at this formative stage in their careers left apprentices insufficiently inspired

56. Smith, WN, 292 (IV.ii).
57. Ibid., 299 (IV.ii).
58. Ibid., 120 (I.x).
59. Ibid., 117 (I.x).
60. Ibid., 124–25 (I.x).

to pursue life-long diligence.[61] Most importantly, it artificially kept the number of urban trade workers low, thereby making them more highly paid than they would be under conditions of "perfect liberty." This gave the "skilled" jobs of the town an unfair advantage over the "unskilled" (that is, un-apprenticed) jobs of the country.

This dislike for rules and regulations stems from a central component of Smith's humane economy, which is the division of labor—a function of free individuals using their sympathetic imaginations to make decisions about how they will engage others in the marketplace. He believed that individuals left at liberty to make their own work choices would naturally and effectively divide labor among themselves, in ways that fostered overall happiness. Whereas a lone individual would have to be a jack-of-all-trades in order to survive, people in advanced states of society learn to specialize. In doing one thing well, each individual's skills become lucrative commodities that can be exchanged for anything else one needs or wants. The brewer trades with the baker, the hunter with the trapper.[62] His famous pin-factory example marvels that, while virtually no one on her own can manufacture even one pin in a day, ten people doing specialized tasks on specialized equipment can make up to 48,000 (4,800 each) per day.[63] (Even the academy divides into "tribes of philosophers" to everyone's advantage.[64]) The more advanced a society becomes in terms of material comforts, the more specialized its workers become. Human nature and the presence of the invisible hand mean that coercive structures (such as guilds) are unnecessary to achieving even the most complicated and beneficial material advances, and indeed even hinder them. Economies more complex and efficient than any bureaucrat or church hierarch could ever conceive of are born of simply letting people follow their own creativity, loves, and ambitions, letting them live where they want, buy what they want, and work where, when, and for whom they want.

Having insisted on individual liberty, Smith also moved toward liberalization at the level of European economic policies, releasing markets' natural flexibility and creative potential from the grip of government

61. Ibid., 121 (I.x). Eric Schlosser highlights similar problems with American teenagers in the fast food industry. Schlosser, *Fast Food Nation*, 67–71.

62. Smith, WN, 21 (I.ii).

63. Ibid., 12-13 (I.i).

64. Ibid., 18 (I.i).

policy, which he saw as existing largely for the purposes of enriching the monarch or protecting powerful business interests. This included ending the setting of prices, which would be more properly reached naturally through consumers' evaluation of how much toil could be saved by buying rather than manufacturing certain goods.[65] It also meant ending the setting of wages, which should be left to arise naturally from laborers' and employers' evaluations of the relative desirability, difficulty, and trust related to certain jobs.[66] Smith encouraged freedom of trade on all levels, which he believed would result in a more widespread distribution of wealth and other benefits.

Smith also insisted upon freedom with regard to colonization, which he saw as another misguided project of greedy monarchs and business people. "To found a great empire for the sole purpose of raising up a people of customers . . . is . . . a project altogether unfit for a nation of shopkeepers; but extremely fit for a nation whose government is influenced by shopkeepers."[67] Tariffs on imported goods do not benefit a nation as a whole (the citizens of which end up with higher costs of living[68]), but benefit only those few individuals and companies who profit from the lack of competition. Freer importation of foreign goods creates competition and drives down prices, thus benefiting the poor masses as well. In the place of tightly controlled trade, governed by politicians whose laws and tariffs responded to "momentary fluctuations of affairs" affecting "certain classes of our people," Smith proposed leaving things well enough alone.[69] He recognized that sudden shifts in economic organization would affect certain populations adversely, so he advised legislation that would gradually wean these people from their artificial benefits; but he was convinced that over time, through the process of countless individuals making their own self-interested decisions,

---

65. Ibid., 36 (I.v).

66. Ibid., 96–102 (I.x).

67. Ibid., 358 (IV.vii).

68. Evensky, *Adam Smith's Moral Philosophy*, 197.

69. Smith, WN, 296–97. He does however note that, if a country has heretofore had tariffs and other protectionist policies, its citizens have a right to demand that the freedom of trade be restored slowly and not all at once. Were modern-day France, for example, to suddenly drop tariffs on wine imports altogether, its own producers would surely suffer a major blow, though in Smith's mind even this would not be permanently fatal to most of them.

the common good would mysteriously surface without the help of any institutional mastermind.

By now it should be clear that Smith, contrary to certain mainstream stereotypes, did not set out to make the world safe for business. As Polanyi writes, "There is no intimation in his work that the economic interests of the capitalists laid down the law of society; no intimation that they were the secular spokesmen of the divine providence which governed the economic world as a separate entity."[70] In fact, Smith's free market was crafted *in response to* what he saw as corporate abuses, *not* for the sake of enabling them. Business and free trade were, in Smith's mind, not ends in and of themselves, but were means to the greater end of widespread human happiness, which comes from the experience of mutual sympathy. In so far as economic systems are not shaped (at least in the main) by mutual sympathy and do not enhance human happiness, they are open to scrutiny and ripe for reform.

Thus Smith does not promote an utterly anarchistic, *laissez-faire* system (or non-system, as the case may be) as the best policy. Even in the best-case scenario of perfect liberty, the invisible hand does not work to the exclusion of cultural and governmental constructs but alongside them. Smith was indeed suspicious of civil government, on the idea that it was constructed by the rich to protect themselves and their stuff from the poor, and was therefore biased toward injustice.[71] But he still saw legislation as a necessary corrective to the force of individual self-interest run amok. Thus government for Smith is one of the world's "self-correcting mechanisms" that helps guard against failures of other mechanisms. It can, for example, undertake such tasks as providing public education to counter-balance the "mind-numbing effects" that the division of labor inflicts on some unskilled workers.[72] The sovereign is also there to protect "every member of the society from the injustice or oppression of every other member of it" (not to mention from outsiders who wish to invade).[73] Moreover, as we saw in *Theory of Moral Sentiments,* natural human self-interest—if it is to become virtuous—requires refining, which comes from the societal context within which one learns to approve certain behaviors and reject others. Freedom, it

70. Polanyi, *Great Transformation*, 112.

71. Waterman, "Economics as Theology," 327.

72. Hill, "Hidden Theology," 309.

73. Smith, WN, 407 (V.i).

seems, is a human "right" only in so far as individuals do not offend com-munally-held human sympathies.[74] In the context of personal happiness and wholeness, freedom is an end in itself; but when it comes to human economic communities, each individual's "freedom to choose" must be seen as a means to the greater freedom. Thus governmental intervention, while it should impinge upon individual liberty as little as possible, is warranted for fostering peace among large groups of individuals.

Even in a "free" market, then, government is a necessary piece of the puzzle. Waterman likens Smith's political philosophy to St. Augustine's theology, in that human government is a function of original sin. "The state and its institutions are a self-inflicted *punishment* of human sin," he writes. "Moreover, without *justice*, the state is an unmitigated evil," but "God allows the self-regarding acts of sinful human beings to bring the state into existence because its institutions—especially those of private property, marriage, and slavery [sic]—are also a *remedy* for sin."[75] For Smith, as for Augustine and Calvin, human nature and understand-ing have been significantly deformed through sin; government, like the market, is part of Providence's plan to keep social evils to a mini-mum. Smith's faith in the natural human market mechanism does not consist in self-interest alone but includes equal parts imagination and sympathy—both individual and institutionalized—which effectively prevent self-interest from imperializing the market to such an extent as to kill it. Joseph Stiglitz writes, "In a market economy with imper-fect and asymmetric information and incomplete markets—which is to say, every market economy—the reason that Adam Smith's invisible hand is invisible is that it does not exist. Economies are not efficient on their own. . . . This recognition inevitably leads to the conclusion that there is a potentially significant role for government."[76] Whether or not we agree with Stiglitz's claim that the invisible hand (representing

74. This goes for the sovereign as well—proper institutions are needed to make sure that the sovereign is not corrupted by having the power to fulfill her own private inter-ests. Waterman, "Economics as Theology," 329.

75. Ibid., 330.

76. Stiglitz, "Ethical Economist," 3–4. Michael Novak, who generally favors a free market, also acknowledges that both government and markets provide checks and bal-ances on one another, together with a third part of the "trinity" of social spheres, the moral; Novak, "Economic System." Evensky, *Adam Smith's Moral Philosophy*, 262–63, highlights that external dictates, which are there to keep a check on self-interest, ideally become internalized over time, so that the mature individual ultimately governs herself without the need of government.

God or Providence[77]) does not exist, his point that economies do not operate in a political or moral vacuum is important. If we take Smith's own moral philosophy seriously, we see that not only does government play an important role in his understanding of a healthy and humane economy, but culture does as well. A culture shaped by the twin qualities of freedom and sympathy—both of which restrain the vicious pursuit of self-interest while encouraging the benevolent virtues—is one that can foster an economic atmosphere in which humans can, not merely subsist, but even flourish.

CRITIQUE OF SMITH

We have sought to give Adam Smith a fair reading, in order to discover whether or not he has earned his mottled reputation among Christian ethicists. One of the most frequent complaints about Smith is also the most basic, namely having to do with his attempt—common among "Enlightenment" thinkers—to express his theory in secular or religiously neutral language, rather than in explicitly theological terms. In doing so, Smith's narrative about human nature lacks a certain clarity that the book of Genesis provides for Calvin and others. John Milbank, for example, argues that Smith relies on "a fiction of unrelated individual starting points—persons and properties sprung from nowhere" and "supposes an individualist view of knowledge, purpose, and responsibility."[78] Without an explicit narrative that derives human origins and humanity's telos from God, Smith seems to sacrifice spiritual goods for material ones, and happiness for utility. "Smithian theodicy all too clearly tended in a direction which legitimated an endless hedonism and luxury and envisaged the long-term 'good outcome' of progress as the *only* human destiny."[79]

While I agree that Smith's work, like any theology, has sometimes been taken in unfruitful directions, I give him more credit than does Milbank. Like Calvin, who started with the knowledge of God as good, Smith also built his ideas upon his understanding that God (or "God-Nature" in Milbank's terms) was good, and that human individuals do not spring from nowhere. Smith was persuaded that the human desire

77. Hill, "Hidden Theology," 303, writes: "By what other means [than Providence] could Smith possibly have reconciled his claim that universal happiness and prosperity results from the free play of avarice and other voluptuous desires?"

78. Milbank, *Theology and Social Theory*, 40.

79. Ibid., 44.

for happiness and capacity for sympathy were universal and God-given; at the same time, he also saw that these very universals ensured that each person was deeply and importantly shaped by her context. In *Wealth of Nations* he writes, "The difference between the most dissimilar characters, between a philosopher and a common street porter, for example, seems to arise not so much from nature, as from habit, custom, and education. When they came into the world, and for the first six or eight years of their existence, they were, perhaps, very much alike."[80] Thus, even if the market model assumes a relative degree of creation *ex nihilo*, Smith also knows that genesis is conditioned by such things as location (near a coast or river vs. inland; in a town vs. the country), intellect, dexterity, gender, custom, and the like. To believe that the division of labor occurs "naturally" does not exclude the knowledge that historical conditions and human inter-connections matter.[81]

Moreover, it is not difficult to discern Smith's ethical judgments over the players in his scenario. Although he paints the butcher, the baker, the mercantilist, and the king with the same brush—all are united in their human tendency to truck, barter, and exchange—he clearly prefers the butcher and baker to the mercantilist and king, precisely because he sees the market claims of the former as more legitimately human than those of the latter. The mercantilist and king work against the natural flow of things that God-Nature intended. They leave their self-interest unchecked by sympathetic imagination, becoming wealthy by using their ever-increasing power to bend the economy unnaturally toward their own interests, crushing the butcher and baker (who presumably act in greater accord with nature) in the process. Smith well knew that, in McCloskey's words, "An economic actor must have a social stage," since no individual or community "can be explicit about every aspect of a difficult transaction."[82] Smith may not spell out the social stage he assumes

---

80. Smith, WN, 23 (I.ii).

81. Polanyi, *Great Transformation*, 112, writes, "Nature in the physical sense was consciously excluded by Smith from the problem of wealth . . . [it depends on] the skill of labor and the proportion between the useful and the idle members of society. Not the natural, but only the human factors enter." Nevertheless, Smith's decision not to declare his own context (e.g., in the church or other particular tradition) made "nature" the mediating context. Since nature is not self-interpreting, Smith's work was easily interpreted according to an anti-religious, "morally neutral" understanding of nature that resists critique on account of its self-proclaimed naturalness.

82. McCloskey, "Other Things Equal?" 478.

in *Wealth of Nations*; but it would be unfair, particularly in light of *Theory of Moral Sentiments*, to say that he saw hedonism or luxury as God's intended purpose for human life, whether individually or communally.

Nevertheless, I share Milbank's concern about Smith's sacrifice of particularity for generality. In isolating the "economic" sphere in *Wealth of Nations* from other areas of human society addressed in *Theory of Moral Sentiments*, and appearing to make the butcher and the baker paradigmatic for all humans in all times and places, he privileges economic exchange over other types of human exchange. This has the effect of forcing all human interactions—including friendship, erotic love, parenthood, and aspects of neighbor-love like justice and compassion—into an economic narrative ("this for that") that may or may not be a good fit. Furthermore, he privileges the individual (male and British) economic actor, thus externalizing the concerns of women, children, animals, the earth, the elderly or disabled, families, and non-European communities. At best, he views these from the perspective of the solitary trader; at worst, he renders them virtually invisible. In adopting the view of the solitary trader, Smith does not go so far as to reduce marriage to a fancy form of prostitution, or parenthood to a father's shrewd business investment. But later economists will be able to do so without any sense of irony, simply by walking through the door Smith opened by removing the economic questions of life from other questions.

It would be unfair to judge Smith's ethics as a whole based entirely on his economic work. But though it is not till *Wealth of Nations* that a rational, calculating sensibility plays an obvious anthropological role, we also saw it surface in *Theory of Moral Sentiments*. In his consideration of humans and their sympathetic imaginations, Smith acknowledges that sympathy has its dangers. For one, humans desperately want it; he notes that it appears to be of such "mighty importance" that the desire to be in a position to attract sympathy is "the end of half the labours of human life; and is the cause of all the tumult and bustle, all the rapine and injustice, which avarice and ambition have introduced into this world."[83] Because Smith sees sympathy as being most easily garnered by fame and fortune, we do not have to leap very far to conceive of fellow-feeling as both a currency and a commodity for sale. The wealthy (or happy) put themselves and their wealth (or happiness) on display as a way of purchasing the sympathy they crave, while the poor—who receive little

83. Smith, TMS, 57 (I.iii.2.8).

sympathy themselves—direct their own sympathetic imaginations toward the wealthy as a way of borrowing the happiness they could not otherwise afford.

As we also saw, Smith observed that humans do not like to sympathize with the unfortunate, because the imagination of another's pain brings the observer pain as well. Suffering and grief are unwelcome sensations, so humans gravitate away from those who require such sympathy. It is worthy of note that Smith—who tries to approach his inquiry as an observer rather than a judge—offers no critique of this human trait. He assumes that, because humans generally dislike being around society's losers, the loneliness of losers is a given fact of life. (Misery may love company, but it will be hard to find.) While he may view this as a moral failing, he neither hopes that humans can learn to sympathize differently, nor exhorts them to try. He does discourage people from becoming too ambitious (i.e., beyond the degree with which one's neighbors can approve), but he does not scold them for avoiding the poor, the miserable, the sick. To do so would perhaps be to interfere with the natural workings of human freedom—a risky proposition, since interference by even the well-intentioned often has unintended consequences. This comes back into play in *Wealth of Nations*, because he sees the desire for temporal wealth as a deception that keeps the economy growing, thus "inadvertently" promoting "the good of the poor."[84]

Smith's bland acceptance of unsympathetic behavior toward the unhappy is especially puzzling in light of his stated conviction that sympathy follows understanding, which is in turn shaped through cultural education. He does not seem interested in the possibility that the right tradition could transform human sympathies away from their natural aversion to pain and suffering. It is here that his lack of an explicit theological narrative becomes most troublesome, due to its incapacity to make moral judgments or imagine alternative human societies. Christian and other religious narratives generally teach that fallen humans must *learn* to have compassion for their neighbors, especially for the poor, the sick, the imprisoned, the unattractive, the enemy; such love is not "natural" to humans in a corrupted state but is nevertheless to be desired. (One is reminded of the rich man in Luke 16 who seems utterly oblivious to poor

---

84. "Smith believed both that this sympathy for the rich was a form of corruption based on a moral mistake, and also that it provided an important underpinning for social stability." Ashraf et al., "Adam Smith, Behavioral Economist," 142.

Lazarus sitting at his door; even his education in Moses and the prophets was not enough to convince him to look.) By forfeiting theological norms in favor of "natural" ones, Smith lost (or perhaps willingly abdicated) the power to criticize human motivations in anything more than an offhand way. (Or as Frank Knight might put it—and as we will see in the next chapter—he chose to focus on the "form" of human behavior rather than its content or value.) Human failings in Smith's work are accepted as givens not to be risen above, rather than contingencies open to change. He chooses instead to remain at the level of concrete, observable effects, judging all human behavior according to "neutral" material criteria, in particular the growth of national wealth. In Christian theology, of course, the vision of human destiny is not a simple matter of material progress in aggregate—although this is certainly one important element—but rather of redemption and transformation into God's image.

In not encouraging humans to stretch their sympathetic capacities toward those in pain (which might also cause the market to grow, though in other directions), he is not only overly optimistic about the ability of markets to reduce human misery, but he also lessens the possibility of hearing voices from the margins. Societally-informed sympathy is only humane if the society itself is humane. If society has perpetuated a lack of sympathy for people in pain (through habits such as racism, sexism, classism, nationalism, and other ways of justifying the consumption or marginalization of other human beings) the individuals within it will bear the burden of its inhumanity.[85] A particular society may encourage men to withhold sympathy from women, or free citizens to withhold sympathy from the imprisoned, treating their sentiments as unformed or "indecent" and therefore unworthy of sympathy, as adults sometimes do with children. As Smith himself acknowledges, sympathy, like every-thing else, must be molded and shaped by understanding and discipline. Without such social discipline, humans' desire for sympathy can become an obsession—or the lack of it can become a communal wound—that is a society's own undoing.

This tendency toward the status quo is a flaw that Calvin himself could not easily have corrected, advising sufferers as he did to bear their lot with patience. But a narrative theological tradition that emphasizes

---

85. For the sake of simplicity, this book is primarily concerned with intra-human relations. However, I am keenly aware that the rest of creation also makes claims on human beings, and thus it can and must also be brought into the conversation.

human equality and shared destiny, as well as the idea that God gives wealth to be shared, is eminently preferable to Smith's impersonalized theodicy of efficiency. Smith leaves out a truly impartial spectator—God—under whose gaze alone both adversity and prosperity are put into clear perspective. Calvinist economics can draw on affirmations that all wealth is God's, and that all humans are equal sharers in both God's image and God's gifts. Our neighbors are, in a way, ourselves; therefore neighbor love (even of losers who seem to bring on their own misery) must be every bit as passionate as one's self-love. A humane economy does not stop at one-way sympathy toward the happy and successful; freedom-oriented practice requires that natural sympathy be stretched to include those who are suffering as well as those who are prospering.[86] Christian theology insists that humans can and must learn compassion to such a degree that they will not rest while others, their human siblings, suffer needlessly. Such a goal is not mere optimism, but hope; and hope demands that humans live according to what they *truly* are, not merely according to corrupted perceptions of them.

The problem remains that, in Smith's attempt to "rid [economic science] of metaphysical illusion by no longer ascribing to things or persons an inherent 'striving' towards their appointed goals," leaving "empirical science free to confine itself to traceable and provable efficient operations,"[87] he removes humans, however provisionally, from their bed of tradition. It is fair to assume that Smith (at least in theory) would not have been in favor of a "monopoly" on sympathy by any group, any more than he was in favor of mercantilist monopolies of certain industries. All humans are equally in need of sympathy, and true freedom therefore entails its widespread production and distribution. But while Smith could encourage lawmakers to change policy so as not to foster material monopolies, he did not have any authority to which he could appeal for a change in the direction of natural human sympathies. An ap-

---

86. While this is not the same as a "preferential option" for the oppressed, it actually assumes it. Much as Calvin says that it was not necessary for God to prescribe any law for humans to love themselves, it is also not (usually) necessary to convince people to admire the happy. Thus, even to insist on viewing the poor as equal to the rich is already to ask something that is possible only through grace. Because it is not obvious or universally accepted that all humans are equal, it requires a lowering of the status one ascribes to the powerful (as well as to oneself) while raising the lowly in one's own estimation; it asks that the last be treated like the first, the first be treated like the last.

87. Milbank, *Theology and Social Theory*, 39.

proach geared toward liberation and transformation, on the other hand, may appeal to the Christian goal of reforming fallen human sympathies such that those who suffer and those who prosper come to receive the equal attention that is their due as equals under God. Only a tradition regarding *why* (to what end) God-Nature gave humans sympathy makes it possible to judge when sympathy has gone awry. Only a tradition regarding virtue makes it possible to discern which moral sentiments are constructive (and worthy of cultivation) and which are destructive (and worthy of censure). Thus, for Smith's economic science to be truly fruitful for humankind, it must be placed in the service of human freedom and happiness—the communally determined measuring stick by which economic practices are judged.

Still, Smith's emphasis on liberty in the economic sphere is something that twenty-first-century lovers of freedom cannot ignore. Smith started with a problem—monopolies in Great Britain forged by the cooperation of greedy governors and businesspeople—and he offered individual freedom as a solution to it. One need look no farther than the United States to see that, for many people, the policy of freedom has brought a large degree of happiness. In the American workforce, immigrants or descendants of slaves can be millionaires; women can be college presidents instead of seamstresses or wet nurses; youngest sons are not required to become soldiers or clergymen;[88] immigrants can own businesses. American consumers do not have to produce our own tofu; most of our children do not have to die in childbirth or infancy; and most people reading this book have probably had (or are in the process of acquiring) at least a college education. We cannot blithely assume, as Smith sometimes seems to do, that every job or product or liberty is equally open to every individual in the system as it really exists (though he does acknowledge inequalities even under conditions of "perfect liberty"). In the real world, a disproportionate number of descendants of slaves are in prison; many immigrants are servants without human rights; countless women take care of other women's children and rarely get to see their own; and youngest sons do become soldiers in hopes of making a better living. Those who start out with more freedom seem

88. Smith expressed concern over scholarships for British clergy in a strange example of how "the competition of the poor takes away the reward of the rich"; he argued that in the Christian churches, impecunious would-be clergy who are able to receive scholarships for their education reduce both the honor and salaries of those who could pay for their education in full. Smith, WN, 130 (I.x).

to get more and more, while those born into less often end up serving twenty-five to life. As a norm, though, Smith's assumption of sympathy-shaped, culturally-specific individual freedom is praiseworthy, both in the marketplace and in broader social life.

CONCLUSION: ECONOMICS AS A MORAL SCIENCE

"Adam Smith would not be surprised by the finding that markets are often built on motivations of fairness, altruism and trust—rather than on self-interest alone" in the way that some critics read him.[89] In seeking a humane economic order, a Christian theologian need not think Smith perfect in order to find him helpful. While Smith (like most scholars) does indeed exhibit a bit of hubris with regard to his ability to see life in all its fullness, and although he does eschew the specificities of theological language in favor of finding a broader audience, his approach is not entirely divorced from theology, even on a conscious level. Smith treats humans as neither monkeys nor machines; he knows they have some anti-social, selfish tendencies, but he also has faith that they are sympathetic, social beings who need each other in order not just to prosper materially but also to realize their humanity fully. Even more, he does not deem it necessary to pretend, even for the sake of scientific generality, that the selfish tendencies are all-encompassing. A freedom-oriented Calvinist approach can therefore learn from Smith in so far as his "universal" economic theory can help us make sense of certain human behaviors, however provisionally. Where we must go farther is in reminding Smith that, because human behaviors are context-specific and never ineluctable, they require critical engagement that insists on justice. The ideal economy reflects Christ-like neighbor-love rather than merely "natural" causes and effects. It does so because the players within it are shaped by the idea that *all* of their neighbors are of equal worth to themselves, instead of by the idea that only people instrumental to their happiness are valuable.

In spite of this shortcoming, economic freedom for Adam Smith's human is decidedly not a simple freedom from governmental interference in her choice of career or in the price of the corn she buys. It is not a freedom to maximize her own happiness selfishly without regard for the happiness of others. It is not a relativistic freedom in which all eco-

---

89. Ashraf et al., "Adam Smith, Behavioral Economist," 137.

nomic behaviors are permissible; on the contrary, Smith expects well-formed (and well-informed) observers to make moral judgments that keep individual actors in check. In all things it is a contextual freedom, the perimeters of which are dictated by nothing other than human sympathy and approbation—originating both within and externally to the individual—and this is no less true in economic ethics than in political, social, or cultural ethics. If the *telos* of the universe in Smith's mind is human happiness, which in turn is fostered by human sympathy, then true human freedom is also directed toward that ultimate end (God's or Nature's purpose), not merely toward the short-term purposes of individual utility. The kind of freedom Smith envisions is not formal or devoid of specific, narrated content, though his appeal to "nature" does leave plenty of room for diversity. It is rather a freedom that is agreed upon by members of the human community (or communities) and shaped through their mutual sympathies; a function not only of loving one's neighbor but also of expecting the neighbor to reciprocate.

Where a Christian approach to economics has the advantage over Smith's is that it can rise above "nature" in a way that he could not, by *openly* incorporating specific, normative content rather than attempting a neutral or universal perspective for all places and times. The freedom it offers is also greater, in that it can distinguish when the market is working justly and humanely and when it is not. This type of approach can look at self-interest without either romanticizing it as a cure-all or throwing up its hands in despair, because it takes seriously the interplay between self-interest and sympathy. Even the most mathematical of modern economists know, every bit as well as Smith and Calvin did, that self-interest and preferences are not the end of the story; if self-interest gives way to excessive greed or "rent-seeking" the market cannot function properly, so discipline and self-denial are always necessary factors. No market, even in an imaginary model, is truly *laissez-faire* because no market arises out of nothing. All markets are contingent, arising amidst pre-existing natural resources and co-existing human cultures in which motives combine and conflict, even within the heart of the single individual. Only in a culture where trust and order are already valued can a free market avoid becoming a destructive free-for-all.[90] The market as-

90. Smith notes that, in spite of England's tariff policies (and apart from that pesky matter of the extermination of prior American inhabitants, 350), the American colonies became one of the most splendid examples of a market economy, *not* because it

sumes that individuals with a healthy concept of freedom will limit their self-interest, if not for its own sake then at least according to incentives and disincentives, which are sometimes provided by law (in the vein of Calvin's second use), other times provided by social approbation and disapproval (Smith's sympathy). We can take from Smith the lesson that human economies will not conform to abstract principles, but will take distinctive shapes according to the societal sympathies in which they operate. Moreover, as people and contexts change, economic practices must be reformed as well. The ongoing problem is to discern *which* ways are most appropriate to human flourishing within which contexts.

When compared to our prior reading of Calvin, and put in the context of my attempt to develop a freedom-oriented Christian economic ethics, Smith appears to be more of a potential ally than an adversary. Smith can be read as knowingly conducting his scientific economic inquiry from a culturally shaped position with an explicitly normative goal. While he did indeed seek to observe "natural" economic phenomena (such as the human tendency to exchange and the consequent division of labor) without theological judgment as much as possible, Smith did not forget that these phenomena had prior ethical underpinnings and potentially dire consequences. Well-formed human sympathy—that is, other-interest and the desire for reciprocal human love—is not only the most fundamental of human motivations for Smith; it is also the only human trait which can properly shape a *humane* economy. Smith never insinuated that "self-interest" was an ethically-neutral term that could be equally applied to the desire for offspring as to the desire for peanut butter. Not every self-interested desire can be substituted for any other in an economic model; a self-interest that is unlimited by sympathy will lead to a corrupt economy of the sort Smith was fighting, whereas a socially-approved self-interest is the building block of any healthy system. To this the Calvinist economic thinker adds that social approbation *itself* is in need of redemption and reform according to the contingent, embodied norms of self-denial and neighbor love.

---

was "free" in a way other economies were not, but because—in addition to there being plentiful lots of good land—the colonists arrived there with prior beliefs about freedom that were suitable to the kind of market economy he proposed. Meanwhile, Valdes' study on the influence of Chicago economics in Augusto Pinochet's Chile, *Pinochet's Economists,* is a poignant reminder of how market economics requires a particular kind of social context.

As the economic tradition moved on, economists increasingly began to push such qualifications into the margins. If Smith saw economics as a subset of ethics—a moral economics—later economists first separated the two tasks (Frank Knight), and finally flattened the remaining task of economics into a utilitarian calculus (the Chicago School). To these later economists we now turn in chapters 4 and 5, before we seek to explore some twenty-first-century visions of obedient freedom and sympathetic self-interest in chapter 6.

4

SPLITTING THE ADAM

Frank Knight's Division of the Human Being

A S A REPRESENTATIVE OF "classical" or "liberal" economic theory, Adam Smith makes a fruitful conversation partner for Christian ethics in that he does not seek to bifurcate economic science from its parent science, moral philosophy (ethics). Smith was cognizant of the fact that economics was a *normative* endeavor; more than that, he intended it to be so. His attempt to explain the "nature and causes of the wealth of nations" was something he undertook because he had a particular understanding of how human nature and freedom played out in social and economic behavior; more importantly, he believed Europe's current economic system offended this understanding and was in need of reform. Smith presents us with a moral economics; whether one reads his theory as based on God or Nature does not change the fact that he saw humans as socially embedded, dependent creatures rather than abstract, autonomous individuals. Like Calvin, he saw humans as "not our own," though if asked to specify *whose* we are, he might have said humans naturally belong to one another.

In this chapter I will introduce Frank Knight, an economist who is somewhat marginal from a twenty-first-century perspective, but whose theory is representative of an important conceptual shift at the University of Chicago in the mid-twentieth century. Perhaps most important for his role as professor to Milton Friedman and other economists who would become more famous (and win more Nobel prizes) than he, he can be considered among the first generation of neoliberal economists now known collectively as the "Chicago school." (We will encounter the second and third generations in the next chapter.) Knight diverged from Smith's moral economics and attempted to separate scientific economics from ethics altogether. Knight aspired to an economics that was about understanding for its own sake, made of perfectly abstract models and free from any particular normative interests or political ideologies. By isolating *homo economicus*—the human whose sole activity is choice, and who chooses based on a calculation of pure self-interest—the economist is able to both explain and predict individual human choices in the abstract. Crucial to understanding Knight, however, is his belief that economists' knowledge is always *only* in the abstract; it has almost nothing to do with real human beings or their real-world problems, where universals necessarily give way to particulars. For this reason, Knight insists that specific questions of policy and weighty matters such as "freedom" are better left to ethicists and politicians.

UNDERSTANDING *HOMO ECONOMICUS*, NOT THE HUMAN BEING

Frank Knight claimed that the importance of economics was not necessarily in its potential social uses or contributions to policy (goals he saw as external to the primary goal of explanation or discovery), but simply in its ability to make scientific sense of human conduct—in particular, the conduct of "economizing," or "[using] resources wisely in the achievement of *given* ends."[1] For Knight, the "simple" underlying assumption of neoclassical economic theory could be summed up thus: "individuals rationally pursue their preferences within the constraints of the available means and knowledge."[2] Ends, means, knowledge, and preferences are all determined prior to the beginning of the economist's work; economics purportedly does not deal with the evaluation of constraints (social, intellectual, or otherwise) on individuals, and cannot help in defining or promoting the particular ends that motivate humans to act. But Knight believed economics could be helpful in understanding the relative use-

---

1. Knight, "Ethics and the Economic Interpretation," 34.
2. Emmett, "De Gustibus *Est* Disputandum," 3.

fulness of certain means that humans adapt in order to achieve the certain ends already identified through other modes of inquiry.

This tradition of economic speculation, he noted, is dependent upon a conception of the "economic man," who provides the subject of the "study of means" (economics). His description of the assumptions economists make about individual actors is enlightening:

> The economic man is the individual who obeys economic laws, which is merely to say that he obeys *some* laws of conduct, it being the task of the science to find out what the laws are. He is the *rational* man, the man who knows what he wants and orders his conduct intelligently with a view to getting it. In no other sense can there be laws of conduct or a science of conduct; the only possible "science" of conduct is that which treats of the behavior of the economic man. . . . A scientific principle necessarily takes the form that under given conditions certain things can be counted upon to happen; in the field of conduct the given conditions are the desires or ends and the rationale or technique for achieving them.[3]

Though Knight sees himself as a scientist, not a theological or philosophical ethicist, he nevertheless begins his economic thinking, like Calvin and Smith, with a foundational understanding of the human being. Each writer strips down his human being to what he sees as the bare bones. In Calvin's case, his theological task led him to present the human as created in God's image, fallen into sin, and being redeemed by God. For Smith's philosophical approach, the human is a sympathetic animal who, because of his need for the fellow-feeling of his community, tends toward truck, barter, and exchange (rather than solitude, murder, or theft).

Knight went farther than Smith in his pursuit of scientific lenses, in which the human individual could be set adrift of any community, becoming an abstract entity who makes rational choices about how to achieve given ends. In this attempt to separate the human from her human context for the specific purpose of understanding how economies work, Knight's anthropological model differs markedly from the earlier two writers. His "economic man" comes across more like a computer (plug in parameters, get a calculated response) than a complex human being with a body, family members, geography, aspirations, or work to do.

3. Knight, "Ethics and the Economic Interpretation," 35.

Many twenty-first-century readers (not unlike some of Knight's own contemporaries) may find this objectionable, but there is a method to Knight's madness. In fact he had little patience for protests against his economic man, because he believed they grew out of a gut reaction against the seemingly mechanistic anthropology underlying it, combined with a misunderstanding of its purpose and limitations:

> Under the first banner are those to whom the "economic man" is a caricature or a calumny or both. . . . Others insist on a degree of freedom and spontaneity or of realism in detail that would exclude any treatment except the recording of events as they happen and their imaginative interpretation [i.e., history]. Of some of these protesters it must be said briefly that they do not understand either the logic or the purpose of the [economic] utility analysis.[4]

In other words, though some economists surely do have the unfortunate tendency to aggrandize the role of their science in understanding all areas of human life, Knight is willing to concede that a purely economic human being, an abstract "decider," does not exist in reality. To begin with, wants or ends in real life are not givens but are a matter of ongoing discussion and constant change, and thus are not truly "data" in the same sense that gravity or temperature are. Moreover, he argues, because no one has perfect knowledge, no human can act with perfect intelligence or rationality. Even the freest person (whom he idealizes, not surprisingly, as a young man without family constraints) is "in large measure a product of the economic system" that has formed him in its image and controls his opportunities, making even him unfit as an "accurate mechanism of desire-satisfaction."[5] Though he does not here refer directly to Smith, Knight is reminiscent of him in that he wisely recognizes that every human is importantly shaped by her particular context, and is open to a variety of impulses and responds differently to given stimuli, meaning that no individual's actions or responses are perfectly generalizable or predictable for all times and places.

Nevertheless, Knight does not see these limitations as liabilities. None of them precludes the possibility of a scientific study of human conduct, with one important caveat: *the reach of economic science must self-consciously reflect and declare its inherent limitations.* Economic science, he sought to assure critics, was not about creating norms for human

4. Knight, "Marginal Utility Economics," 159.
5. Knight, "Ethics of Competition," 49.

behavior, nor about prescribing policies based on a mechanistic view of the person. Rather, economics offered the possibility of understanding, if not all human behavior, at least that narrow slice of it that could be regarded as the adaptation of means to given ends. Economics "treats of conduct *in so far* as conduct is amenable to scientific treatment, in so far as it is controlled by definable conditions and can be reduced to (natural) law. But this, measured by the standard of natural science, is not very far. *There are no data* for a science of conduct in a sense analogous to natural science."[6] Economics can study the behavior of choosing between options, but only when all the options are already given—a limitation that would put economics at the mercy of history and/or ethics, were economics interested in making concrete recommendations. He goes on to explain:

> Economics deals with the form of conduct rather than its substance or content. We can say that a man will in general prefer a larger quantity of wealth to a smaller (the principal trait of the economic man) because in the statement the term "wealth" has no definite concrete meaning; it is merely an abstract term covering everything which men do actually (provisionally) want.[7]

The beauty of economics for Knight is that one does not need to know *what* certain people consider to be "wealth" to know that they will desire it, and to know that they will do their best to attain it through the rational adaptation of whatever means they have available to them. Even those who renounce wealth can arguably be said to do so in pursuit of other "higher" goods, such as God's favor, which may also be considered wealth for the purposes of economic study.

In his desire to limit the ability of economics to assessing only "the selection of means to given ends . . . in terms of its instrumental rationality," he essentially releases economics from dependence on ethics, insisting that economic models have no import for "value-seeking" or "value-defining" behavior.[8] It is the job of other disciplines—such as psychology, philosophy, theology, chemistry, or history—to determine what the definition of "wealth" is, what it should be, and why. This view is integral to Knight's assertion, in no uncertain terms, that *policy is not*

6. Knight, "Ethics and the Economic Interpretation," 36. Original emphasis.

7. Ibid.

8. Asso and Fiorito, "Waging War against Mechanical Man," 17.

the job of economists. The utter inability of economics to address "value" or norms makes it ill-suited to any simple application of its scientific "laws" to actual social organization. Unlike Smith, for whom policy was both the impetus and the goal of his economic task, Knight disowns it as either impetus or goal, and tries instead to move toward a science not contingent upon context. He recognizes that social and economic policy must from the beginning be conditioned by social values impressed upon it by non-economic sources, such as tradition and culture. Social scientists cannot avoid the fact that, when discussing policy, even terms as apparently cold as "efficiency" involve unscientific judgments:

> Even in physics and engineering, "efficiency" is strictly a value category; there is no such thing as mechanical efficiency. . . . The efficiency of any machine means the ratio between the *useful* output and the total output. . . . [Thus] the necessity arises for having a measure of usefulness, of value, before efficiency can be discussed.[9]

Economic policy—as distinct from economic science, he thinks—has no choice but to begin with prior values or beliefs, determined through non-scientific means, about what constitutes efficiency. It follows then that any given economic system may be criticized "chiefly [on the basis of] its value standards," which are "prerequisite to any intelligent criticism of social processes or results."[10] Only the form, not the content of value, lends itself to economic analysis.

It is worth pausing here to consider the immensity of Knight's apparent self-restraint. He is essentially saying that economists' work belongs in the ivory tower and nowhere else; that economic reasoning is merely one small factor in the utterly complex job of real-life decision-making; that economic man is not the sum total of human nature but only a rather shallow slice of it. He is not interested in what "real" people "really" do, but rather what the hypothetical person does when given a problem to solve through the adaptation of means to ends. It is not difficult to give him this much; it seems reasonable to assume, after all, that if a person values orange juice more than grapefruit she will buy more orange juice than grapefruit. But Knight admitted that such a choice does not tell us all we need to know about human behavior in general, human economic

9. Knight, "Ethics of Competition," 42.

10. Ibid., 43–44.

behavior more specifically, or even about that single individual's economic behavior. It tells us nothing about why she likes juice in the first place (perhaps because it is what her mom gave her before she was old enough to speak), why she prefers orange juice (perhaps because the orange industry has the most successful ad campaign), or why she believes it is more "efficient" to buy her juice than to steal it (perhaps because she believes theft is bad for one's karma).

And Knight appreciated the difficulties posed to economics not only by the human subject matter, but by the human *observer* as well. Significantly, he acknowledged that there is no such thing as a neutral point of view; "the brick-and-mortar world cannot be constructed for thought out of purely objective data. . . . Apparently we are incapable of picturing anything as existing without putting a spark of our own consciousness into it. Behind every fact is a theory and behind that an interest."[11] He saw that every human observation bears the mark of the observer's own experiences, training, and desires, making every observation laden not only with theory, but specifically "with what the behaviorists have discarded as metaphysics"—including such things as our current topics of theological anthropology and freedom.[12] As Asso and Fiorito put it, "The freeing of thought from emotion and metaphysical entities would mean its annihilation. It is impossible to perceive or imagine the real world without recognizing the equally real character both of purposes and intellectual concepts."[13] All science in Knight's mind was *human* science, a "linguistic community,"[14] subject to the limitations of human persuasion and consensus. Economic theory is as much a projection of those who practice it as it is reflection of those they study.

But in spite of the idea that the interests and goals of the scientist were subject to internal and external change, he did not consider this complication a problem for economics. His affirmation that human beings (unlike rocks, sound waves, or cells) do not lend themselves to a positivist approach, does not change his argument that economics can objectively study human conduct with regard to those *very few* behaviors that can be observed formally, namely the adaptation of given means to given ends. However, economists who overstepped the boundaries of

11. Knight, "Ethics and the Economic Interpretation," 38–39.

12. Asso and Fiorito, "Waging War against Mechanical Man," 19.

13. Ibid.

14. Ibid., 23.

economic science and tried to explain more than their tools would allow met with Knight's harshest criticism.

THE DANGERS OF THE "ECONOMIC ENTERPRETATION" (OR, WHY ECONOMISTS CAN'T EXPLAIN EVERYTHING)

Frank Knight had at least two audiences in mind when he wrote about the discipline of economics. First, as we saw in the last section, his justification for the scientific pursuit known as economics was directed toward outsiders, particularly those who (perhaps unnecessarily) feared it. A second audience that emerges is the economic insider who oversteps the proper boundaries of the discipline. Even more vigorous than his defense of general economic theory—and more important to our focus on anthropology—was Knight's attack against what he saw as economic theory gone awry. In response to the popular movement among institutionalist economists of his time, Knight "embarked in a personal campaign, against the adoption of behaviorist psychology in economics."[15] The behaviorist approach to psychology, which blossomed in the 1920s, emphasized (in contrast to an abstract *homo economicus*) the embeddedness of human individuals among institutions, as well as the importance of an individual's past on her future choices. It "viewed human action as more instinctive than reflective" or rational; humans did not make rational calculations, in other words, but simply reacted to their surroundings like Pavlov's dog.[16] While such an approach admirably brought economics back into the world of contingency, in its extreme version such embeddedness was seen as not only conditioning but actually determining a person's behaviors. In Knight's mind, this determinist approach incorrectly portrayed the human being as a helpless product of circumstances, the result of a convergence of accidents of history, as a means of both *explaining* all past behavior and *predicting and controlling* all future behavior.

Some economists jumped on the behaviorist bandwagon, attracted by the expansive (some might say imperialistic) power of such an approach, which stood over and against the "perceived narrowness of 'orthodox' economic theory" that could not explain *everything* about human life, such as that of Knight.[17] Behaviorism not only promised

---

15. Ibid., 7.

16. Freeman, "Images of Human Nature in Economics," 634.

17. Asso and Fiorito, "Waging War against Mechanical Man," 1.

fuller explanatory power for all things human, but also seemed to offer great possibilities for policy making. If human beings' behavior could be entirely explained and predicted, it could also be controlled (e.g., crimes prevented, laziness eradicated, productivity increased) by means of the proper laws and institutions. Needless to say, this offered a tempting "new scientific rationale of government intervention."[18] One institutionalist expressed it this way:

> Where it [neoclassical economics] fails, institutional economics must strive for success. It must find the roots of activity in instinct, impulse, and other qualities of human nature; it must recognize that economy forbids the satisfaction of all instincts and yields a dignified place to reason; it must discern in the variety of institutional situations impinging upon individuals the chief sources of difference in the content of their behavior; and it must take account of the limitations imposed by past activity upon the flexibility with which one can act in future.[19]

Rather than leaving certain questions unanswered, institutionalist economists (like biologists or anthropologists) sought to analyze the influence of past policies and institutions on human behavior. In so doing they could also alter, with relative confidence, the course of the future— presumably for the better—through the use of economic incentives for what they deemed beneficial behavior, and deterrents against what they deemed harmful behavior.

This approach to economics, what he called the "doctrine of the 'economic interpretation,'"[20] was in Knight's estimation entirely unacceptable, largely because it overstepped the boundaries of economic science and ventured out into the foreign territories of ethics, psychology, policy, and history. It overreached by involving itself in the *content* and *criticism* of human behaviors, rather than merely in its single, abstract *form* of means adaptation. Knight felt that economic method rightly treats human wants as facts or data, rather than as values or norms, positing a simplified (and admittedly fictional) view of human life "as a process of satisfying desires."[21] For Knight this was a necessary and

18. Ibid., 5.

19. Ibid., 3 (citing Walton H. Hamilton [1919] from his paper, considered the "institutionalist manifesto," delivered to the American Economic Association in 1918).

20. Knight, "Ethics and the Economic Interpretation," 19.

21. Ibid., 21.

important endeavor, in so far as human life provides such data, but he found that believers in the economic interpretation took the simplification too far. No longer satisfied with the old-fashioned, now apparently sentimental goal of understanding for its own sake, Knight felt that modern economic scientists tended to "subordinate the desire for *understanding as such* to a *desire for control*."[22] Knight put himself in the former group of scientists who recognized that human life does not lend itself easily to statistics or mechanical fixes, whereas he thought the latter were so motivated by the search for solutions that they were willing to overlook this fact.

Though in some ways the behaviorist approach rightly complicated the view of "economic man" and his pursuit of maximization by acknowledging that his choices were affected by outside conditions, it also insisted that "the course of history is 'determined' by 'economic' or 'materialistic' considerations"; that is, all history is a product of human conduct, which arises from human motives, which are at bottom economic in nature—a view Knight believed to be false.[23] This new model human, "behavioristic man," "seemed to have no historical specificity, sharing an odd destiny with his neoclassical counterpart. He simply was 'the result of an over-emphasis upon the non-pecuniary and the neglect or under-emphasis upon the pecuniary motives, as the old economic man was the result of the opposite tendencies."[24] If "economic man" was an abstract chooser stuck in a timeless moment of want satisfaction, "behavioristic man" was the cumulative total of viewing *all* of life as a process of cost-benefit analysis over a period of time. Knight argued that seeing life as a matter solely of economics is "a very inadequate view of the truth," one that works only within certain narrow, methodological boundaries.[25] The process of choosing was not the only frame through which to view human life, and to conduct social business as if it were so would have dire consequences.

Even behaviorists themselves acknowledged the difficulty of making data out of human behavior, since the temptation to interpretation was inevitable. Their answer was to attempt to avoid subjective interpretation

22. Knight, "Limitations of Scientific Method on Economics," 107. Emphasis added.

23. Knight, "Ethics and the Economic Interpretation," 21. In this statement he critiqued Marxism (which he considered as useless as Christianity).

24. Asso and Fiorito, "Waging War against Mechanical Man," 6. Quoting T. N. Carver.

25. Knight, "Ethics and the Economic Interpretation," 21.

and instead account for "purposive action" only "in terms of more basic properties of behavior. . . . [E]xplanations of human conduct based on 'teleological' terms like *motive, intent, purpose, aim, desire, urge,* and so on, should always be carefully avoided in scientific analysis."[26] The behaviorist had to view the human being as a process of stimuli and responses that had no reason for being, no final goal. Even human consciousness had to be denied if economics was to be truly scientific: "So long as man's behavior is conceived to be volitional and purposive," so long as a person actually has a degree of freedom to choose, human behavior "must escape experimental and scientific study, for it is a non-repetitive occurrence and has no antecedent which can be objectively studied."[27]

Knight's vehement reaction to the "economic interpretation" might surprise economic outsiders, who may see it as quibbling over shades of gray. Both Knight and the behaviorists he criticized sought to discover general truths about human behavior through the use of abstract models; and both he and the behaviorists recognized that genuine humanity lent itself somewhat unwillingly to scientific generalizations. But crucial to understanding Knight is attention to the word "interpretation"—something to which he believed his own economic methods to be immune. While he did indeed seek to discern how "economic man" functioned in a theoretical economy, he believed he could escape the next step of interpreting all of human life according to the maximizing moment. Knight argued for the inevitable and constant change involved in human consciousness, such that it could not be reduced to a "mechanical" process of the sort analyzed in physics. "The 'desire' which prompts the act of purchasing," for example, is not parallel to gravity, or to the "'attractive force' among planets."[28] Because of such complex human conditions as introspection, intuition, communication, and language, human behavior escapes the susceptibility to objective study that, for example, water molecules may provide. Human choices are not simple physical events (hormones notwithstanding) but are influenced by inward and ever-mutating purposes that elude definitive categorizing and understanding. What is true for one person at one moment can simply not be assumed to be true for her at the next moment, or for the next person; exact replication—a mainstay of scientific inquiry—is always impossible with human consciousness.

26. Asso and Fiorito, "Waging War against Mechanical Man," 9. Original emphasis.
27. Ibid., 10.
28. Ibid., 12.

The replacement model of "behavioristic man" offered a great challenge to neoclassical economic thought. If the behaviorists were right that the conditions in which an economic agent found herself determined all her future economic choices, and the institutions causing those economic choices in turn determined history, seen as a mere "evolution of economic actions and reactions,"[29] then, Knight conceded, economics could truly be considered an all-encompassing approach to life. The more pragmatic institutionalist view could take over from the overly abstract and possibly useless "mystical attitude"[30] of which Knight felt himself wrongly accused, in fact eclipsing any need for any other social or human science whatsoever. (After all, Knight had bravely admitted that his own style of economics went "not very far" in explaining truths about human economic life.) History, psychology, and ethics alike could rightly be considered "glorified economics," superfluous and lacking in any unique contributions. Knight's insistence that policy making is an art form rather than a scientific experiment would have to give way to supposedly amoral technicians who misguidedly believe they have no axes to grind.[31] In spite of his protests, such was indeed to be the fate of neoliberal economics at Chicago and elsewhere.

THE DANGERS OF "THE CHRISTIAN ABSTRACTION" (OR, WHY CHRISTIANS DON'T UNDERSTAND ECONOMICS)

One of Knight's main complaints about behaviorism was that its emphasis on determinism offended his belief in human autonomy. As a defender of liberal ideals, he upheld "economic and ethical individualism," which gave way to the "political negativism" of *laissez-faire* policies in which each individual "shall be free to use his own resources in his own way to satisfy his own wants."[32] In addition to fighting what he saw as the big-government ideology of the behaviorists, Knight's battle against determinism also went in another direction, namely against ideologies other than liberalism. While he considered his own ethical individualism to be scientific fact rather than an ideology to which his economic

29. Ibid., 7.

30. Ibid., 22.

31. Ibid., 26. See also Knight, "The Limitations of Scientific Method on Economics," 134–35.

32. Knight, "Ethics and Economic Reform," 48.

theories and methods naturally conformed, he saw others' pre-scientific commitments as cause for the greatest alarm.

Knight identified three main enemies to his liberalist ideal of individual autonomy, two of which I will address only briefly. The first, idealism, which he called "groupism," had the benefit of being able to address the ethical defect of liberalism regarding those cultural issues that self-interest did not cover, such as society's care for the weak. But, he feared, it also lent itself to the deification of the collective in the form of the state, which required military power and authoritarianism to make it work.[33] His second enemy, Marxism, a "gospel of hate," which he called "romantically immoralistic, destructive, diabolical" and "monstrous," suffered in Knight's estimation, like utilitarianism, from the fundamental problem of ethical nihilism.[34] Marx's vision of a revolution in which the world, made up of exactly two classes of people, would be turned upside-down went against what can only be described as Knight's "faith" in history, especially that the human community could reform itself over time and benefit from what it had learned in the past. "Man is a social animal," he wrote (in a noteworthy echo of Smith), "a product of history. All that is good in him is obviously a reflection of social discipline and the product of age-long travail," which he feared Marxists wanted to wipe clean in favor of a once-and-for-all revolution, followed by a new dictatorship of the proletariat.[35] Knight believed that this kind of "dialectical determinism"[36] over which individuals had no control effectively destroyed the possibility of worthwhile ethical action, making individual freedom a superfluous luxury.

Of particular interest to our project of thinking about economics through freedom-oriented Calvinist lenses is Knight's attitude toward the third enemy he identified, Christianity, which received treatment almost as unequivocally harsh as Marxism. Religious morality, in Knight's mind, is not only *unnecessary* to social or political action but worse than that:

> evil rather than good seems likely to result from any appeal to Christian religious or moral teaching in connection with problems of social action. Stated in positive form, our contention

33. Ibid., 75–86. Knight did not observe that groupism's opposite—free market capitalism—was in equal need of military power for its stability.

34. Ibid., 87.

35. Ibid., 99.

36. Ibid., 101.

> is that *social problems require intellectual analysis in impersonal terms* but that Christianity is exclusively an emotional and personal morality; and this, while unquestionably essential, does not go beyond providing or helping to provide the moral interest, motive or "drive" toward finding solutions for problems. . . . [T]he teaching that it does furnish solutions has results which are positively evil and decidedly serious.[37]

Instead of offering viable, concrete political solutions, Knight understood Christianity (in contrast to Calvin's world-transforming approach that we saw in chapters 1 and 2) as teaching that political life, much like the physical or natural world, is to be taken deterministically as a given condition under which human beings have to live. He cites repeated commands in the Gospels for helpless people to pay their taxes or remain servants if they are servants.[38] Because an individual's moral life takes place within these given boundaries, he thinks it is only in this *individual* realm that Christianity may have some benefit. Moreover, he observes (echoing Calvin), history teaches that ignorant Christians have been unable to run the world any better than non-Christians. The world therefore needs policy makers with technical rather than religious expertise, much in the same way as it needs architects. Or, as one reader of Knight put it, the world needs "earthbound realism," on which Christianity "has no monopoly."[39]

Knight's overriding critique is the profound lack of realism he sees in the Christian ideal of love, which as he understands it makes Christianity useless for any effort to create freedom-based policy. The golden rule, for example, which encourages Christians to "do unto others as you would have done unto you," reveals its deep flaws when trying to turn it into law. "In most real situations," Knight argues, "intelligent people know that the 'other' not merely does not want what we would want in his place, but also that what he wants is not what is good for him, or for the world, and that to give it is not the right course of action. . . . The solemn fact is that what people most commonly want for themselves is their 'own way,' as such, or especially power."[40] Freedom to exercise power, it seems, is not always a good, and individuals do not have the

---

37. Ibid., 103.
38. Ibid., 104.
39. Heyne, *World of Economics*, 84.
40. Knight, "Ethics and Economic Reform," 109.

right to evaluate their fitness for such freedom (mainly because they do not have the ability to do so properly). Knight does not acknowledge his underlying anthropological assumptions regarding the separative individual who exists without a community that shapes him, or his assumption that freedom essentially involves a self-evident, self-aggrandizing will-to-power rather than the power to love one's neighbor.[41] Such are his generalizations that Knight sees Christian freedom as utterly antinomian; law in his mind can have nothing to do with love, and freedom bears no particular shape of the kind law provides. In Knight's imagination (and he is of course not alone in this), laws arise to curtail a *previously existing* freedom (in the sense of a will-to-power), as opposed to Calvin's vision in which human freedom is co-created and of one piece with God's gift of law.

To those who wondered whether Christianity could at least provide "ideals which might serve as a moral leaven and indirectly work for the transformation of social institutions and relations," Knight responds in the negative.[42] (He does not, of course, consider the possibility that his own liberalist commitments might be, in large part, the remnants of the Christian cultural norms in which he was raised.) The problem has to do with the Christian commands to love God and one's neighbor as oneself. "If Christianity does not mean this," he insists, "there is nothing that it can be said to mean."[43] The ideal Christian human being, he thinks, is as abstract and frightening as the human being who lives only to maximize. What kind of monster, after all, loves everyone equally?

> [I]f this idea [of undifferentiated love] can be formed, it is surely neither attractive nor helpful as a moral ideal. It would seem that a "Christian" who tried to practice such love would have no friends—being in that respect like the famous economic man. He would not be human. Hospitality as well as friendship would lose its meaning, to say nothing of "love" in any accepted interpretation.[44]

41. Theologically speaking, even "tax collectors" have the power to love others (Matt 5:46, 7:9), though perhaps not as many others as the redeemed can love (in theory if not in practice).

42. Knight, "Ethics and Economic Reform," 105.

43. Ibid.

44. Ibid., 106. It is unclear whether Knight's orientation toward abstractions causes him to draw from Jesus's *words* about love for his model of Christianity, or whether he was describing Jesus of Nazareth *himself* when he argued that someone who loved

Moreover, Knight observes, real-life families are poignant proof that love is not a cure-all. "Very commonly," in fact, "it appears that the presence of love complicates the concrete problems rather than contributes to their solution."[45]

On a global level, Knight views the Christian ideal of "love" as part of an antinomian plot that bodes poorly for the real world. Knight shares a concern with liberation theologians and other Christian ethicists that if all human woes are viewed as spiritual rather than material, the reality of human suffering is trivialized. It is one thing for a universally-directed religion like Christianity to claim that nations and their borders have no moral relevance, but it is quite another to insist that individual Christians should love foreigners equally to their own compatriots, and in concrete ways. Human beings cannot love everyone, at least not without differentiating, for example, between one's own children and complete strangers. Such an idealized world cannot exist among real individuals. Moreover, he thinks, love is a feeling, and since feelings cannot be compelled by law, and since law necessarily involves compulsion, "Christianity may be said to point toward . . . a society of antinomian anarchism."[46] Its apparent desire for the abolition of order actually offers *too much* freedom for Knight's comfort, to such a point that absolutely *no* rules can be made for human social life. (In this he echoes sixteenth-century critics of Calvin and Luther.) Interestingly enough, Knight's reduction of "love" to an inward emotional state, rather than a norm or a way of life, does not lead him to conclude that Christianity has no social or political implications. On the contrary, it causes him to fear that the application of Christianity's love to the real world is politically dangerous—at least as dangerous as the wrongful application of economic science's findings about means adaptation.

Knight rightly argues that, when treated as an abstraction, Christianity is as one-dimensional as the economic interpretation. In fact, it is so entirely unrealistic with regard to human tendencies as to end in anarchy, if turned into policy. If all individuals were bent on loving one

---

in an undifferentiated way would quickly become a social outcast. Many a Christian, after all, have balked at Jesus's apparent rejection of his mother in the Gospels, and his own Jewish contemporaries seem to have been dismayed at Jesus's willingness to love Romans and Jewish law-breakers in the same way he loved observant Jews.

45. Ibid., 108.

46. Ibid., 115.

another as they loved themselves, he thinks, no one would work and all would be beggars. The "parasitic saintliness" of Christianity may at best provide a model for contemplation or admiration (although it is difficult to see what, if anything, Knight sees as admirable in it), but it is not a model that any real human being could or should emulate.[47] Even the "golden rule" can be boiled down to the individualistic command that people should "mind their own business and let us alone," a common sense truth (at least common to Knight) to which love is an unnecessary and sentimental additive.[48] All of life is about the exercise of one's own will-to-power; we don't need Christianity to tell us that. "The point here," he concludes:

> is the negative one, that the Christian teaching not only has nothing to say about this whole problem-field of change in social organisation, i.e., about law-making and constitution-making, which involve constitutional change, but that it positively diverts attention both from a correct view of the problem and from the fundamental facts of social life out of which the problem arises.[49]

Since Christianity and economics are both exercises in abstraction, they can have nothing to do with each other; economics is about the rational adaptation of means to ends and Christianity (as Knight sees it), with its emphasis on ends alone, is utterly mute regarding such adaptation. Knight seems to think that economics' focus on the form of human means adaptation makes it substantially different than Christianity's focus on the form of its given end, love; moreover he sees this difference as giving economics the potential to be more truthful than Christian love, which is necessarily caught up in the particularities of individuals' lives in a way that (he thinks) means adaptation is not.

I raise Knight's treatment of Christianity as a way of bringing to light the fine line he sought to walk as an economic scientist. On one side were social scientists who, he thought, misunderstood the limits of the economic abstraction, believing every human question could be answered and every human problem solved through creating and controlling social structures and institutions based on an understanding of human decision-making. On the other side were Christians and

47. Ibid., 116.
48. Ibid., 109.
49. Ibid., 114–15.

other religious meddlers who criticized the economic abstraction and answered it with an equally harmful abstraction, refusing to understand the nature of reality and insisting that love would fix everything. The former raised before Knight's terrified eyes the specter of centralized authority, the latter of anarchy. We must acknowledge (briefly for the moment, but we will return to it in our critique) that Knight's portrayals of both groups are somewhat reactionary, to say the least, and his own self-awareness was not particularly keen. Nevertheless, it is informative to see that he attempted to carve out an extremely narrow bit of territory within which the economist could be seen as authoritative. In "minding his own business" (i.e. sticking to economic models) and "letting others alone" (i.e., letting politicians, priests, and others do their jobs) he sought to obey the golden rule as he understood it.

FREEDOM FOR ECONOMIC MAN?

The task remains to extrapolate the vision of the human being and her freedom that arises from Knight's thought. We learned, first, that Knight did not see "economic man" as an actual human being but a provisional ideal that symbolizes merely one aspect of human behavior, namely the behavior of rationally choosing how to adapt means to given ends. This model person, while enabling scientists to study human wants scientifically, at least in the abstract, should by no means be taken as an attempt to sum up human life in its fullness or to provide ethical norms. On the contrary, most people who are not "monsters or imbeciles"[50] have a natural (if irrational) aversion to the kinds of answers economics would give to questions other than narrowly economic ones. The economic person, he insists, is by no means anyone's ideal person; a human who calculated everything strictly according to self-interest would be "worthy of moral condemnation. . . . [T]he intolerable repugnance of the idea that . . . all effort, aspiration and sacrifice are delusions [mere covers for self-interest] is after all [a good reason] for believing that they are not."[51]

Knight affirms that there is a place for human virtue, that there is a difference between doing something because it is prudent (the highest virtue of economic man) and doing something because it is good

50. Asso and Fiorito, "Waging War against Mechanical Man," 26.

51. Knight, "Ethics and the Economic Interpretation," 39.

(something he sees as foreign or irrelevant to economic man).[52] But with regard to determining *what is good* for the human being, he calls others to acknowledge that economics is not able to go the distance. Knight here exhibits a divided anthropology that pits the economic man (the abstract form of human motivation) against the rest of the human being (the actual content). Scientific economic anthropology touches *only* on the single human characteristic of choosing how to achieve what one desires given available resources. As we have seen, he does not approve of the behavioral economist's attempt to flatten the entire human being into this one aspect. The real individual is much more than a chooser, and the fact that economics cannot help determine the given ends (nor even the given means) in the choosing scenario is Knight's main defense for the distinct exercise known as ethics.

Accordingly, he also offers a twofold description of freedom for this two-fold human being, which distinguishes economic freedom— the naked ability to wield power that is merely a means to an end—from ethical freedom, which is an end in itself. His awareness of the historical roots of utility theory gives him a certain caution about the way it defines "freedom." Classical economic thought (like Smith's), in its move away from feudalism and the "stupidity of governments," upheld the idea that "the essentially negative ideal of *freedom*" would be more likely to achieve the greatest good for the greatest number of people than would governmental bureaucracy.[53] But Knight argues that this kind of "freedom theory," in which the individual is allowed the maximum amount of freedom that is compatible with equal freedom for one's neighbors, is actually a misnomer. In actuality, utility theory necessitates the assumption that the free individual will obey certain universal laws; this includes the natural law that an individual who is left "free to choose" *must* maximize pleasure through whatever means are available, while at the same time not abusing her freedom.[54]

Knight therefore claims that utility theory confuses "freedom" with "power" in its social doctrine. When economists insist that economic policy must leave individuals "free," they are in fact not talking about freedom in any ethical sense (specifying neither the teleological good

52. In chapter 6 we will dwell more fully, with Deirdre McCloskey, on the question of whether prudence is the economic actor's only virtue.

53. Knight, "Freedom as Fact and Criterion," 2–3. Original emphasis.

54. Ibid., 4.

for which, nor the evil from which, they must be free) but rather in a purely utilitarian sense of being able to use whatever power is theirs. The distribution of power, he notes, has little or nothing to do with individual freedom, but is rather determined by the cumulative effects of one's own and others' past actions. Those with more income to spend, usually by virtue of inheritance rather than their own effort, have more power to wield. Equal freedom, as conceived of by naïve economists who would too quickly jump to create policy norms out of theory, can therefore not lead to economic justice. On the contrary, he notes ruefully, the "doctrine" of equality to which economists subscribe is there to provide justification for the inequalities that already exist.[55] Because he rejects this doctrine, as well as the mechanistic behaviorist mindset that envisions all human actions as determined by outside institutions, he concludes that economists would be wise to keep away from terms like "freedom," which have no real meaning in the scientific study of cause and effect. Freedom is an ethical category, one which rests on a community's prior agreement and approbation—something he wants economists to exclude from their calculations. With regard to economic policy, freedom of choice can be seen only as a *means* to given ends, which are themselves dependent on the prior moral judgments of individuals and communities.[56]

Economic science is not therefore unimportant; a general law of supply and demand that is based on historical observation is possible and of limited value.[57] But for *real* (not hypothetical or theoretical) human problems we need ethics—what he calls the "Criticism of Values"—because in dealing with them "we are constantly thrown back upon categories still more remote from the scientific, upon relations which cannot be formulated in logical propositions at all, and we must admit that a large part of our 'knowledge' is of this character."[58] As mere mortals, humans must resort to figurative language. "[I]t is impossible to describe the world in terms which mean definitely what they say," which is where ethics comes in; ethical discussions "run in terms of suggestion rather than logical statement, in figurative rather than literal language, and principles will be available through sympathetic interpretation rather than intellectual

55. Ibid., 10.
56. Ibid., 14.
57. Rutherford, *Chicago Economics and Institutionalism*, 13.
58. Knight, "Ethics and the Economic Interpretation," 39.

cognition."[59] Ethics addresses and critiques the ends toward which human wants are directed, and it critiques means, not only according to efficiency, but according to the kind of propriety that Smith explored. Compared to this heroic (and risky) task, the job performed by economics seems small indeed. Likewise, "economic man" seems rather dim and incapable of shedding much light on genuine, complicated human beings, at least without the kind of interpretation Knight himself abdicates.

A major difference between economics and ethics for Knight is in the ability to divide up life into discrete categories; economists can do it, ethicists cannot. When ethicists claim that their interest is in *non-economic* human motivations (for example, those not related to wealth or material survival), Knight skeptically notes that they are usually unable to demonstrate to economists' satisfaction that such motivations exist. Close examination "fails to show any definite basis for [the distinction between economic wants and other wants] or to disclose the possibility of any demarcation which is not arbitrary and unscientific."[60] When ethicists try to distinguish those wants that are merely "economic," such as those related to survival or to self-sufficiency, they find themselves having to make judgments about which wants are necessary and which are not. In reality, Knight rightly claims, it is impossible to identify the boundary at which economic concerns end and ethical concerns begin, since life is not so easily dissected:

> If by [making] a living we mean life as it is actually lived, every-thing is included, recreation, culture, and even religion; there is no basis for a distinction between the economic and anything else, and the term has no meaning . . . [The idea that economic activity] includes everything which involves the making and spending of money or the creation and use of things having money value . . . [is true, but this] directly or indirectly covers virtually the whole life activity of a modern man.[61]

Any attempt—whether by economists or ethicists—to categorize the necessities of life as "economic" while reserving "moral" value for anything over and above bare subsistence is frivolous, since Knight's observation shows that this is not how humans live. Humans do not experience wants as essentially different from needs; "For any practical social purpose," he

59. Ibid., 39–40.
60. Knight, "Ethics and the Economic Interpretation," 24.
61. Ibid., 24–25.

notes, "beauty, play, conventionality, and the gratification of all sorts of 'vanities' are more 'necessary' than food and shelter."[62]

But Knight does not declare that the reverse as also true—that it is frivolous to address "economic" forms as if they were not also moral. The *form* of desire for beauty or friendship, or social approval is, he insists, the same as the *form* of desire for water to drink or air to breathe. A preference is a preference is a preference, without regard to its content. The normative significance of such a perspective is not hard to see. If the desire for Manolo Blahnik shoes operates according to the exact same principles as the desire to have one's children immunized against an impending outbreak of swine flu, then one mechanism (personal want satisfaction) and one kind of market (the market built around personal want satisfaction) will sufficiently take care of both. The deceptively simple shoe mechanism becomes normative for the immunization market, which is no more complex in economic terms (wealthy children live, poor children die). Put this way it may seem absurd, and yet this is precisely what economics does.

In the final analysis Knight seems to intuit what Adam Smith also knew, namely that economic science is decidedly ill-equipped to explain anything that exceeds the self-fulfilling paradigm it prescribes for itself. General laws of rational choice or supply and demand are not without value; the discovery of such laws has indeed played an important role in bettering the living conditions of much of humankind, but it has at the same time worsened conditions for some others. For real human problems we also need ethics or the "Criticism of Values," because in dealing with people on the ground we discover complexities of context that no generalized model can embrace in full. Knight wisely admonishes ethicists not to give in to the extreme abstractions of either economics or Christianity when trying to define freedom, the definition of which is open to dispute and change. He thinks neither can provide a universal picture of the human being or offer a realistic, defensible basis for concrete social action. An abstraction can have only limited value— whether, as in the case of science, for discovering basic laws, or, in the case of religion, for providing ideals for contemplation. But real ethics (upon which policy is dependent) for real people (for whom policy ex-

62. Ibid., 28. The flip side of this non-boundary, of course, is what we will see in the later Chicago school's treatment of all aspects of human life in terms of want satisfaction or means adaptation.

ists) must give an account of goods or values which can be identified
only through discussion and criticism.

CRITIQUE OF KNIGHT

Readers approaching Frank Knight's economic thought with a pair of
Protestant lenses may find themselves feeling somewhat ambivalent. At
a basic level, his single-minded pursuit of discovering the laws of human behavior through scientific methods is one that Calvin himself
might have approved, affirming as he did that God has created and
continues to provide for the world—including the social world—with
an order that is at least partially accessible to fallen human understanding. Christian theology generally affirms that humans have reason, that
they can partially distinguish right from wrong, that they generally seek
what they understand to be good, and that they are capable of making
wise (or foolish) decisions based on their understanding. It affirms the
sciences as being gifts of God for the promotion of human flourishing;
Christians who choose to ignore the sciences are not only fools, they are
poor stewards of the gifts God has given them. The "freedom" enjoyed
by Christians does not mean freedom from the laws of nature or the laws
of human society—Christians cannot walk on water; neither can they
escape responsibility for wisely and lovingly adapting their (God-given)
means in order to attain their (God-given) ends. Moreover, political
leaders, whose (God-given) ends include the good of those over whom
they have authority, have a responsibility to make use of economic science *if* it can indeed achieve such ends.

Christian theology can likewise affirm Knight's attempt not to be
hubristic with regard to the explanatory power of economics. His adamant non-imperialism with regard to the reach of economic science is
worthy of admiration; his view that economic knowledge was purely
abstract and therefore not immediately useful for the real world can be
characterized as a highly rare disciplinary humility. It is not often that
one hears a scholar admitting that the discoveries of his field are virtually
useless without extensive translation and adaptation by those outside
the field—everyday folks who are better equipped to deal with real-life
issues like ethics or policy.[63] He rightly insisted that the isolation and

63. Robert Nelson is a current economist who has a similar view; see, for example,
Nelson, "Scholasticism v. Pietism," in which he argues that mathematical economics

identification of general laws, even relatively common-sense ones (such as supply and demand), is a worthy endeavor. Like mathematics, which relies on simple axioms and offers conclusions that "are descriptive of reality and are indispensable in predicting and controlling the phenomena of the physical world," economics, too, has its simple axioms that are ignored at great peril; "the broad outlines of social policy depend upon them and are quite commonly misguided through the failure of legislators and administrators to understand and follow them."[64] Furthermore, he says, it is not the laws themselves that are normally in dispute—in fact such laws generally arise because "the mind has not the creative power to imagine a world fundamentally different from that in which we actually live"[65]—but rather it is the conclusions reached by the *use* of those axioms that is where the real controversies lie.

In these statements, however, Knight reveals the inevitable connections between theory and policy that he usually tries so diligently to avoid. Try as he might, the wall between description and prescription cannot hold. Where the Christian ethicist must part ways with Knight is at the point of his lack of understanding about the connection between explanation and norms. Knight's awareness of the contingencies involved in economic policy does not cause him to question his own assumption about the neutral position of economic science itself. He narrates economics in such a way that he does not have to acknowledge rational means adaptation as a "value" or norm that economic science inherited and perpetuates. His modernist faith in ahistorical "abstracts" and their sterile usefulness (as well as his unquestioned, twentieth-century American ideology of "political negativism"[66]) leads Knight to overestimate his own ability to be objective. Economics does *not* seek, as he puts it, to "find out what the laws" of human behavior are; it rather *assumes* these laws to begin with and, because it can imagine nothing different, makes them normative. He has more faith, for example, in the economic abstraction than in other abstractions such as Christian love. That the "economic man" makes "rational" choices is assumed; it is not open to

(designed mainly to impress mathematical economists) misses an important opportunity to share economic wisdom with non-economists, who might then apply and make use of it.

64. Knight, "Limitations of Scientific Method on Economics," 137.

65. Ibid., 136.

66. Knight, "Ethics and Economic Reform," 48.

discovery or critique and it therefore wholly determines the findings of economic inquiry. Yet in what sense can even the form of human rationale be taken as a given? His failure to address in what sense utility analysis can be said to have a "logic or purpose" and not be considered a normative endeavor is what will help him create the wings on which his successors will venture toward heaven. Some of them, as we will see in the next chapter, place economics in the service of freedom (Friedman); others supersede freedom with economics (Becker).

Frank Knight was, to some degree, at war with himself over the task of economics. He attempts to have his cake and eat it too—believing strongly in the importance of models based on ahistorical assumptions, trusting that such assumptions could yield certain limited, but useful, truths; but at the same time resisting the behaviorist "economic inter- pretation" of human life largely because of its application of ahistorical truths to contingent humans. He seems to be saying that, even though rational action is non-negotiable for economic science, economic *policy* can throw it away if it values other (necessarily *irrational*) action more; in other words economic science is in no way normative for economic policy. This, of course, is not the case, and the "behaviorist man" Knight hated was the inevitable trajectory of the "economic man" he liked, since (as he himself acknowledges) the human mind can hardly be satisfied with understanding as such. Moreover, understanding as such cannot truly exist since (as Knight again acknowledges) even the "scientific" hu- man observer has a finite imagination. His decision to practice econom- ics from the starting point of abstract assumptions, rather than from particular historical questions or problems, meant that he was unable to stop the speeding train once it gained momentum.

But Knight is not the only one who tries to have it both ways. In Christian theological terms, "economic man" (the self-interested choos- er) represents humans at their worst, while Jesus (the lover of God and all humankind) represents humans at their best. If genuine human beings— fallen, but still good—tend to fluctuate somewhere in between, any eco- nomic "science" built on the image of them at their worst (thus creating the only norm by which they can hope to succeed in the marketplace) puts an unacceptable weight upon their shoulders, which prevents them from aspiring to something better. Yet many Christians in America take the untenable position that public policy should be based on a greed- motivated economic person, while personal and church life should be modeled on Jesus-style neighbor love. As even most economists—few of whom are anarchists—acknowledge, such an economy is not only un-edifying, it is impossible. Ultimately, those who would shape a fruitful and humane economy in the here and now must place their faith either in institutional checks and balances (such as government) or in the other-interest and self-limitation of individual human beings (or better yet, both); without these God-given graces, even the "perfect" market will not function.

Before moving on, the Christian ethicist must also consider Knight's tirade against Christian love. Theologians seeking a freedom-oriented economics can whole-heartedly agree with Knight's critique of Christianity, in so far as it remains an abstraction and a superflu-ous additive to "real" life. No less than "economic man," a "loving hu-man" that somehow floats ethereally over concrete human suffering is of little value to human social, political, and economic life. But it must be said that his understanding of Christianity is woefully limited, his attack being against the "social gospel" movement of his time on the one hand, and the imperialistic Roman Catholic Church on the other. It is a significant liability to Knight's thinking (due to his own church experience and his reliance on authors such as Reinhold Niebuhr, who prescribe separate rules for "moral man" and "immoral society"[67]) that he appeals mainly to the Gospels in this regard. And within the Gospels he appeals to certain *words* attributed to Jesus, rather than to Jesus' embodied, political actions such as rejecting earthly power, eating with sinners and tax collectors, or "cleansing" the temple. An interpretation of the Christian scriptures more like Calvin's—which sees the Gospels as part of the New Testament; and sees the New Testament not as an isolated book of pithy sayings but rather as a narrative embedded in the diverse context of the community of Israel, the Hebrew Scriptures, the early church, and Christian historical theology—would necessarily have led Knight to different conclusions.

Moreover, Knight seems to understand little of Christian theology other than the golden rule. His fixation on abstractions caused Knight to cast a blind eye on certain central tenets of the Christian worldview—such as the incarnation and the church, which together mean that love is never abstract and is always and everywhere embodied, historical, and contingent. Ethics, which in his mind is about *applying* scientifically-

67. Knight, "Ethics and Economic Reform," 113n.

discovered data to achieve whatever effects society considers good, remains impervious to Christianity because of its perceived status as the monolithic and vapid recommendation to love everyone equally. He demonstrates no historical perspective on Christianity, in which one can find embodied recommendations in the biblical examples of the patriarchs and matriarchs, or of Christ and his disciples. He also demonstrates no understanding, for example, of Calvin's teachings on law or freedom, which are insistent that the Christian's inner life (characterized by knowing God as good) has specific and concrete manifestations, none of which involve distinguishing one's private faith from one's social and political life. The freedom that comes from obedience to God sets the pattern for human social policy, though it is admittedly followed only imperfectly by sinful humans. Christian neighbor love is not an abstraction but is rather embodied in time and space, in the same way the incarnate God demonstrated it in Palestine in the first century CE. Had Knight forsaken his modernist insistence on abstraction and ethical individualism, his shallow caricature of the Christian tradition might have given way to a vision of Christianity's potential for "earthbound realism."

His fierce disregard for Christianity actually undermines his argument about the importance of ethics as separate from economics, and actually makes clearer the way in which his vision of ethics is, unbeknownst to himself, a glorified economics. Like economics, he claims that Christianity is ill-equipped to talk policy because it is too abstract. But not all Christian theology is abstract, and if Christianity, in spite of its narrative framework and normative practices, can offer nothing beneficial to human social life then it is unlikely that any model other than a utilitarian cost-benefit analysis can. Indeed, it is likely that all metaphysical systems would be equally harmful according to Knight's perspective, due to their lack of realism. His assertion that orderly social life is necessarily dependent upon "intellectual analysis in impersonal terms" seems to put the ball back in science's court, despite all his protests to the contrary; policy is no longer an art, it is a science that only those free of religious or ethical sentiment can execute. In spite of his insistence that ethics is not a matter of glorified economics, he reduces it from an all-encompassing narrative to a stripped-down process of choosing what to do when. And although he sees religion (not so much tradition and practice, but mainly a worldview) as providing the "moral interest, motive or 'drive' toward finding solutions for problems"[68]—in other words, the *given ends* that economic decision-making satisfies— he sees no role for religion in the "criticism of values" with regard to means adaptation. The means are also given, but in this case they are given by economic science.

Knight's lingering problem seems to be his unwillingness to admit that method itself is at least partially determinative of results. His defense of realms for ethics and religion that are independent of economics stems from his underlying desire to protect a sphere in which truth or "fact" is released from the messy context of real life. He argues that science deals with "literal" matters (such as the unattached male of economic fame) while ethics deals in the "figurative"; the former is "logical" while the other "suggests." He does not see that, because the whole world is subject to human interpretation, each field should be seen as possessing *both* its own logic *and* its own suggestion, even as each one addresses *both* concrete *and* conceptual issues. Moreover, in characterizing ethics as the "criticism of values," Knight gives the economic term "value" priority over traditional ethical terms like "norms," "virtues," or "goods," thus reducing ethics (even as he seeks not to) to an accessory to economics at best, if not an afterthought. Ethics in his mind is comparative economics; it is a content-full cost-benefit analysis, rather than habits of narrative, description, and praxis that go beyond the simple adaptation of means to ends. Such a view does not do justice to Christian ethics, whose job (impossible in Knight's mind) is to "imagine a world fundamentally dif-ferent from that in which we actually live."[69]

Freedom-oriented Calvinism not only imagines a different world through the gift of revelation, but seeks to embody it as well. The "loving human" is Christianity's answer to "economic man"; where economics posits a self-interested model it supposedly does not believe in, Christian ethics insists that human love really is possible because Jesus the hu-man has already done it, and because the Holy Spirit continues to enable humans to do so. The Christian teaching that human nature has been redeemed in its totality—both body and spirit, both its mortality and its eternity, both individual and communal—gives it a decisively concrete character. While economics must shy away from ethical matters such as "freedom," Christianity can boldly offer not only a "moral leaven" but an

68. Ibid., 103.

69. Knight, "Limitations of Scientific Method on Economics," 256.

embodied pattern. Economics cannot declare its principles to be "law" simply because it chooses (self-interestedly) not to think more creatively. The lesson of the incarnate Christ—gendered, ethnic, political, yet "heavenly"—is that where nature fails, God's gifts do not.

CONCLUSION: ETHICS-FREE ECONOMICS?

Frank Knight stands as a theoretical way station between Adam Smith's deliberate attempt to create liberty-fostering socio-economic norms for his culture, and later economists' attempts to explain the entirety of human life as if normative interests were irrelevant to their inquiry. Knight sought to pursue economic understanding for its own sake, treating it methodologically as a natural science, even while admitting that human beings as a subject of scientific study do not permit of simple analysis. While his attempt to isolate economics from ethics and other fields was ultimately futile, Knight is at least to be admired for his nascent self-awareness. He made a purposeful and explicit decision to stay out of policy-making because he understood that economic abstractions—such as the sheer *power* of "economic man" to choose according to his own self-determined preferences—could not be applied without troublesome consequences. He saw that in the world of historical contingency, *freedom* is a norm in need of both description and protection. Because he felt ill-equipped (or perhaps simply disinclined) to do so, he did not try to set goals for economics, nor did he try to draw vast conclusions about human social life. Instead he left the heavy lifting to ethicists and politicians.

His tragic mistake, however, was in his belief that the sciences could be undertaken apart from normative human interests. As it turns out, knowledge for its own sake is not merely a sentimental idea but a self-deceptive one. He claims that the economist's endeavor is for knowledge pure and simple, but it is finally impossible for a person, even a scientist, to seek knowledge without some reason for doing so. The economist's very quest is, at a minimum, undertaken in response to one's sense of curiosity as to how the universe works. (Economists will also note that the hope of job security can be a major factor.) In science knowledge is considered "instrumental," worthy based solely on its ability to get practical results.[70] As Judith Butler puts it, "Knowledge and power are

---

70. Knight, "Limitations of Scientific Method on Economics," 108.

not finally separable but work together to establish a set of subtle and explicit criteria for thinking the world."[71] Economics, no less than theology, "thinks the world," and along with it, human beings and their freedom. Knight was perhaps naïve to hope that economics could stay in its cage and resist the imperialist urge, just as it would be naïve to think that theology could do so.

Knight is also to be critiqued for his faith in the amoral quality of theoretical abstractions. His belief that economics could usefully study a fictional abstraction known as "economic man," even while admitting that a real system based on economic man would be a disaster for human life, allowed him to evade any responsibility that he and his colleagues might incur for the consequences of their studies. His unwillingness to admit normativity renders his economics less fruitful for a liberative and transformative approach. He knows that without ethics there is no freedom; and because he refuses to speak of freedom his economics loses any explicit connection to the goal of human flourishing. He must settle instead for a supposedly more abstract "power" to make choices regarding the adaptation of means to ends. But an economics that has lost sight of freedom will inevitably tend toward oppression of the powerless. Economics, like theology, "is contextual and inevitably intertwined with the interests and desires of a particular culture or social class."[72] If it is not purposefully directed toward the interests of the weak, it will reflect instead the interests of both those who write it for tenure and those who depend upon it for re-election.

Knight's insistence on academic and scientific rigor in the field of economic inquiry seems to have been a necessary conceptual step toward economists' authority in the public eye. He represents a narrow bridge between two vast territories. The first, occupied by thinkers like Adam Smith, is the territory in which economic behavior can be seen as one facet of human moral existence. The human tendency to truck, barter and exchange can be provisionally isolated for the purpose of examining it, but must in the end always be seen as part and parcel of its historical and cultural context of interlocking sympathies. This approach was unsatisfying to Knight because of its contingency, so he sought to isolate human economic behavior even further into the moment of choice, an abstract form that he hoped would be respected as truly scientific in a

71. Butler, *Undoing Gender*, 27.

72. Ibid., 154.

way that Smith's approach could never be. Knight actually succeeded in persuading some people of the validity of economic insights, but ironically it had the opposite effect of his stated goal. The territory on the other side of Knight's narrow bridge is one in which economists, drunk on the authority derived from their scientific rigor, went back to caring about the historical and cultural contexts of economies, but this time without any respect for the limitations of their own abstractions. All the world became the playground of economics; human complexity was now open to economic simplification and moreover, economists came to view themselves as uniquely qualified to offer advice on how best to organize human material society. To a certain extent, economics ended up exactly where it began, only with greater rhetorical power and less self-awareness of the ways it was embedded in a particular tradition. A great reversal then took place: if Smith's economy was built on *homo sympatheticus*, later economists' sympathy would be built on *homo economicus*. Sympathy, in the economic view, is nothing more than a matter of personal preference.

Without tradition to allow social science to critique itself, later economics eventually gave up "engagement with empirical and concrete economic realities" and, along with it, social responsibility.[73] Knight's thirst for a scientific knowledge of human conduct could not be prevented from morphing into a pragmatic thirst not only to *explain* the world but to *control* it by the laws one discovers. In its intolerance of ambiguity, orthodox neoliberal economics would eventually dictate a unified theory of the human being. His successors in the later Chicago school would internalize Knight's abstractions without his self-limitations. As I will show in the next chapter, Friedman would promote freedom as the given end of all humankind, an end which only neoliberal economics could ensure; while Stigler and Becker would bring an end to discussions of freedom altogether.

73. Knight, "Ethics and the Economic Interpretation," 40.

5

"THE CHARMING CONCEIT"

Chicago Economics and the End of Freedom as an End

IN THE LAST CHAPTER I suggested that Frank Knight's wall of separation between the theoretical abstractions of economics and the concrete norms of ethics could not withstand the pressures of intellectual imperialism. His faith in the limited power of economic science to explain and predict the form, if not the content, of human conduct gave his successors at Chicago a taste (so to speak) for even greater explanatory power. To leave complicated questions about human motivations, goals, and values to other modes of inquiry would prove, as he himself predicted, "intellectually unsatisfactory" to many economists: "The scientific mind can rest only in one of two extreme positions, that there are absolute values, or that every individual desire is an absolute and one as 'good' as another. But neither of these is true."[1] Knight's willingness to live with some tension (not to mention to leave room for the unique and important contributions of ethics and other academic fields) was not shared by the majority of his colleagues and students, and therefore although he was arguably one of the main founders of the Chicago school, "much of what Knight believed would later be rejected by his disciples."[2]

1. Knight, "Ethics and the Economic Interpretation," 31.
2. Nelson, *Economics as Religion*, 115; see also 139.

The Chicago school is generally thought to include three identifiable generations of thinkers.[3] Knight (along with Jacob Viner and Henry Simons) represents the first; Milton Friedman and George Stigler, Knight's students, represent the second; and the third is formidably represented by Gary Becker. Whereas Knight imposed a cage upon his own economic inquiry, believing that "the utility description of behavior as an affair of comparing and choosing is valid only in so far as men compare and choose" and that "no one in his senses has thought of it as the exclusive form of all activity in all historical time,"[4] we will see that his successors at Chicago disagreed. They did not try to avoid the sort of "economic imperialism"[5] Knight abhorred; instead they pursued an aggressive agenda of analyzing the entire world of human experience in terms of economic choice, and then encouraged the use of this type of analysis to control human behavior. The later Chicago school embodies Polanyi's observation regarding *laissez-faire* thought that what was born in the eighteenth century (with Smith) as "a mere penchant for non-bureaucratic methods" eventually became "a veritable faith in man's secular salvation through a self-regulating market."[6]

My goal here is not to explicate all of Chicago economics, but to uncover and critique the concept of "freedom" as it occurs in one particular branch of the family tree. This chapter will focus special attention on those sections of their writings in which these second- and third-generation Chicagoans reveal their beliefs about the human being, human freedom, and the economic system best suited to these. When reading economic theory, it is both possible and necessary for the ethically minded reader to be deliberate about discerning the anthropological and normative

3. Ibid., 117.

4. Knight, "Marginal Utility Economics," 159. This is a not-so-subtle slam against Marxism.

5. Shulman attributes the coining of this term to Swedberg in 1990. See Shulman, "Metaphors of Discrimination," 7. Backhouse concisely describes economic imperialism as the application of economic methods of analysis to new areas of human life; Becker is (here as elsewhere) the proverbial poster child. See Backhouse, *Ordinary Business of Life*, 311. George Stigler wistfully expressed economics' aspirations thus: "Even if it does not achieve this imperial status, I am wholly confident that it will become a powerful theme guiding much work in the social sciences in the next generation." Stigler, "Economics or Ethics?" 191.

6. Polanyi, *Great Transformation*, 135. He applied this statement to the "liberal creed" of the mid-nineteenth century in particular, but the sentiment still holds among many libertarians in the twenty-first century.

claims that support its scientific claims, for the obvious reason that economic analysis always carries with it both "behavioral and even policy implications."[7] Those who find the *economic description of the human being* flawed are unlikely to favor the sorts of *policies* that flow from it. When approaching the topic with the type of freedom-oriented Calvinist lenses we have adopted here, what becomes painfully evident in reading the later Chicago economists is the incremental draining of the term "freedom." In chapter 3 we saw that, for Smith, freedom was of ultimate importance and an economic end in its own right; he emphasized freeing individuals from rulers with feudal and mercantilist interests in hopes of creating a humane economy that served more than just the powerful few—an attitude that Friedman preserves, in some ways. By the time we get to Stigler and Becker, we will see that freedom—if indeed such a term can even be used with relation to their thought—has been emptied and reduced to a mere means in service to other unspecified ends.

MILTON FRIEDMAN: FREEDOM AS SOCIAL POWER

Milton Friedman was a thinker of both unfailing conviction and deep contradiction. On one hand, the Nobel laureate is remembered as:

> [p]erhaps the most notable economist endorsing the view that economics is value free. . . . Friedman (1953) argued that economics as a positive science is concerned exclusively with the factual and predictive. As such, it is independent of any particular value position or normative judgment. Positive economics is an objective science, in the same sense that the physical sciences and engineering are objective.[8]

But at the same time, in spite of his insistence in the positivist or non-normative character of market science, Friedman evangelically holds a prior commitment—a value not derived from economic analysis itself—that human beings must be free. This is no small detail; in his life and death, he has been called "Freedom Man" and "an intellectual freedom fighter."[9] Freedom, in Friedman's mind, is not only the pre-condition on

7. Shulman, "Metaphors of Discrimination," 5. (The "even" here is fascinating, as if it were a novel idea that economic analysis might be intricately connected to concrete policy recommendations.)

8. Henderson and Pisciotta, *Faithful Economics*, 2–3.

9. Klein, *Shock Doctrine*, 22. Citing Margaret Thatcher and the *Wall Street Journal*, respectively.

which a *laissez-faire* economy can function; it is also the goal toward which market mechanisms are directed—a goal they will naturally achieve as long as no government wrenches are thrown in.

In the preface to Friedman's *Capitalism and Freedom*, he acknowledges those—including Frank Knight (from the last chapter) and George Stigler (from this chapter)—in whose intellectual tradition he stands. "I ask their pardon," he writes, "for my failure to acknowledge specifically the many ideas of theirs which they will find expressed in this book. I have learned so much from them and what I have learned has become so much a part of my own thought that I would not know how to select points to footnote."[10] Thus he plants his roots firmly in Chicago school soil. But if Frank Knight (who viewed economics as being useful for explaining certain phenomena in abstract terms, but of extremely limited power with regard to direct, real-life applications) was the original charismatic force that consolidated the various minds at Chicago into a tightly-knit group of scholars, it was Friedman who would not only determine the research program of the school for years to come but also spread his view outside the walls of the university.[11]

Perhaps due to a number of years he had spent working in governmental agencies before joining the Chicago faculty,[12] Friedman showed unabashed faith in the direct political applicability of economic theory. He was convinced that the knowledge economics could provide held the key to nothing less than ultimate human freedom, and upon joining the faculty in 1946 he "swiftly took over the intellectual leadership of one faction of the Department and energetically attacked the views and proposals of the others. His vigor in debate and the content of his arguments set the tone and public image of Chicago economics for at least a quarter century."[13] Friedman's unique talents in economic analysis and application, combined with his missionary-like "zeal" for economic progress and his willingness to proselytize and convert the economic "heathen,"[14]

10. Friedman, *Capitalism and Freedom*, xi.

11. "Before the arrival of Knight and his student Simons, it would have been hard to identify a particular intellectual style among Chicago Ph.D.'s." Reder, "Chicago Economics," 5.

12. In Gary Becker's article on Friedman he notes that Friedman spent several years working for the National Resources Commission, National Bureau of Economic Research, and the Treasury. See Shils, *Remembering the University of Chicago*, 138.

13. Reder, "Chicago Economics," 10.

14. Shils, *Remembering the University of Chicago*, 145–46.

are what allowed him to spearhead Chicago's ascent, both in the intellectual leadership of the economic community and in policy-making significance.[15] Friedman seems to have achieved particularly deftly the Chicago school's desire "to influence the teaching of economics to non-economists . . . to have other social scientists, lawyers, judges, legislators, bureaucrats, voters thinking about economics in terms of 'correct' models; make the 'right' assumptions; ask the right questions; etc."[16]

Where others saw boundaries and limitations, Friedman saw possibilities and invitations to expand economics' uses. Unlike some of his predecessors and colleagues, he was not satisfied with the idea that "policy-advising activity . . . is not what professional economics is about"; instead Friedman, like Smith, took an explicitly policy-oriented stance of the sort Stigler would later (with tongue-in-cheek) label "preaching."[17] Running the economic machine takes some expertise, however, and Friedman was not satisfied with preaching alone. Economic historian Robert Nelson characterizes Friedman as an "economic technician" and "the most brilliant American economist of the twentieth century" as well as the most influential.[18] Friedman exhibited the attitude (not impossible to defend on Calvinist grounds, as I will explain in chapter 6) that if economists are the technical experts on human maximizing behavior, then society would be as foolish to ignore them as it would be to build a bridge without the help of qualified engineers. Moreover, it would be positively irresponsible and even selfish for economists to keep their knowledge to themselves. He, along with his wife, Rose Director Friedman, went so far as to translate neo-classical economic theory into a capitalist manifesto of sorts—longer than Marx's pamphlet, but nevertheless written in layperson's terms.[19] Friedman as preacher dem-

---

15. Nelson, *Economics as Religion*, 140.

16. Reder, "Chicago Economics," 18.

17. Stigler, "Economics or Ethics?," 147.

18. Nelson, *Economics as Religion*, 141; 148.

19. Friedman and Friedman, *Free to Choose*. Lucidity seems to be one of Friedman's special gifts. Becker notes that even in economics classes, Friedman, unlike other professors, "developed the theory in a clear, systematic, logically consistent fashion. He also gave numerous illustrations and applications." Shils, *Remembering the University of Chicago*, 141.

onstrated a deep faith in the idea that economic truths, persuasively argued, would set people free.[20]

The results of Friedman's efforts were gratifying, and would almost surely have caused Knight to shudder had he lived to witness them. While his public success was not immediate,[21] Becker notes that Friedman's accomplishments eventually included "the adoption of many of his ideas by professional economists and the introduction by governments the world over of many of his programs—such as flexible exchange rates, flatter tax schedules, and privatization of many government activities."[22] He attributes this to Friedman's noteworthy confidence—not shared by all economists of his generation, at least in Becker's memory—in both the explanatory power of economic theory and its relevance for applications in the "real world." (For this reason, Becker credits Friedman with teaching the most influential course—price theory—he ever took, a truth that will become clear when we return to Becker in the coming pages.[23])

Friedman's Human Being, and What Freedom Is Not

Friedman enables the task of uncovering his views on human freedom, in that he helpfully begins his 1962 work, *Capitalism and Freedom*, with an entire chapter devoted to his reflections on "Political Freedom and Economic Freedom." Undeterred by Knight's caution that freedom was an ethical matter on which economics could not shed light, Friedman goes boldly into this territory, combining political and economic (and, to a lesser degree, theological) ideas to create a lofty, yet practical and seemingly achievable, vision of material human life. His argument for neoliberal economics is persuasive and appealing (at least at first glance), in large part because of his personal conviction that it is the only system that truly respects humans' essential dignity. "As liberals," he writes, "we take freedom of the individual, or perhaps the family, as our ultimate

---

20. He saw it as his job to keep these truths alive in the realm of intellectual conversation, until such a time as they reached a tipping point in popular thinking. Friedman, *Capitalism and Freedom*, viii–ix.

21. Ibid., vi–vii.

22. Shils, *Remembering the University of Chicago*, 140.

23. Ibid., 142–43. Becker also remembers Friedman's harsh criticism of the prose in his original analysis of discrimination for being virtually unreadable, a trait Becker seems successfully to have weeded out of his own writing, 144.

goal in judging social arrangements."[24] Who among us, in the twenty-first century, wishes to argue that human dignity does not require a large amount of individual freedom? Christian ethicists and others who believe individual freedom is part of humans' God-given nature, the respect for which is therefore a necessary component to genuine human flourishing, must take Friedman seriously even if we do not entirely subscribe to his rationality.

But Friedman's theological anthropology—his understanding of the human individual for whom freedom is the ultimate goal—is not immediately apparent; it is not the explicit starting point for his thinking on freedom. Instead, his political ideology is; individual human freedom of the type associated with the intersection of democracy and competitive capitalism is where he begins. It acts not only as the foundation for his economic theory but also as its task. Readers must glean his views of the human being from brief comments that arise here and there, almost as afterthoughts, in his musings on other topics. In the context of his explanation of liberalism's valuation of the individual, for example, he writes, "The liberal conceives of men as imperfect beings."[25] By this he means that they are capable of doing "harm" to one another (though he notes that harm is a matter of perspective). These imperfect beings must therefore be protected from the potential harm others may inflict upon them, and prevented from doing harm to others, while also being enabled to do the "good" of which they are also capable (but which is also a matter of perspective).

The reason humans are prone to harming one another if left to their own devices, or to disagree about what constitutes harm, is because they are, at their core, disconnected individuals. They are "a collection of Robinson Crusoes, as it were,"[26] each of whom lives for himself ("or perhaps the family"). Each person has a certain amount of power and controls a certain amount of resources. Acts of "self-denial" are very rare among these imperfect beings;[27] once people have a taste of power and control, they are highly unlikely to give it up and are likely to desire even more. Human individuals have no built-in incentives to limit themselves in any way. Any peaceful (non-coercive) interaction or "co-operation"

24. Friedman, *Capitalism and Freedom*, 12.

25. Ibid., 12.

26. Ibid., 13.

27. Ibid., 16–17.

between more than one Robinson must therefore be achieved from out-side, through persuasion, bargaining, and mutually-beneficial exchange —and finally, when all else fails, by government. (While humans do in-deed need to be prevented from harming one another, they must not be prevented from harming themselves if they so choose. Such paternalism is unacceptable to the liberal mindset, as we will see below.)

In spite of their imperfection, or perhaps because of it, Friedman is unwavering in his conviction that these human beings must be "free," by which he refers to *individual power placed in the context of social life.* "Freedom as a value," he writes, "has to do with the interrelations among people; it has no meaning whatsoever to a Robinson Crusoe on an iso-lated island (without his Man Friday)."[28] The human being in isolation is, like any other animal, simply a power-wielding entity. It uses its natural powers to take actions according to self-interest, though in the case of human animals these actions are (he assumes) informed by reason and not a simple matter of instinct. Only when human beings are exercis-ing their natural powers in close proximity to one another, when their individual powers may come into conflict with others', does it become necessary for them to begin speaking of freedom. And since Adam Smith seems to have been correct in his observation that human beings are social creatures in constant need of their fellow humans, freedom is a natural outgrowth of all human interactions. Friedman writes, "Literally millions of people are involved in providing one another with their daily bread. . . . The challenge to the believer in liberty is to reconcile this widespread interdependence with individual freedom."[29]

In spite of his deep commitment to human freedom, or perhaps because of it, Friedman largely agrees with Knight that ethics is not the economist's job. An economist is no more qualified to make prescrip-tions for other people than the policymaker is. Because the liberal sees people as imperfect beings, he writes, "a major aim of the liberal is to leave the ethical problem for the individual to wrestle with. The 'really' important ethical problems are those that face an individual in a free society—what he should do with his freedom."[30] Liberals of Friedman's

28. "Robinson Crusoe on his island is subject to 'constraint,' he has limited 'power,' and he has only a limited number of alternatives, but there is no problem of freedom in the sense that is relevant to our discussion." Ibid., 12.

29. Ibid., 13.

30. Ibid., 12.

ilk are able to assume the worst of people without seeking to prevent every flaw. Institutions for the organization of human society are there not for any positive purpose of improving human beings, but simply for the negative purpose of preventing individuals from impinging, intentionally or unintentionally, on others' freedoms. Where Friedman differs from Knight significantly is that Friedman does not see "freedom" as being itself an ethically loaded term on which the economist/preacher is unqualified to make broad pronouncements. Instead, he takes freedom-as-power to be an empty form that everyone can relate to, and also a non-negotiable human right. "[I]n a society," he writes, "freedom has nothing to say about what an individual does with his freedom; *it is not an all-embracing ethic.*"[31]

Unlike Calvin's example, in which freedom contained within it both a particular narrative about the human being and specific norms for her life; and unlike Smith, who saw freedom as an integral piece of human happiness arising from the ongoing interplay of natural human sympathies, Friedman attempts to speak of a "thin" or content-less freedom that is not bounded by any narrative and contains no prescription of any consequence. He will offer some minimal direction as to what freedom is not (namely centralized power), but will not intentionally offer any "all-embracing" definition of what it is. For him, the power to choose is not an ethical norm but simply a means to greater material prosperity in both individual and aggregate terms. And yet, Friedman's zeal for spreading this gospel of individual power makes it plain that his investment in freedom was more than purely scientific.

Why "Political Freedom" Cannot Exist Without "Economic Freedom"

The negotiation of freedom that must take place among countless interdependent individuals, all concerned primarily with themselves but also in need of one another, gives rise to the need for government. In a world of imperfect people, after all, "absolute freedom is impossible."[32] Thus social freedom for Friedman is something that largely takes its shape in relation to the state—the manifestation of concentrated power—whose unnecessary intervention is the antithesis of his brand of liberalism. Although he cannot explain why, Friedman assumes that the possession

31. Ibid. Emphasis added.

32. Ibid., 25.

of freedom is a necessity; social life should therefore be organized in such a way as to guard it from invasion, and the primary purpose of government is to protect its citizens from both outsiders and insiders. This requires a government that can make laws and support a military, but in the final analysis these duties exist primarily for economic reasons, namely the purpose of protecting autonomous exchanges among its citizens. "It is widely believed that politics and economics are separate and largely unconnected," he writes; some believe that political freedom can exist without economic freedom, as in "democratic socialism."[33] Friedman sees such a concept as an oxymoronic "delusion"; how can a person be considered free politically if she can vote but must work in a certain state or a certain factory, or may not own property, or may not vacation in Cuba due to sanctions? Such contradictions are, he believes, the inevitable end of centralized economic power.

For Friedman the freedom to exercise power should be applied in equal measure to all rational persons in a society. It is individual power, not government or collective power, that leads to advances in arts and sciences. Individual power is the engine of both individual and communal human progress, and this power is most effectively harnessed by the market—a system of interlocking, autonomously motivated exchanges. Thus, Friedman makes the extraordinary statement that economic freedom, in the form of competitive capitalism, is not a *result* of but is actually "a necessary condition for political freedom."[34] In other words the free market in which individuals exercise their own power of choice—with regard to where, with whom, and for what wage they work; where, with whom, and how they live; what they consume and how often they consume it—is the only path to freedom of other kinds. Even an *elected* socialist government is incompatible with individual human power of choice because it treats individuals as "separately short-sighted and improvident," and thus in need of paternalistic government care.[35] This is not only unjustified from the standpoint of freedom, he thinks; it is also an inefficient way to try to achieve the goods that he thinks all societies desire.[36]

33. Ibid., 7–8.

34. Ibid., 4.

35. Ibid., 187.

36. As we will see, Stigler questions this assumption. If a group of individuals consistently elects socialist leadership, it must be because socialism *is* the most efficient

But governments, it seems, cannot help but expand themselves; they naturally demand conformity and reduce individualism, leaving the specter of collectivist totalitarianism ever on the horizon. "Freedom is a rare and delicate plant," he writes. "Our minds tell us, and history confirms, that the great threat to freedom is the concentration of power. Government is necessary to preserve our freedom, it is an instrument through which we can exercise our freedom; yet by concentrating power in political hands, it is also a threat to freedom."[37] Because government is so dangerous, the competitive capitalist form of economic organization is especially necessary. Economic freedom is, on the one hand, "an end in itself," in that liberals believe humans must have control over the material aspects of their lives (though he does not say why); and on the other hand it is "also an indispensable means toward the achievement of political freedom," in that it fills a need for checks and balances on government.[38] Competitive capitalism, or the market system, is built on the dispersion of power (theoretically, power is shared by every player in the system) and it also contributes to the dilution of power (theoretically, monopolies cannot stand long against competitors).

Like Smith's appeal to individual freedom as a more effective economic engine than hierarchical planning, Friedman claims that individual freedom rather than government bureaucracy is the best way to achieve the greatest material prosperity for the greatest number of people. (He assumes that material prosperity is a worthy goal, largely because he believes it results in increased freedom to exercise power; those who prosper have more choices.) Because he sees freedom mainly in terms of *choice*, he also sees the economic sphere as the place where human freedom begins. While he therefore declares with pride that the political and economic freedom enjoyed by Americans is virtually unprecedented in human history, his doctrines still cause Friedman to see barriers to freedom in several places. For example, he takes a page out of Smith in arguing that a person who would like to be a doctor, but is

---

means to *some* good that *some* voters desire, even if it is not the production and distribution of material goods that is the economist's general rule of valuation.

37. Friedman, *Capitalism and Freedom*, 2. (He reiterates some of the historical experiences that he believes have proven this on p. viii of the Preface.)

38. Ibid., 8. Friedman also connects economic freedom to religious freedom, and cites as an example the Amish, who did not wish to be part of the nation's Social Security program, and whose livestock were later confiscated by government, in a direct curtailing of their material freedoms (9).

prevented by law from practicing medicine without a license, is a victim of freedom deprivation.[39] Not only should consumers have the freedom to choose any doctors they want (including unqualified ones), any and all would-be doctors should have the freedom to hang up a shingle without government interference. The American Medical Association represents, in Friedman's mind, an unjust union monopoly, supported by misplaced governmental legislation, which conspires to restrict the number of doctors in the market and thereby keep doctors' wages unnaturally high.[40] Both patients *and* doctors need economic freedom in the sense of non-interference by government, as a means to further their political freedom (or non-interference by government in other, "non-economic" areas of life). The separation of individual economic power and political or collective power, Friedman argues, is key to the goal of human freedom as such.[41]

Because economic freedom is seen as a building block of political freedom, Friedman's style of liberalism believes that in a market-organized society, government's job is first and foremost "to ensure that markets operate effectively."[42] A secondary purpose of government— and one that Friedman acknowledges somewhat begrudgingly—is to take care of those very few things that might be considered "public" goods; that is, "to accomplish jointly what we would find it more difficult or expensive to accomplish severally" or through markets, such as the building of roads or the cleaning of public spaces. But he sees this second purpose, not as a natural outgrowth of human community, but as a necessary evil in large groups of people. It is highly risky since government leaders, having once tasted power, inevitably want more and expand their roles accordingly.[43] Thus the power originally intended to accomplish something good will almost invariably be twisted

39. Ibid., 9; see also 149–60.

40. Friedman and Friedman, *Free to Choose*, 238–41. This continues to be a timely issue, and not only for economists. A recent film documentary, *Business of Being Born* (2007), argues that medical doctors have systematically pushed midwives out of the American birthing market, such that most American women have no option but to give birth in hospitals where they have little control over their experiences, thus leading to doctor-directed overuse of pharmaceuticals and surgical techniques (especially Caesarian sections).

41. Friedman, *Capitalism and Freedom*, 9.

42. Blank and McGurn, *Is the Market Moral?* 43.

43. Friedman, *Capitalism and Freedom*, 2–3.

into the power to harm. Moreover, Friedman notes what all citizens of diverse communities know intuitively, namely that "what one man regards as good, another may regard as harm," thus making even "good" centralization problematic for those who find themselves at odds with its definitions.[44] His fear of government self-aggrandizement and his trust in individual humans' ability to make choices that are in their own best interests, means that the best power in Friedman's mind is diffuse power—in particular, *individual* power to create, learn, mature, and in turn contribute to societal progress overall.

Friedman resents the "corruption" of the name "liberal" by people who, although they retain electoral systems, prefer to rely on a centralized government rather than on individual transactions for their quality of life. He locates himself instead in the tradition of eighteenth- and nineteenth-century liberalism, over against the modern, "welfare state" liberalism of government safety nets. He sees liberalism as:

> the intellectual movement that . . . emphasized *freedom as the ultimate goal* and the individual as the ultimate entity in the society. It supported *laissez faire at home as a means* of reducing the role of the state in economic affairs and thereby enlarging the role of the individual; it supported *free trade abroad as a means* of linking the nations of the world together peacefully and democratically. In political matters, it supported the development of representative government and of parliamentary institutions, reduction in the arbitrary power of the state, and protection of the *civil freedoms* of individuals.[45]

Accordingly, he also resents the term "conservative" applied to people like himself, since he has no wish to conserve the big-government policies that he sees prevailing in his day. Those who lobby for greater individual responsibility, he argues (rather than allowing people to leech off the body politic), are more properly in line with "liberalism in its original sense—as the doctrines pertaining to a free man."[46]

Friedman comes to his economic convictions with an admirable desire to allow for the flourishing of variety in the human community. He repeatedly advocates for diversity, and against the tyranny of ma-

44. Ibid., 3.

45. Friedman, *Capitalism and Freedom*, 5. Emphasis added; here we can see the way freedom acts as both an end in itself and as a means to other ends in Friedman's thought.

46. Ibid., 6.

jority rule. His stated concern, which arises largely from his historical location during the Cold War era, is that government's natural tendency is to demand conformity to majority rule; it prefers to enforce a standard of mediocrity rather than to allow excellence and weakness to coexist; and if not stopped, it will end in totalitarianism. While Friedman acknowledges that unanimity among members of a community can never be fully achieved, and thus some forced conformity to majority rule is inevitable,[47] most of the tasks that centralized governments take on, he thinks, "can be justified, if at all, only on grounds of paternalism," or the idea that most citizens cannot be trusted to make wise decisions on their own. This is an argument that he thinks true liberals "will be inclined to reject" because of their faith in human reason.[48] Indeed, even today's liberals (people like me, who Friedman believes have stolen the name from its rightful owners) would likely affirm that minorities need to be protected from majorities when it comes to coercive lawmaking. They likely also agree that individual adults have dignity, are capable of decision-making, and need to be free, to a large extent, to make their own choices, even if they are choices of which we disapprove—at least in the areas of religion, sexuality, reproduction, voting, and the like, and maybe also in the areas of health care, education, smoking, nutrition, child-rearing, and so on. And yet, the one point at which today's liberals are consistently likely to argue with Friedman (and today's conservatives are likely to back him up) is economics. We will continue to explore why this might be in the remainder of this book.

Critique of Friedman

In spite of his protests, a non-ethical description of freedom (necessarily based on a non-ethical description of human beings) ultimately eluded Friedman. As Knight noted, "freedom" without ethical content is merely the naked ability to wield power, and this is not particularly interesting. Although he is unable to see it, Friedman's version of freedom is pregnant with a number of ethical judgments that require explanation. Take for example his deceptively simple claim that humans are "imperfect" (or that they are like "Robinson Crusoe" in their individuality); how does he know? What would perfection look like? Where does he get

47. Ibid., 24.
48. Ibid., 178.

this picture of perfection? The imperfection of humankind is not a matter of common sense but of moral judgment, and this anthropological assumption places Friedman in a camp with Smith and even Calvin, a similarity not surprising given the Judeo-Christian traditions from which they all spring.

Likewise, the apparently obvious idea that individuals' transactions "should" be voluntary—a matter of personal choice—and that government "should not" coerce citizens (except so as to protect individual freedom of choice) demonstrates a prior commitment to a Western ethic of human dignity out of which liberalism and neoliberal economics grow. Like Knight, Friedman begins with an ideological commitment to individual choice and self-determination that his economic methods then support. He shares this faith with Knight because, like Smith, they both fear the concentration of power, and they believe individuals' selfish and potentially destructive uses of power can be more effectively harnessed by the market than by the state in terms of protecting the greater good, though Friedman and Knight attribute this to the scientific workings of nature rather than to Smith's invisible hand of providence.

The ethic of freedom as individual choice is normative for Friedman's economic thinking, in that his desire to protect it provides the impetus for his studies and the goal of his pronouncements. Not surprisingly, the freedom that Friedman's theory protects is that of educated and wealthy individuals with access to the financial means and information that enable good choices through the provision of multiple options.[49] This is not to say that Friedman is unaware of poverty. He writes quite persuasively about why neoliberal policies are better for poor people than are those policies modeled on socialist paternalism. He points, for example, to disastrous examples of public housing projects, arguing that it would be more fruitful for the government to give poor people a cash allowance that they could spend as they wished, rather than offering free housing in poorly-built and overcrowded government apartment buildings. Giving them cash would create a market for low-income housing in which landlords would have to compete for renters' dollars, thus forcing landlords to improve their properties and keep prices down. (The Earned Income Tax Credit program, which provides cash back to working families, is based on Friedman's models.) The choice not to give poor people cash, he argues, reflects a paternalistic attitude on the part

---

49. See Schwartz et al., "Is Freedom Just Another Word for Many Things to Buy?" 14.

of wealthy politicians and voters, who simply do not trust poor people to spend their own dollars wisely (e.g., they might buy drugs instead of pay rent!). Public schools, he argues similarly, are crippled by heavy bureaucracy and regulation, and the fact that individuals lack the freedom to attend whichever schools they want. Bad schools in poor neighborhoods grow worse and worse because they do not have to compete for students; those who attend these schools are a captive audience. The government requires parents to send kids to school, usually the one closest to them if they cannot afford a private option, so there is no individual accountability for teachers (whose union "monopolies" he bemoans) or administrators. Poor children are forced by legislators to go to the bad school in the poor neighborhood instead of being able to choose whichever school they want.

The socially-minded reader who does not wish to see poor children forced to live in dilapidated housing projects, or to attend overcrowded and under-achieving schools, will find it difficult not to at least consider that Friedman may be onto something. For Christians and others who value human self-determination, Friedman surely seems correct to argue against a degrading paternalism that sees poor people as thieves, imbeciles, and/or bad parents—people who are incapable of making rational choices that will benefit themselves, their families, or their communities. Christians who see *all* human beings as *equal* bearers of God's image—creative, loving, and desirous of the good—must question our own assumptions about people's inability or unwillingness to work, to parent, or to practice self-discipline. We can learn something from Friedman's insistence that every human being is fully capable of improving his or her life, as well as the lives of others, through the choices he or she makes.

But in spite of his high estimation of the choice-making facilities of poor people, Friedman's abstract model for economic choice remains *the person with sufficient means, resources, and power to achieve his or her desired ends.* Such means include not only money (or at least the ability to get a bank loan), but also efficient infrastructure such as transportation. The poor person who wants to work, for example, may "rationally choose" to travel from his low-rent neighborhood to the high-rent district in which service jobs are plentiful; but in order for this choice to come to fruition there must be cost-effective and timely transportation available to him. (Most Americans know all too well that owning a car is expensive, but that other efficient options for getting to work are virtually non-existent outside of the country's few biggest cities.) Friedman likewise assumes that the poor child who wants a good education has parents who will rationally choose to send her to the best school available; but again, the cheap but terrible school down the block may be the only viable option for her if other schools are too expensive, if there are no education loans available to her parents, or if there is no cost-effective transportation to the good school across town.

His emphasis on the norm of free choice allows Friedman to be blithely oblivious to the fact that many people—even if they are fully *capable* of rational choices—have options that are extremely limited by finance, geography, family histories, brain chemistry, politics, or education. Those who do not enter social life with the material resources they need may have to make "rational" choices that actually harm them, simply because the opportunity for genuinely beneficial choices is not there. (In many cases, only harmful options are available.[50]) For example, with regard to his argument that the American Medical Association represents an unfair monopoly on the practice of medicine, it is not difficult to see that people with greater means will be able to seek out doctors with good reputations who are in high demand, while those of lesser means will be more likely to fall prey to well-meaning incompetents or unscrupulous fakers. They may "choose" the less competent doctor over no doctor at all, but this does not mean they "choose" to be harmed. One need not believe the government and the AMA to be entirely devoid of cynical motives in order to acknowledge that they may have some value to most of the public, if for no other reason than that they provide helpful information that saves individuals the time (and money) required to do full research on all their medical consumer options. Another example is in the realm of nutrition; those who live in depressed urban centers know that there is often no supermarket for miles around (much less a farmers' market), and that fast food is the only affordable option people have for putting food in their children's bellies, contributing to America's current epidemics of obesity and diabetes. Yet another option is banking; people in such areas usually do not have access to savings or checking accounts and must instead rely on check-cashing establishments that take inordinate portions of their paychecks. The free-to-choose model, in short, rings a bit hollow

---

50. Albino Barrera writes, "unceasing changes in prices and market opportunities . . . expand or contract economic agents' sphere of autonomy and welfare. These pecuniary externalities can precipitate 'very hard choices' among unappealing alternatives." Barrera, *Economic Compulsion and Christian Ethics*, 42.

when placed next to real human beings and their real lives, which may or may not allow them to choose from among genuine options.

Friedman also downplays the prevalence of both private monopoly and "neighborhood effects," or externalities, in the free marketplace. With regard to government, he makes a compelling case that those who are lucky enough to find themselves in positions of power are likely to expand that power as far as they can go. Yet when it comes to private business, he dismisses the potential for danger because of his faith that competitors will arise to keep corporations honest. One company may enjoy a monopoly for a time, he argues, but if government can resist interfering with any foolish legislation, he is certain that a private monopoly cannot last. Friedman is not particularly interested in who may suffer while private industry works these kinks out ("the believer in freedom has never counted noses"[51]); compared with public monopoly or public regulation, private monopoly is the least of the evils. While he admits that circumstances do matter, and that choices about policy cannot "be made once and for all, independently of the factual circumstances," he nevertheless errs (as do his disciples) on the side of giving private corporations free rein to ride rough-shod over others with less power than they have, until some other individual or corporation is strong enough to stop them.[52]

Sometimes such monopoly results in neighborhood effects, when "actions of individuals have effects on other individuals for which it is not feasible to charge or recompense them."[53] When someone pollutes a stream, he says, forcing his neighbors downstream to "exchange good water for bad," it is simply too difficult to pay these neighbors for their trouble. Friedman does not admit that preventing people from polluting water that they share with others might be an appropriate role for government. His reigning philosophy is, "If I do not like what my local community does, be it in sewage disposal, or zoning, or schools, I can move to another local community, and though few may take this step,

51. Friedman, *Capitalism and Freedom*, 9.

52. Ibid., 29.

53. Ibid., 30. Neighborhood effects or externalities provide much of the impetus for the controversial "free market environmentalism" or "enviropreneur" movement, in which limiting governmental action to the protection of individual property rights (such as the right to clean water or soil) is seen as the key to protecting the earth. See, for example, PERC's web site (Property & Environment Research Center).

the mere possibility acts as a check."[54] As always, Friedman assumes that every individual controls all the resources she needs to live her life exactly how and where she wants to. Material wealth is apparently no object for *homo economicus*, and any sentimental connection to location that might keep a person in a particular place is her own fault. Such assumptions again reveal Friedman's ethical orientation, though he believes what he is saying is purely scientific.

While my focus here is mainly to look at Friedman's writings about freedom, rather than his personal actions, it is important to note at least briefly that his economic preaching extended far beyond Chicago, and even beyond the United States. His was not necessarily "a peaceful battle of ideas against those who believed that governments had a responsibility to intervene in the market to soften its sharp edges."[55] To the contrary, Naomi Klein argues forcefully that Friedman's "fundamentalist form of capitalism has consistently been midwifed by the most brutal forms of coercion, inflicted on the body politic as well as on countless individuals."[56] She, along with others such as Juan Gabriel Valdes, highlights in particular Friedman's controversial involvement with Pinochet's rule of Chile.[57] Friedman and other Chicago school economists were so committed to their brand of economic "freedom" that they were willing to join hands with even a brutal dictator, who regularly violated basic human dignity through disappearances, torture, and murder, in order to bring about a capitalist system. The ends—free markets that are often highlighted as role models for the developing world—apparently justified the means (despite Friedman's insistence that, "Desirable or not, any end that can be attained only by the use of bad means must give way to the more basic end of the use of acceptable means").[58] Such actions have obvious ethical motivations and significance, and can only artificially be viewed separately from Friedman's science.

Although he believes that choice or freedom-as-power is a universal "value"[59] in need of little explanation or defense, Friedman makes little attempt to hide the preaching in his teaching. There is a "clear and reasoned

54. Ibid., 3.

55. Klein, *Shock Doctrine*, 21.

56. Ibid., 22–23.

57. Valdes, *Pinochet's Economists*.

58. Friedman, *Capitalism and Freedom*, 22.

59. Ibid., 12; freedom is a "value" relevant both to "relations among people" and to individual ethical action.

recommendation" contained within Friedman's economic science—a prescription within his description—that is not merely incidental.[60] The fact that Friedman entitled his books *Capitalism and Freedom* (and *Free to Choose*) rather than *Capitalism and Power* (or *Power to Choose*) is an important rhetorical choice with the particular ethical goal of winning readers over to his way of thinking. Presumably, Friedman intuited that readers would be more likely to approve of a cry for greater freedom than a cry for power; presumably, Friedman believes that what he himself longs for is greater freedom, not greater power, and yet he cannot account for this in economic (or non-ethical) terms.

Friedman's emphasis on freedom becomes especially important when seen in the overall scheme of the twentieth-century Chicago school, namely because he represents a dying breed or, perhaps more precisely, a brief throw-back to Adam Smith in his prescription for liberty. Friedman's science, like Knight's, would undergo inevitable changes in the hands of other Chicago economists. Friedman's evangelical call for economic (and concomitantly political) freedom was to be replaced by a cold utility of the sort that would have made Jeremy Bentham proud. As Stigler writes about classical economics, "In Smith's time and for a few decades thereafter the argument for efficiency was embellished with a rhetoric of sacred and inviolable rights of natural liberty. But if the concern with natural liberty was ever strong, it had disappeared by the mid-Victorian age."[61]

In spite of their close working relationship, Friedman's defense of freedom as a valued (if merely formal) human *telos*, not only as a means to other ends, quickly became irrelevant even to many economists among his own cohort, such as Stigler. (Indeed, one might think Stigler had never met Friedman!) The "sentimental" gilding of maximizing behavior with words like "liberty" or "freedom" fell out of favor as heuristic hindrances to scientific inquiry. To one economist's question, "Is there any reason to disentangle our explanatory relationship as economists from the other human sciences by an artificial assumption if doing so impoverishes our characterization of human action?"[62] the late Chicago school answers, frankly, "yes." When taken to its natural end, the separation of the discipline of economics from disciplines such as history,

---

60. Stigler, "Economics or Ethics?" 146.

61. Ibid., 151.

62. Emmett, "De Gustibus *Est* Disputandum," 6.

theological ethics, and moral philosophy would result in a perspective in which even the "liberal" in neoliberal could be considered an unwelcome value statement.

GEORGE STIGLER AND GARY BECKER: FREEDOM AS MEANS TO OTHER ENDS

In the 1930s, around the time that Gary Becker was born, Frank Knight expressed the sentiment that would alienate him philosophically from later Chicago thinkers, beginning with Friedman:

> [M]an's relations with his fellow man are on a totally different footing from his relations with the objects of physical nature and [economists must] give up . . . the naive project of carrying over a technique which has been successful in the one set of problems and using it to solve another set of a categorically different kind.[63]

Knight's insistence that human-human interactions were qualitatively different from human interactions with gravity or chemistry was not long in favor in the Chicago school he initiated. Friedman's unabashed application of economic analysis to political questions (rather than humbly limiting himself to the narrow selection of topics approved by Knight such as price or production) quickly set him apart from his predecessor. His economics became more powerful than Knight's because it reached outward from the university and made the whole world its laboratory. In addition, the fact that government and union bureaucracy seem to be Friedman's most feared enemies lends a slant to his interests that is distinct from Knight's, whose main fears were fascism and communist dictatorship. Ultimately Friedman's world-transforming approach—that "the mark of good science is [the] empirical adequacy of its predictions, not its assumptions"[64]—won out at Chicago, and others would take his theory even farther and "boldly go" where no economist had gone before.

Stigler: From Freedom to Efficiency

Friedman's contemporary, George Stigler, helped lead the charge toward all-encompassing predictability. As noted earlier, Stigler wanted

---

63. Knight, "Limitations of Scientific Method on Economics," 147.
64. Emmett, "De Gustibus *Est* Disputandum," 4.

to extend economic theory as Friedman did, but without the "embel-lishment" of superfluous terms like freedom. It was *efficiency* that was king in economics—a simple ratio between cost and benefit, neither of which, in Stigler's mind, require any actual content—and this was some-thing virtually no other field could touch, least of all moral philosophy. He writes,

> The attack on the efficiency of public policies will only be appro-priate and convincing [to economists] when achievement of the goals and costs of the policies are undisputed. If one policy will achieve more of *a given goal* than a second policy with the same cost in resources, the former policy is clearly superior, and there is no room for argument over ethics.[65]

The result, rather than the process, is what interests him. We see that, if Stigler leaves any room for ethics, it is with regard to the "given goal"—that is, the ethicist may worry herself about the goodness or rightness of the production of guns versus the production of customized teddy bears, but the economist's only interest is in which methods of production create the most guns or teddy bears with the least cost. The economist "needs no ethical system to criticize error"[66]; if she criticizes anything, it will be merely to point out that there are cheaper ways to put a weapon in every hand. Importantly, and perhaps unsurprisingly, Stigler also does not see fit to specify how "cost" is defined; questions about "externalities" such as *Cost in terms of what?* or *Cost to whom?* are neither asked nor answered. The pollution created by a particular teddy bear factory, for example, is of no interest to him as long as the factory does not need to factor pollution taxes into its equation.

Later in life, however, Stigler came to the realization that even what economists think of as "inefficiencies" may have their benefits for some people.[67] He became convinced that certain policies that hindered the efficient growth of national wealth were in fact very efficient at produc-ing *some* specific utility for *some* specific parties. Even if, for example, tariffs or minimum wages did not meet neoliberal criteria for aggregate nationwide usefulness, domestic corporations or union workers—not to mention those legislators elected by these interest groups—found them

65. Stigler, "Economics or Ethics?" 151. Emphasis added.
66. Ibid., 152.
67. Ibid., 155.

very useful in terms of those things *they* valued.[68] Indeed, Stigler recognized, if it is not the job of economists to adjudicate among utilities but merely to *explain* phenomena, then they can hardly complain when a union (such as Friedman's bugbear, the American Medical Association) efficiently uses legislation or other legal means to secure permanently higher wages for itself. Rationalities compete with one another, and the economist's rationality is not the same as the doctor's. Having explained how such legislation came into being and persisted in spite of its inefficiency, the only thing left for an economist like Stigler to do is stand back and observe, marveling at the human capacity for maximizing personal utility. Even to call it "inefficient" is no longer appropriate, since that would require the economist to answer the ethicist's question, "inefficient for whom or for what?"

Thus, any human behavior—even irrational or inefficient behavior—is now fair game for economics. Perhaps the definitive breach of any boundary that might have once surrounded economics came in 1977 with the original publication of the article "De Gustibus Non *Est* Disputandum" (there's no accounting for tastes). Written by Stigler and his colleague Gary Becker, the thesis of the article was that any "widespread and/or persistent human behavior can be explained by a generalized calculus of utility-maximizing behavior," without having to qualify the explanation with the disclaimer, "tastes remaining the same."[69] Put simply, the duo asserts that economics can provide explanations for, as well as offer predictions of, virtually any kind of human behavior—not merely the economic (e.g., given the opportunity, more people will buy a cheaper MP3 player rather than a more expensive one of similar quality), but also the previously non-economic, including (in this particular article) heroin addiction. Economists need no longer allow for changes or increases in individual tastes that might result from factors such as advertising, chemical dependency, religious beliefs, or aging. The assumption

68. This is reminiscent of the "double movement" Polanyi describes of *laissez-faire* doctrine and its "collectivist" detractors, in that the latter always develops spontaneously in response to the former. "For if market economy was a threat to the human and natural components of the social fabric . . . what else would one expect than an urge on the part of a great variety of people to press for some sort of protection?" Polanyi, *Great Transformation*, 150. Stigler would agree that reactions against *laissez-faire* policy are governed by the very same rational, self-interested mechanism that *laissez-faire* seeks to harness. The two political philosophies compete because individuals' interests and "values" compete.

69. Stigler and Becker, "De Gustibus Non *Est* Disputandum," 76.

of constant tastes is sufficient for explaining virtually any social question. Emmett writes that Stigler and Becker's "methodological alternative is simultaneously a solution to the scientific economist's problem, and an application of the scientific approach most economists have adopted."[70] Such a solution was there all along; economics just needed some people audacious enough to apply it.

This collapsing of individual and specific tastes into a single utility function for the purpose of analysis is made possible by an equally one-dimensional anthropology; the human being is a rational actor (that is, forward-looking, maximizing, and consistent in consumer choices.)[71] What the rational actor maximizes is utility, the content of which is ostensibly left empty by economists; actual utility (what classical utilitarians called "pleasure") is different for every individual and depends greatly on things like context and upbringing. But these specifics are unnecessary for explanatory purposes. Whether (and why) a person has a taste for fair-trade chocolate or a taste for sport-utility vehicles is irrelevant; both persons will maximize according to the same human mechanism of rational choice. Even the assumption that humans are "rational" is said to be free of content, to the extent that behavior heretofore labeled "irrational"—like drug addiction or altruism—can be incorporated. The person who gets pleasure from potentially deadly drugs makes a rational choice to consume more of them, while the person who gets pleasure from giving money away makes a rational choice to give away more money. The same basic narrative works for all situations: humans are pleasure- or utility-seeking animals; humans have the capacity to rationalize; humans rationally figure out how to use whatever means are available to them in order to maximize the amount of pleasure they consume.

Becker and the Economic Interpretation

Stigler and Becker adopted Knight's belief that economists study the *form* of human behavior, not its content; this allowed them to limit the types of questions they needed to ask in order to conduct their economic analyses, while at the same time giving them a wide-open field of unlimited behaviors to analyze. Whereas Knight resisted the lure of an "economic interpretation" of traditionally non-economic areas of life based on an overly-simplified anthropology, Stigler and Becker welcomed the

70. Emmett, "De Gustibus *Est* Disputandum," 4.

71. Becker, *Accounting for Tastes*, 23.

economic interpretation as scientific progress.[72] Where they differed importantly was in what they regarded as the normative purpose or goal of economic science. Knight argued that "understanding as such" should be the economist's highest goal, but inevitably this gave way in later generations to the more enticing goal of applying economic science to practical matters. Becker in particular embraced his calling as preacher. He wrote a column in *Business Week* for years in which he made recommendations for governmental and business policies based on economic assumptions and principles.[73] These later Chicagoans shared the desire of the behaviorist-institutionalists to leave the ivory tower and effect changes in the real world, and in doing so, they stretched economic science's reach as far as it could go. In giving up Knight's qualms about engaging in policy discussion, economists made not only *economic* policy their business but *all* policy. Everything in human life became fair game. (We are reminded of Knight's warning that there is no aspect of life that is truly non-economic, no part of "making a living" that is not intertwined with every other human interest.)

In addition to the question of drug addiction raised in this groundbreaking article, Gary Becker has famously extended rational choice theory to a number of other political and social problems. (He and Stigler argue that something can be considered problematic or "harmful" if it is characterized by inelastic demand—that is, if the consumer absolutely must have it.[74]) Four of his most influential analyses—racial discrimination, crime, human capital, and family structure—are crystallized in his 1996 Nobel lecture, "The Economic Way of Looking at Behavior." In it he explains that, by treating such phenomena as racism, theft, and children as "tastes" comparable to tastes in food or fashion, economics is able not only to explain why racism persists or why some people have more babies

72. See especially the second part of Emmett's paper, in which he offers (what he thinks might have been) Frank Knight's response to "De Gustibus" had he been alive to read it; Emmett, "De Gustibus *Est* Disputandum," 8–11.

73. For example, "The sale of government enterprises to the private sector can— and should—be carried much further. Publicly owned enterprises apparently are less efficient and less flexible than competitive private companies because they are unable to separate economic choices from political considerations." See Becker and Becker, *Economics of Life*, 33. Elsewhere, in his chapter, "Crime and Punishment," Becker openly addresses issues such as "how many resources and how much punishment *should* be used to enforce different kinds of legislation?" Becker, *Economic Approach to Human Behavior*, 40.

74. Stigler and Becker, "De Gustibus Non *Est* Disputandum," 33.

than others, but also to predict future behavior on both individual and grand scales. More significantly, economists can advise policy makers on the best way to encourage more desirable behavior and discourage the less desirable—in other words, they can enable social control of the sort free-marketeers fervently disavow. (Again, Becker does not feel the need to define the norms that shape his term "desirable," although reading between the lines it is possible to discern that "undesirable" behavior is that which does not produce wealth or other commodities for which there is a demand; or conversely, that which produces commodities for which there is insufficient demand.[75])

Especially telling—and perhaps most offensive to non-economists—is Becker's treatment of family. While many readers would be willing to go along with the idea that employers discriminate against African-Americans out of economic concerns (i.e., to keep white customers or employees happy so as to keep business profitable), they may be harder pressed to agree with him that people marry (or not) or have children (or not) based on an "economic" calculation of utility. Becker speculates, however, that this is generally a greater hurdle for intellectuals than it is for "the common person," since to most people it is merely *common sense* that humans make choices that they think will make them happier, which frequently entails being wealthier.[76] On the topic of marriage, it must be admitted that Becker is in good company; arranged marriages based on financial concerns remain common in many twenty-first-century world cultures, and even most of Jane Austen's fictional characters are in search of wealthy spouses (with love as a possible bonus for some). The view of marriage as a romantic—rather than an economic, legal, and political—arrangement is a relatively modern luxury.[77] And it

75. Becker, *Economic Way of Looking at Behavior*, 8. On this page he claims that theft is bad not for any moral reasons, but because it is a *forcible*—that is non-voluntary—*redistribution* of wealth, rather than a creation of it. On the other hand, he admits he forgot to count in the industries that would rise up to meet the need for theft prevention, so theft can perhaps be seen as more beneficial than costly, at least in terms of overall economic growth.

76. Ibid., 14.

77. A recent magazine article asks, "What is the purpose of marriage? Is it—given the game-changing realities of birth control, female equality and the fact that motherhood outside of marriage is no longer stigmatized—simply an institution that has the capacity to increase the pleasure of the adults who enter into it? If so, we might as well hold the wake now: there probably aren't many people whose idea of a 24-hour-a-day good times consists of being yoked to the same romantic partner through bouts of stomach flu and

does not take an economist to acknowledge the concrete ramifications of family relationships; for example, middle-aged divorced women often find themselves struggling to remain financially solvent, marriages often split up over financial tensions, and the single greatest indicator of whether or not someone will be poor is whether or not her parents are poor. There is little doubt that family life is integrally tied up with economics.

If readers might be willing to concede to Becker's narrative of marriage as a utilitarian arrangement, his teaching on children might bring the ethical problems with his framework into greater focus. It has two edges, dealing first with the utility or pleasure one gets from being a parent to growing children, and secondly with weighing one's own utility against one's children's utility. First he asserts that, as countries become richer and more productive, the "higher value of time raises the cost of children," thus putting to rest Malthusian fears that wealth leads to an overabundance of children.[78] Time spent parenting is time not spent earning other types of wealth, primarily money. Parents whose time is costly (such as urban, upwardly mobile individuals) will therefore naturally "acquire" fewer children than parents whose time is not worth as much (such as low-level agricultural workers or the un- or under-employed, including stay-at-home parents). Becker sees children as "consumer durables" that, like anything else, parents consume so as to provide utility to themselves. People can be said to have "tastes" for children (or not) that are conditioned by other factors in their economic histories such as religion, age, career, or culture. These histories, however, Becker sees as irrelevant to the general principle that parents consume their children according to their individual, rational calculations of utility.

Secondly, Becker argues that parents' tastes determine not only the number of children they have, but also largely *what kind* of children they will have:

> A family must determine not only how many children it has but also the amount spent on them—whether it should provide separate bedrooms, send them to nursery school and private colleges, give them dance or music lessons, and so forth. I will call more expensive children "higher-quality" children, just as Cadillacs are called higher-quality cars than Chevrolets. To avoid misunderstanding, let me hasten to add that "higher quality" does not

depression, financial setbacks and emotional upsets, until after many a long decade, one or the other eventually dies in harness." Flanagan, "Why Marriage Matters," 49.

78. Becker, *Economic Way of Looking at Behavior*, 15.

> mean morally better. If more is voluntarily spent on one child than on another, it is because the parents obtain additional utility from the additional expenditure and it is this additional utility which we call higher "quality."[79]

The would-be parent must not only calculate the immediate potential costs and benefits to herself of having children; in addition, once she has acquired these consumer goods she must anticipate the potential returns and invest accordingly. She does this not only through spending but also through "hardwiring" certain habits of thought (one might say ethics) into them—even habits that may mean the reduction of the child's ability to take pleasure in her own life. This may mean, for example, instilling in her a sense of responsibility for taking care of her parents as they age: "[G]uilty children provide offsetting advantages to parents. . . . Parents choose the optimal spending on their own consumption and their children. . . . [E]ven very altruistic parents may want to lower the utility of their children if that induces enough old-age support."[80]

In other words, one's children exist not as ends in themselves but rather as means to the ends of their parents. What are commonly thought of as "parenting skills" are in fact, whether consciously or unconsciously, a matter of "rational" calculation as to how best to extract all possible utility from one's children.

While children no doubt gain at least some utility from their parents' "investment" in them, ultimately Becker envisions family life as a competitive marketplace. To an extent, parents' and children's utility functions can be shared; e.g., they *may* both gain utility from the kids going to private schools, eating organic food, watching NASCAR, or taking vacations to Branson, especially because children learn to value what their parents value. And if the parents are financially well-off (or if their society offers a well-funded safety net), their adult children's independence may be the thing that brings them the greatest utility. But particularly for parents of limited means, their pleasure in being cared for when they are old may come into competition with their children's pleasure in living independent adult lives. Or for parents with wealth and status, their pleasure in seeing their children follow in their upwardly-mobile footsteps may compete with their adult children's pleasure in becoming monks, drug addicts, or starving artists. It is the children in this scenario

79. Becker, *Essence of Becker*, 243.
80. Becker and Murphy, *Social Economics*, 149.

who are usually the losers because they are essentially powerless against the patterns they receive from their parents, which become part of them before they are wise enough to notice or care. By the time they are old enough to use their rationality to question their parents' values, their rationality has already been shaped by those very values. Resistance at this point may be futile; the guilt, materialism, or repulsion they have internalized may seem overwhelming and permanent.

Becker's talk about human beings as both consumers and consumer goods brings us back to the all-important question of "freedom," a term that is conspicuously missing from Becker's writing. In a matter of only a few years between Friedman and Becker, Chicago anthropology had been flattened to such an extent that freedom had lost its place as the focal point or goal of market economics. The purpose of the economy is no longer to increase or protect the freedom for humans to be fully human; it is rather about the power to maximize individuals' "utility." This utility need not be defined or qualified because, though it is different for every person, it can be treated universally as a single, content-less function. Moreover "freedom" even in the sense of free choice is no longer needed as a building block of economic theory; it has been replaced by "rational maximizing behavior"—something open to children, the uneducated, the drug-addicted, and criminals alike. Stigler and Becker no longer even have grounds for claiming (as Friedman did) that an economy "should" be structured in a certain way, since such moral valuations are outside the purview of economics to decide. One person's efficiency, they rightly argue, is another person's inefficiency; one person's freedom is another person's bondage. Essentially, *every* market is a free market—whether found within prison walls or a communist state or a capitalist powerhouse—because every market is the product of the rational choices of individual maximizers. For economists to prescribe certain actions would be to wear another hat—that of policymaker or ethicist—for which their knowledge of a value-free economic science does not fit them. Nevertheless, both Stigler and Becker eventually take the step from positivist description to policy prescription, from science to preaching.

Critique of Stigler and Becker

Becker seems to enjoy the shock value of applying a term like "higher quality" to human beings. Though he qualifies it by claiming that he is insinuating no "moral" claims, it is not difficult to see the concrete trajectory of such a powerful narrative. The terms Becker chooses for describing marriage and parenthood come out of his prior belief that the economic way of looking at behavior is both truthful and useful. These terms, moreover, have very real consequences that begin with human *self-perception*; people formed in the context of capitalist wisdom—as are most twenty-first-century American Christians—tend to view themselves primarily as consumers. We are consumers of goods, choosing those items that bring us the most pleasure for the lowest cost. We are consumers of politics, choosing those candidates and policies that promise us the greatest benefits and the least pain. We are consumers of religion, choosing those traditions that bring us the most happiness with the least amount of unnecessary sacrifice.[81] Becker's portrayal of marriage as a contract between mutually consuming partners is not much of a stretch when seen in this context. Though American Christians may disagree on the exact terms of costs and benefits, most would allow that when a marriage ceases to serve one of the customers to his or her satisfaction, the contract may be dissolved. And although we are loath to call our children consumer durables, we might admit that a certain amount of cost-benefit analysis—a measurement of the joys we expected against the concomitant sacrifices of parenthood—went into our decisions to have one child, no children, or many children.

Is there any reason economists should not be able to talk about higher- and lower-quality children as if they were cars? If, as Friedman claims, economics does not provide any all-encompassing narrative, and if, as Stigler claims, economics does not give its teachings any ethical embellishments, what is so bad about reducing everything to utilitarian terms for purposes of simple analysis, explanation, and prediction? One could argue from a Calvinist point of view that what the economist does is akin to what the evolutionary biologist does, uncovering existing patterns without undue interpretation.[82] As long as economics knows its place, is the end of freedom as an end in economics a loss really worth grieving?

81. Research in the economics of religion has found, however, that for certain people sacrifice is precisely what they are looking for. See, for example, Iannaccone, "Why Strict Churches Are Strong."

82. Again, how much interpretation is "undue" is, even in hard sciences, a matter of ethical debate. See, for example, Michael Mann's *1491*, an account of research about the Americas in which he makes clear the many ways that political agendas (both of individual professionals and groups of activists) affect even those scientific findings based on material data.

Perhaps economic utilitarianism would be unproblematic if economists were individuals who lived on deserted islands, who could study economic trends as if they were geometric forms without concrete existence, and who never spoke of their findings to anyone else in the world who might have an expressed interest in (or influence over) actual human lives, or who might "mistake" economists' scientific findings for ethical recommendations. The obvious trouble is that economists do not live in vacuums. They teach in universities, to impressionable undergraduates and/or the future power-brokers of the world. They rear children, shop, invest for retirement, and eat lunch with policymakers. They appear on radio and television news programs, write letters to the editor and blogs, run businesses, the Federal Reserve and the U.S. Treasury, and have psychological and cultural biases (both pre- and post-economic training) about what constitute good and bad choices. Unless they are hermits—a quality not often attributed to economists at the University of Chicago—professional economists, being only human, find that preaching is an ineluctable part of their work. They cannot stop preaching any more than can biologists who favor stem cell research or physicists who think nuclear power is the solution to the world's energy crisis. One cannot explain the world without at the same time judging it. Their understanding *is* their ethic—it is the habit by which they are formed and it shapes (and is shaped by) the way they live and interact with others.

With this in mind, we can see that Becker's utilitarian narrative has consequences for public policy. Take, for example, the idea that there are higher- and lower-quality children in the world—higher being those whose parents invest more money in them, lower those in whom less is invested. Such a concept is not foreign to any of us, mostly because it has been preached to us so effectively by economists, eugenicists, policymakers, and probably our parents. (I can recall my octogenarian grandmother bemoaning the fact that "the wrong people were having babies" while the right people limited their procreation, so that bad people were beginning to outnumber good people.) The most obvious repercussion of such a narrative is that it views children as means rather than ends in themselves. Becker chooses not to address the fact that certain cultures have a "taste" for boys over girls, a kind of calculation that causes some parents of girls not to invest in them (often through abortion or infanticide), in order thereby to invest greater resources in those children (boys) whom they consider more likely to give them a better return. The neoliberal economist has no resources to name this as a problem, apart from demonstrating that it might be an economically and politically unwise economic practice for a nation in the long run. In fact, Becker and Stigler would be forced to say that, according to the economic world view, killing baby girls is simply an act of rational maximization—it is a forward-looking, fully human decision made on the basis of what parents think will bring them greater happiness or utility. Moreover, it is voluntary in that all actions are voluntary, "even if it is compulsory and they face a threat of punishment."[83] Becker might argue that more complete information or more growth-oriented economic circumstances would alter parents' preferences and choices, but the utility-seeking mechanism is always and everywhere the same. The lesson that all human decisions are equally rational may not be one that average people want to learn, but the economist, after all, presents only the scientific truth, without moral embellishment.

Because economics views all human action as voluntary, even under coercion, the non-ethical economist has little interest in seeking to serve freedom or liberation. George Stigler wrote (with regard to economists' interest in issues related to welfare and income distribution) that, "economists have imported egalitarian values into economics from the prevailing ethos of the societies in which they live, and they have not been important contributors to the formation of that ethos."[84] That is to say, the concern for justice (in this case regarding wealth distribution) is not something that comes from within economics proper; in fact he sees it as an unwanted foreign presence that slows the progress of economic theory. Although there seems to be a perennial interest in justice among at least some people in every society, it is not the point of economics to foster it. Things like justice and freedom require ethical evaluation and judgment, whereas economic principles should be straightforward and unencumbered by morality. The economist as preacher, he thinks, must not be overly influenced by the ethical sensibilities of his hearers and must be willing to preach unpopular sermons; otherwise "pulpits should be at the rear of congregations, to make clearer who is leading."[85] Even if unscientific intellectuals in the pews balk at comparing some children to Cadillacs and others to Chevrolets, the economist's job is to preach the cold, hard truth anyway.

83. Becker and Murphy, *Social Economics*, 147.
84. Stigler, "Economics or Ethics?" 159.
85. Ibid.

Again, it is worthwhile to give neoliberals the benefit of hearing them out, assuming (as I do) that Stigler and Becker, no less than Friedman or Knight or Smith, are moral beings who promote economic truths precisely because they value truth, and they value truth because they believe it can make a positive difference in human life (and moreover because they are created in God's image). They have not deliberately set out to tell lies; they seek to offer a true description of human action because they hope that it will also serve as a prescription, though not a prescription for individuals. This distinction is important. Becker does not recommend that individual parents kill their girl babies (indeed, his *Autobiography* notes he is the father of two daughters), even though in his economist's hat he could offer only economic reasoning for this. On the other hand, as an economist Becker could recommend public legislation for nations based on his desire to prevent the predictable, economically and politically imprudent long-term effects that occur when a community's male population far outweighs its female. In this case he would still not be arguing that human girls have any inherent worth, but he could defend their existence on grounds of economic results. The explicit prescription that is inherent to neoliberal economic description is directed toward powers that be—governments, modern-day mercantilists, and *groups* of parents and other citizens typically associated with nation-states. What he can offer is essentially a prescription for effective control—that is, for successfully "harnessing" individual human self-interest in such a way as to achieve *whatever* given ends those in charge aspire to. Freedom is no longer the end goal of economic policy as it was for Friedman; it is not even needed as a building block for an economy. Human choices are voluntary but not free; they are entirely stable and predictable responses, determined (even predestined) by given circumstances and prior behaviors, and as such they are ripe for manipulation.

This requires some explanation, since Becker explicitly claims that social control is not the point of economics. He cites economist James Duesenberry that "economics is all about choices, while sociology is about why people have no choices"; and Becker rightly states that "some anthropologists and sociologists go much too far when they claim that culture so dominates behavior that little room is left for choice."[86] (Such thinking leads back to the paternalism that Friedman feared.) But while neoliberal economics does indeed depend on the existence of human

---

86. Becker, *Accounting for Tastes*, 17.

choice, "choice" is not the same thing as "freedom," as becomes obvious in Becker's writings. As Frank Knight insisted decades before, choice is merely a word that refers to the use of individual power, a new (and unsuccessful) attempt at a value-neutral word on which to model economics. But as he noted, "It is not enlightening . . . to be told that conduct consists in choosing between possible alternatives."[87] The economist's choice is always a choice among givens—A or B—and by limiting choice in this way, economists can *in theory* successfully predict people's choices and in doing so even predetermine them through the right policies. The kind of "freedom" that Milton Friedman sought to protect is really only a collection of options pre-determined for each individual.

An example of this determinism is taste itself, with regard to which humans lack any real choice. Individuals' preferences are always affected by others' behaviors, something that occurs naturally when private interest comes into contact with public (as it always does). For the sake of social stability, "hardwiring" certain values into people (such as honesty) is "preferable" to their having "moral flexibility"—or what some might call freedom. "One way to accomplish this is to have the 'taste' for honesty [or other socially-beneficial habits] built into preferences" which "commit a person to act honestly even when honesty does not 'pay,'" such as when one chooses not to cheat as a matter of principle, even when there's no one watching.[88] Becker acknowledges that while tastes do differ from person to person based at least partially on past choices they have made, tastes also differ largely based on choices that have been made *for* them. Religion, for example, may foster a taste for future (rather than this-worldly) utility,[89] and one's religion is generally determined by one's upbringing; thus one's parents "help account for" one's religious tastes.[90] In addition, one's social network plays a large role in the formation of human tastes, in that it encourages people to have a certain kind of taste that will be more beneficial to them socially. "Once

87. Asso and Fiorito, "Waging War against Mechanical Man," 4.

88. Becker and Murphy, *Social Economics*, 144.

89. Becker, *Accounting for Tastes*, 11.

90. Take Becker's view on church involvement: "M [a non-rich minority whose interests conflict with R's] would not attend churches where they acquire norms promoted by R [a rich minority] that lower M's utility unless they are sufficiently compensated in other ways. Otherwise, M would not go to church, or would find churches that promote more congenial values. R subsidizes clergy, buildings, and other church expenses if they promote norms that are favorable to R, such as the interest of rich families in fostering respect for private property." Becker and Murphy, *Social Economics*, 146.

a social network is given, people have little control over the production of their social capital, for that is mainly determined by the actions of peers and relevant others."[91] Culture, tradition, and ethics also are "preferences handed down from one generation to another through families, peer groups, ethnic groups, classes, and other groups."[92] A taste for crime might be beneficial to someone in a particular social context where it increases social capital, whereas it would be harmful to someone else in a different context. (Readers may glean here that Becker's social capital is anonymously but closely related to Adam Smith's social approbation and sympathy that we saw in chapter 3.)

But while Becker acknowledges that tastes are in large part inherited or cultivated for people by the social contexts in which they find themselves, he seeks to demonstrate that economic analysis works because all individuals still have some element of "choice" in all of their actions. Take again addiction; the choice to try heroin for the first time is presumably a choice an individual makes of her own volition. At the same time, the economist can include in her calculations that a person may be more or less likely to make such a choice depending upon her upbringing, religion, socio-economic status, culture, and so forth, thus removing any nuance of freedom from the term "voluntary" (much like the sociologists he criticizes). Once she has made the original choice and becomes addicted, the choice to feed her addiction may also be considered a "rational" and voluntary choice in economic terms, except that now her choice is conditioned by the taste or hardwiring she has acquired through her past choices. Thus an individual is not really free when she chooses to take another hit; she is rather living out the destiny that was set in motion when she made the first fateful decision. Conversely, if an individual does manage to break her habit, there is certainly a reasonable economic explanation for this as well, related to utility maximization; she "chose" (given certain, pre-determined hardwiring) the benefits of non-addiction over the benefits of addiction, based on her rational understanding of her options and their predicted effects. Becker's attempt to differentiate economic choice from sociological determinism is thus unpersuasive.

To what end neoliberals seek to analyze the human world in this way is a matter requiring discernment, but the ability to explain and predict

91. Becker, *Accounting for Tastes*, 13.
92. Ibid., 16.

all things human seems inevitably tied to the desire to control them as well. To manage human beings—rather than to set them free—ends up being the task of neoliberal economics. Such an end points economists in a direction opposite to the trajectory set by Calvin. In Calvin's theology, freedom is the goal of Christian ethics, including economics; he sought to set people free, such that they could become more fully themselves by being re-formed in God's image and serving their neighbors. Chicago, to the contrary, seeks to harness and *use* people's freedom (that is, their power to make choices) as a means of social control, albeit under the power of banks and businesses rather than a Consistory or other government bureau. Economics' apparent superpowers of both explanation and administration make economists the much-sought-after "priests" of market cultures, even when these priests do not necessarily have all the answers.[93] As one writer puts it, "If we look beyond economics there appears to be no other discipline with a mainstream tradition that enjoys anywhere near so great a degree of dominance (or so little relative explanatory success)."[94] The influence of economics has formed a culture of lawmakers who see it as their job to understand and predict (with the help of economist-preachers, whether right- or left-leaning) the rational maximizing behavior of their particular constituents. Once they know why people choose to park illegally or murder people for fees (or to vote Democratic or Republican), they can then turn to the task of creating institutional incentives and disincentives to discourage certain behaviors. They might increase the likelihood of being caught when parking illegally in a given neighborhood, while in a different neighborhood they might increase the amount of the parking fine; both tactics are designed to prevent particular types of people from breaking the law—an objective presumably justified in some prior calculus made by lawmakers of yore whose tastes moderns have inherited.

One example of how economic principles work their way into lawmaking is provided by Marriage Protection Week, declared by George W. Bush in 2003. His brief "proclamation" declared that the "sacred"

93. Nelson, "What is Economic Theology?" 3.

94. "How has this mathematising project risen to such a position of dominance in modern economics, and managed to maintain this position over a longish period of time," given its explanatory failures?, asks Lawson, *Reorienting Economics*, 247–48. He argues that its dominance is mainly a case of Darwinian selection (though he notes some recent rebellion in France), due perhaps to a human psychological need for "explanatory coherence" and (even the illusion of) predictability and control, 281–82.

institution of marriage is a necessary part of "good" and "responsible" parenthood. More importantly, he claimed the government had a stake in protecting it (through taxation and other economic means) so that, down the road, children would "fare better" and thereby offer "benefits to our people, our culture, and our society."[95] An article published by the Heritage Foundation fleshed out the political reasoning behind this initiative. The government, it argued, had a duty to "promote marriage" as a "public concern"—specifically by encouraging fathers to marry the mothers of their children[96] and encouraging unmarried women, especially those of low income, not to become mothers.[97] The latter document makes it obvious that the government's main concern is an economic one: government subsidies for low-income, single-parent families have become "too expensive" relative to their perceived social benefits.[98] It is telling that "marriage promotion programs" are targeted toward "at-risk" (code for "low-income") adolescents in the form of high school programs.[99] Future adults being educated in wealthy school districts are apparently seen as less problematic for society. Meanwhile, it also seeks to tie economic assistance to marriage, lest government provide economic incentives for people to become single parents. Programs like government-funded job training have so far "had no apparent effect on increasing marriage"; thus in the future, "any job training must be linked to marriage-skills training."[100] Single parenthood, especially among the poor, is as much the government's business as any other disease; to say the government should stay out of marriage "is like arguing that the government should pay to sustain polio victims in iron lung machines but should not pay for the vaccine to prevent polio in the first place."[101]

Economists may protest that their work is not normative because they do not tell governing bodies *whether* they should encourage marriage; they merely tell them *how* to do it. But this "healthy marriage" initiative offers one example of clear evidence of the way the economic mindset—in which human beings are essentially consumers—has been

95. Bush, "*Marriage Protection Week.*"

96. Rector and Pardue, *Understanding the President's Healthy Marriage Initiative*, 2.

97. Ibid., 5.

98. Ibid., 7.

99. Ibid., 5.

100. Ibid., 8.

101. Ibid., 9.

absorbed as a cultural norm. On one hand we have the image of parents (often children themselves) as consumers who choose to have children (or not) based on economic incentives and disincentives. As Traci West rightly infers, this frames women (especially poor women on welfare) as prostitutes, in that "it is taken for granted [by policy makers] that cash is the primary motivation for sexual/procreative activity."[102] While it is acceptable for a woman to choose to procreate for a sum of money provided by a *private* buyer (usually a husband), it is unacceptable for *public* money to pay for a woman's procreation. Also at work here is Becker's issue of higher- and lower-quality children. Children whose parents do not invest in them prudently—either because the parents are imprudent, or because the absent father denies his children and their mother his vast average income of $17,500[103]—are more likely to grow up and become criminals or other economic drains on society. Government would therefore be wise to prevent these low-quality children from ever being born, rather than trying to repair the damage when it is already too late.[104] Higher-quality children are seen as being good for society, while lower-quality children are seen as a hindrance to overall productivity and therefore not worth the life they are given.

Even John Calvin acknowledged that "the majority of children are not always a source of joy to their parents," but are often predominantly a source of "tears and groans."[105] But he did not therefore declare that the birth of troublesome children should be prevented. To speak solely in terms of cost-benefit analysis betrays an *internalized economic ethic* in which children are either commodities deserved only by those who can afford them (who, as Becker noted, seem to want fewer of them) or liabilities to be minimized, especially if their cost to taxpayers may outweigh their contributions. But such a narrative is one to which Christians have no business subscribing. In direct opposition to Becker's investment model, a freedom-oriented Calvinism begins with the affirmation that all human beings bear the image of God, making them equal in dignity (and quality) apart from any external "values" attributed to them

102. West, "Policing of Poor Black Women," 144.

103. Rector and Pardue, *Understanding the President's Healthy Marriage Initiative*, 2.

104. Ibid., 5.

105. Calvin, *Psalms*, 111. Calvin himself fathered one son who died in infancy, followed quickly by his mother. After her death, Calvin raised two step-sons from his wife's previous marriage, and also fostered boarding school students in his home.

culturally. According to this view, life—especially human life—is a gift, and thus in the words of Karl Barth, "even the unmarried mother" is the recipient of a great honor.[106] Traci West observes that fertility, or "the spreading of life," once seen as a good, has been twisted by economic rationality until it is seen (as in Rector and Pardue's polio analogy) as "the spreading of pathology, of . . . a disease of catastrophic potential."[107] Placing children back into a Calvinist framework of gifts arising from "the singular kindness of God"[108] will not solve every parent's (or government's) problems, but it is a powerful antidote to the utilitarian view that a human being's value is dependent on the relative utility supplied to those affected by their existence, rather than being inherent to the person. Economists *are* preachers, and Christians and others who are unaware of this are likely not only to absorb the "economic interpretation" uncritically, but also to be shaped and formed by it in ways of which they are unaware.

CONCLUSION: THE END OF FREEDOM AT CHICAGO

In Friedman, Stigler, and Becker, the "charming conceit"[109] as to the clear-sighted, unsentimental, unembellished truths of economics comes into focus. Like Knight, they claim that ethics and freedom are unscientific and are therefore not the economist's tasks. But also like Knight, they are unaware of the norms inherent in their scientific methods—such as that humans are "rational" in so far as they seek the good as they understand it, or that "efficiency" and "cost" are things that can be measured objectively. Against the claim of ethical neutrality, the self-consciously ethical thinker points out the inseparable connection between understanding and ethics. As Calvin taught, the job of the will is "to choose and follow what the understanding pronounces good, but to reject and flee what it disapproves" (I.xv.7). Because the economists we have been looking at are moral beings with a sense of right and wrong, good and bad, they have not been able to resist going against Knight's admonition to stay out of policy discussions. They naturally pursue that which their understanding tells them is good (anything pertaining to economic growth

---

106. Barth, *Church Dogmatics* III/4, 277.

107. West, "Policing of Poor Black Women," 141.

108. Calvin, *Genesis*, vol. II, 208.

109. Weintraub, *How Economics Became a Mathematical Science*, 269.

or material progress as they see it), and flee what they see as worthy of condemnation (anything hindering growth or progress).

To a certain extent, Protestant theologians can affirm with Calvin the economic view of humans as rational beings who choose according to their preferences, in so far as "shunning or seeking out in the appetite corresponds to affirming or denying in the mind" (I.xv.7). The idea that humans' self-interest directs them toward that which they understand to be worth desiring is not wrong. Indeed, Becker even nuances this type of understanding—showing its similarities to Calvin's views as well as to Smith's vision of social sympathy and approbation—when he "accounts for tastes" according to each individual's parental, institutional, and cultural influences, as well as past actions. Where scientific economists go wrong is in denying their inherent role as preachers, and as preachers, ethicists. While Milton Friedman openly preaches the gospel of power to choose, Becker maintains that his work consists only in "a method of analysis," nothing more.[110] But Becker's deliberate choice to "exclude such abstract social ideals" as freedom from his studies, "in favor of more-real underlying economic calculations" unveils the true nature of his work.[111] Whether he intends to or not, the priority he gives to rational choice undermines any ability to support a vision of freedom that goes beyond the exercise of power. The human being is always and everywhere under the power of a single, uncomplicated sovereign master (to replace Bentham's pleasure and pain): rational self-interest. From such a master, economics offers no escape.

Just as Frank Knight criticized Marx for pointing toward an ethical nihilism that came from viewing all of human life as an economic calculation, the Christian theologian must criticize neoliberal economics for the same reason. As Stigler noted, neoliberalism must view every market as essentially a free market, in that every realm of human exchange (politics, religion, family) involves rational, voluntary human choices made under given conditions, in pursuit of an undetermined, formal utility. Such an interpretation of human social life leaves economists with one of two options. Either they can own up to a desire to *control* the economic behaviors of groups of human beings through the technical manipulation of market forces; or they can do little more than sit back

110. Becker, "Economic Way of Looking at Behavior," 2.

111. Nelson, *Economics as Religion*, 198.

and *observe*, silently, since any pronouncement as to the "efficiency" or "benefit" of certain behaviors automatically turns them into ethicists.

The absurdity of this latter option makes it clear that neoliberal economics is a particular school of ethics, one which provides a powerful and compelling description of human life that has been deeply affected by the cultures from which it arose, and which continues to shape the individuals and cultures that come into contact with it. Its ability to simplify and make sense of vast human complexities makes the economic description highly attractive to people whose minds resist ambiguity and uncertainty. But it is not merely a description; it is always also a particular prescription for how to organize the world. And despite its association with liberalism, the prescription it offers is not particularly *liberative*; it does not tend toward genuine human freedom. While it does describe individuals as having some power of self-determination, it also puts them at the mercy of others' self-determination, which may or may not be limited by fellow-feeling (or government). Calvin argued that economies should be informed and shaped by the love of one's neighbors that comes from knowing God as good—the true state of freedom. Neoliberal economics insists that economies should be informed and shaped (because they always are, whether we know it or not) by the interactions of individuals enslaved to the maximization of their own private utility. Whereas the economist sees this as a more honest view of human life, free of embellishments and sentimentality,[112] freedom-oriented Calvinism sees it as "the pestilence that most effectively leads to our destruction" (III.vii.1).

---

112. Polanyi writes that the social philosophy of economic liberals "hinges on the idea that *laissez-faire* was a natural development, while subsequent anti-*laissez-faire* legislation was the result of a purposeful action on the part of the opponents of liberal principles." The market mechanism is seen as the given, whereas any non-market concern is seen as an unwelcome ethical import. Polanyi, *Great Transformation*, 141.

6

EXPANDING THE CONVERSATION

Possible Steps Toward More Virtuous Market Economies

IN THIS FINAL CHAPTER I wish not to offer any definitive conclusions, but to address two important questions for future studies in Christian economic ethics, namely: Must Christians (or any people of good will) reject the secular, "dismal" science known as economics? and, Must Christians reject capitalism (or market economies) altogether? These questions, of course, could also be alternately formulated: Must Christian ethics *embrace* economics and/or market capitalism? My answer to each question is "Yes and no." On one hand, I am painfully aware of the very real harms to human flourishing that emerge out of an uncritical acceptance of economic "facts," neoliberal "choice," and the capitalist models based on these.[1] But I also believe there is much possible good to be gleaned from these diverse, freedom-based traditions, and to reject them (and their representatives) categorically is to partially blind ourselves in our search for a more just and life-giving global economy. My hope is that critical but respectful Christian theological conversations

---

1. As Dorothy Sayers notes, the very first casualty of economistic thinking is the *enjoyment* of work that was the original inheritance of those created in God's image. With the fall, "work" becomes "employment" and necessity; economic science then often takes this latter necessity for granted as its philosophical foundation. Sayers, "Vocation in Work," 405–7.

with economics can bear fruit, especially for those among us who suffer most from material privation.

In light of this hope, I will spend some time introducing three examples of twenty-first-century economics that suggest potential new directions for Christian economic conversations. These economists (who are only three among countless others) adhere more closely to Adam Smith's connected style of capitalism than to Chicago's individualistic version. In addition to economists, I have also included several references to Pope Benedict XVI in this chapter. Although a Roman Catholic Pope cannot rightly be said to represent the "Protestant ethic," it is important for Protestants to remember two things as we seek a more just world economy. First, in spite of many significant moral differences, Protestants share certain deep-rooted theological commitments with the Church that gave birth to the Reformations. These commonalities shine through when placing Catholic social thought next to a freedom-oriented Calvinist economic perspective. And second, the history of Protestant economic theology is deeply fragmented—often suspicious of government, steeped in an individualistic sense of works-righteousness, and strangely lacking in the neighbor love that Calvin made so central to his social thought.[2] The Catholic tradition of social encyclicals offers a cohesive set of teachings that Protestants, too, may engage for the sake of staying rooted in the distinctive narrative that sets Christian ethics apart from other ethics, even while allowing Christians to remain in conversation with non-Christians.

MUST CHRISTIAN THEOLOGIANS REJECT THE SCIENCE OF ECONOMICS?

Theologian D. Stephen Long has written an astoundingly thorough survey of more than two centuries of conversation between Christian theology and economics, entitled *Divine Economy: Theology and the Market*. In it, he identifies three major ways that theologians have traditionally approached economic science (to which I offer only a cursory introduction here). The first or "dominant" school of thought, he argues,

---

2. A recent example of these moral divisions happened when television personality Glenn Beck admonished his Christian viewers to "run" from any church that preaches "social justice or economic justice," arguing that these were code words for Nazism and communism. Siegel, "Christians Rip Glenn Beck."

tends to accept neoliberal economists' findings as if they were true and then proceeds to "add value" to what is taken as "fact." (He identifies Michael Novak and Max Stackhouse as two well-known examples of such thought.) The second or "emergent" school rejects the neoliberal approach as essentially unjust and weighted in favor of the wealthy and powerful, and instead looks to Marxist social science for its facts. (Gustavo Gutierrez and Jon Sobrino are among his primary examples here.) The third or "residual" school of theologians, Long argues, is superior to both the dominant and liberationist approaches, because this is the only group that begins and ends with theology, eschewing "facts" in favor of narrative and virtue. Rather than taking economic science at face value, theologians such as John Milbank and medieval theological powerhouse Thomas Aquinas rightly view all social science as inherently narrative, theological, and ethical. Moreover, since theology takes precedence over modern social science, this third school discredits economists and others as essentially doing *bad* theology and ethics.

Among other astute observations, Long notes that many Protestant theologians in the unsatisfactory "dominant" school draw from Calvin's theology. This leads to an obvious question: Does Calvin's theology necessarily resign itself to merely *observing, using,* or *adding value* to science, including social science, rather than allowing for genuine conversation, critique, and transformation? On the surface it may seem so. Calvin offers an apology for the natural sciences, which rests importantly on his assumption that all humans are "captivated by love of truth" (II.ii.12).[3] Even after the fall, Calvin goes on, human beings bear the mark of those who have "already savored" the truth, and they cannot help but seek out greater and greater understanding of the world around them. It is this quest for understanding that sets humans apart from "brute animals"; and because God has gifted humans with this unique intelligence (I.xv.2), Calvin allows that not all earthly or non-Christian pursuit of understanding is in vain. There are two kinds of human understanding, he claims, "one kind of understanding of earthly things; another of

---

3. Calvin implicitly argues here that economists do what they do in an attempt to use their God-given gifts to understand the truth; this differs markedly from the economic assumption that economists do what they do in pursuit of maximizing self-interest. Each point of view, of course, is capable of subsuming the other; Calvin could say that the maximization of material self-interest is the way humans mistakenly go about seeking the truth, while economists could say the pursuit of truth serves the self-interest of those who pursue it.

heavenly" (II.ii.13). Although the natural human understanding cannot itself discover truths about God (and is unwise to try, since the attempt inevitably gives way to idolatry or superstition[4]), human nature is instinctually adept at performing certain tasks that "foster and preserve society," and can produce fruitful effects "when it turns its attention to things below": "I call 'earthly things' those which do not pertain to God or his Kingdom, to true justice, or to the blessedness of the future life; but which have their significance and relationship with regard to the present life and are, in a sense, confined within its bounds. . . . [these include] government, household management, all mechanical skills, and the liberal arts" (II.ii.13). The social animal known as the human being retains a God-given common sense of basic fairness and order, such that even reprobates are able to envision and execute efficient and useful laws and institutions, as demonstrated by the ancients (II.ii.15). The few who reject law and order in favor of "let[ting] their lust alone masquerade as law," do so because they stubbornly and selfishly choose not to live by what they know to be fair and orderly, rather than because they do not recognize fairness and order when they see it.

Thus Calvin is clear that, even though many people behave badly, "some seed of political order has been implanted in all men," which proves that "in the arrangement of this life no man is without the light of reason" (II.ii.13). Corrupt as the human understanding may be, the Calvinist may still appeal to at least limited natural understanding of earthly matters. The Calvinist may even admit that certain non-Christian thinkers and scientists know *more* on some topics than most theologians, "because [knowledge of the arts/sciences] is bestowed indiscriminately upon pious and impious, [and] is rightly counted among natural gifts" (II.ii.14). The human mind, though fallen from its original integrity, "is nevertheless clothed and ornamented with God's excellent gifts" and still has some access to "inferior things" (II.ii.15). The Christian need therefore not fear to accept truth wherever it is to be found, even when it emerges from the minds, mouths, and pens of those with non-Christian beliefs about God. Calvin even scolds those Christians who would ignore the possibility of learning something from the "impious":

> [God] fills, moves, and quickens all things by the power of the
> same Spirit [that dwells in believers], and does so according to

4. "[I]dolatry is ample proof" of the fact that human beings have a "certain understanding" of God "implanted" within them (I.iii.1).

the character that he bestowed upon each kind by the law of creation. But if the Lord has willed that we be helped in physics, dialectic, mathematics, and other like disciplines, by the work and ministry of the ungodly, let us use this assistance. For if we neglect God's gift freely offered in these arts, we ought to suffer just punishment for our sloths. (II.ii.16)

From a freedom-oriented Calvinist point of view, if economic science offers genuinely useful tools for the peaceful and lawful governing of human society (although we must remember that such a field was not in existence for another two centuries after Calvin's lifetime), Christians would be fools not to accept it as a good gift of God. As Benedict writes, love on its own is not an economic policy:

> Without truth, charity degenerates into sentimentality. Love becomes an empty shell, to be filled in an arbitrary way. In a culture without truth, this is the fatal risk facing love. It falls prey to contingent subjective emotions and opinions, the word "love" is abused and distorted, to the point where it comes to mean the opposite. Truth frees charity from the constraints of an emotionalism that deprives it of relational and social content, and of a fideism that deprives it of human and universal breathing-space.[5]

Secular economics may be praised in so far as it helps in the pursuit of truths about human social order and fairness. It is analogous to a Christian flood victim accepting a ride in a boat from an atheist, where the latter has proven to be more adept at boat making.

This theological approach partially answers Stephen Long's concern regarding the concession of a relatively autonomous sphere to economics. Like Frank Knight, Calvin believes economists can tell us *something*, even if they cannot tell us everything. Christians who refuse even the limited understanding that the sciences have to offer are being not only overly cautious, but also negligent in terms of loving their neighbors as themselves. Economists—even impious ones—may do human communities a great favor in propagating a few basic ideas about the ways individual maximizing behavior, supply and demand, institutions, and governmental policy affect market workings. If indeed "free" markets promote "growth" by raising more humans above the level of subsistence than do other kinds of economic systems—while also reducing, or at least not aggravating, human suffering—Christians would be remiss in

5. Benedict XVI, *Caritas in Veritate*, 3.

their neighbor love to ignore the wisdom and the potentially great benefit that economists might impart. (Whether and which markets actually *do* accomplish such goods, whether such goods come at an unacceptable cost, or whether those goods are justly distributed, are questions that must remain constantly open to ongoing, broad debate.)

But while Calvin provides ample room for scientists to pursue knowledge of natural or "earthly" truths without the interference of theological know-it-alls, the Calvinist theologian must still join Long in critiquing economists who overreach the boundaries of their wisdom. The human "capacity to understand, with the understanding that follows upon it, is an unstable and transitory thing in God's sight, when a solid foundation of truth does not underlie it" (II.ii.16). Economists who are not in touch with their field's roots in tradition, history, and ethics, and who therefore neglect to account for the real human suffering that capitalist markets can cause and have caused, are doomed to incomplete and even false understandings. Humans are also so corrupted by the fall, Calvin cautions, that their pursuit of truth often deteriorates into "investigating empty and worthless things," thus "tormenting itself in its absurd curiosity" while ignoring the truths that really matter (II.ii.12). It is not that the truth is not available to everyone; God "represents both himself and his everlasting kingdom in the mirror of his works with very great clarity," but due to human "dullness" these representations are of little benefit to most people (I.v.11).

The economic discipline's first mistake is that it claims to deal with only those "natural" phenomena and "factual" findings that can be observed and reported objectively. Then, despite its self-imposed starting limitations, it is tempted to offer all-encompassing conclusions about human economic life. In reality, economists (like all mere mortals) must pick and choose the types of "natural" and "factual" data they collect, and then they must interpret these phenomena according to their prior commitments. Although economics relinquishes claims as to the ethical essence of humankind, it still hopes to be useful, perhaps even to change the world for the better, which is why Frank Knight's stance was ultimately unsatisfying for his Chicago associates. Most economists seek to explain "why" things happen, not merely to state "what" happens. But economic science cannot tell the whole truth about human economies, precisely because it does not tell the whole truth about the nature of human beings. As Benedict puts it, "Fidelity to man requires *fidelity to the truth*, which alone is the *guarantee of freedom* (cf. John 8:32) and of *the possibility of integral human development.*"[6] Moreover, even saying "what" happens is a theologically (or ideologically) loaded business. Life without interpretive description would, after all, be mere chaos to the human mind. People need lenses, paradigms, and metaphors through which to view and make sense of various phenomena, which in turn require decisions of inclusion and exclusion, connection and separation; their hypotheses will be shaped by a well-protected core of assumptions and beliefs to which they ascribe and will, in large part, determine their findings.[7]

Because the phenomena with which economics deals have to do with past and future human behavior (in that it predicts the future based on models that arise from its reading of the past), and because humans in all their fullness cannot be described or analyzed properly without the help of normative claims about who humans are and therefore *should* be, economics might more fruitfully (in terms of human flourishing) be considered a subset of either moral theology or history. As we saw with Smith, economics first emerged as a sub-discipline of moral philosophy that made explicitly normative claims about human nature and the proper ordering of human society, but it has since sought to isolate itself from other disciplines and to operate independently of norms. In doing so, it has robbed itself of any "foundation of truth" that might make it less "unstable and transitory," and it tends toward serving the limited ends of those individuals who promote it. Once it is demonstrated that economics' assumptions are in fact normative in nature, it ceases to appear "scientific" in any ahistorical way.[8] For example, Calvin's teaching

6. Benedict XVI, *Caritas in Veritate*, 9.

7. Mark Blaug writes that Kuhn's term "paradigm," when applied to economic science, "retains a function in the historical exposition of economic doctrines as a reminder of the fallacy of trying to appraise particular theories without invoking the wider metaphysical framework in which they are embedded." But ultimately he thinks Lakatos's idea of a "hard core" of knowledge/faith surrounded by a protective belt is more appropriate. Blaug, "Kuhn versus Lakatos," 233–34.

8. In this they may suffer only because they aspire and fail to measure up to standards of the "harder" sciences and mathematics, as the following joke illustrates. An economist, a logician, and a mathematician see a cow through their train window. "And the economist says, 'Look, the cows in Scotland are brown.' And the logician says, 'No. There are cows in Scotland at least one of which is brown.' And the mathematician says, 'No. There is at least one cow in Scotland, at least one side of which appears to be brown.' And it is funny because economists are not real scientists, and because logicians think more clearly, but mathematicians are best." Haddon, *Curious Incident*, 143.

on the first use of the law calls into question the economic assumption that self-interest, utility, and preferences need not be defined or qualified in order for economic models to work; without the law constantly tutoring humans in the knowledge of good and evil, all self-interest (which economists approve) would give way to rent-seeking (which they do not). Economists therefore assume a need for law that parallels, at the very least, Calvin's second use, in that they agree on the fact that humans need some external motivation to do the right thing.

This is not to say that the methods employed by economics cannot ultimately be unique among academic disciplines. It is not to say that certain mathematical formulations might not yield helpful information for the making of effective, life-affirming economic policy. It is only to say (as many theologian-ethicists have said before me) that economists cannot operate from an ethics-free position, without any culturally and historically conditioned assumptions, or without any ulterior motives. In Calvinist terms, no human can claim access to a reason unmarred by sin. The human community may benefit greatly from the insights of economics, but where the freedom-loving theologian must exercise some suspicion is with regard to the given parameters and assumptions that underlie various predictions, since these can often be self-fulfilling—particularly when the predictor lacks a self-critical eye. Economists can predict what they predict only by focusing on narrow questions that interest them, and by deliberately ignoring vast amounts of data as irrelevant to those questions.

Thus, while the Calvinist theologian rightly denies the truthfulness of any economist (or any scientist, historian, or philosopher for that matter) who might claim to speak from a neutral or objective point of view, or who might be unwilling to engage non-economists in conversations about economics, she should have no problem at all allowing some space for the discipline known as economics, any more than she should forsake the many other modes of inquiry. On the contrary, thinks the Calvinist, such fields are signs of God's diverse providence and worthy of admiration! The shortcoming of economics (as with any science) is not that it cannot tell us anything; it is that it sometimes aspires to tell us everything. Economists may rightly observe, for example, that humans generally act so as to better (rather than harm) their own conditions; what they may not do is offer a convincingly amoral answer as to *why* they act this way. Nor can they make amoral claims as to whether some human actions are better or more fruitful than other human actions.

From a Calvinist point of view, this is simply because economists cannot learn the *whole* truth from nature; what *is* is not necessarily what *must be*. At best, they have lightning flashes of brilliance, which cannot be tied together sensibly without the aid of grace. To a certain extent, Pope Benedict echoes this sentiment:

> In the list of areas where the pernicious effects of sin are evident, the economy has been included for some time now. We have a clear proof of this at the present time. The conviction that man is self-sufficient and can successfully eliminate the evil present in history by his own action alone has led him to confuse happiness and salvation with immanent forms of material prosperity and social action. Then, *the conviction that the economy must be autonomous, that it must be shielded from "influences" of a moral character, has led man to abuse the economic process in a thoroughly destructive way.* In the long term, these convictions have led to economic, social and political systems that trample upon personal and social freedom, and are therefore unable to deliver the justice that they promise.[9]

The economic science that exists for the perpetuation of markets requires constant dialogue with those "critics of human values" (as Knight called ethicists) who believe the "economic sphere" of life is as ethically important and morally fraught as any other.

Such critique may also come from within economics itself. Calvin writes confidently that, "while men dispute among themselves about individual sections of the law, they agree on the general conception of equity. In this respect the frailty of the human mind is surely proved: even when it seems to follow the way, it limps and staggers" (II.ii.13). The fact that rational-choice economists cannot agree even among themselves on economic policy is evidence that their science is deeply intertwined with personal narratives and prior ethical criteria that exist outside the market assumptions they share. Economists may agree on the existence of human self-interest, but they cannot agree on the line past which self-interest ceases to be beneficial and becomes harmful; or on which kinds of policies and institutions most efficiently harness self-interest (largely because "efficiency" itself must first be defined); or on what counts as a

---

9. Benedict XVI, *Caritas in Veritate*, 34. Emphasis original.

"market failure" or an "externality." Their disagreements are not due to a *lack* of understanding of economic principles, but rather to *differences* in understanding that arise from prior beliefs and commitments that guide their understandings.[10] To be sure, the morally condemnable image of *homo economicus*, a machine of efficiency whose every move is a mere cover for naked self-interest, has its roots in tradition as well. Bernard Mandeville's "Grumbling Hive" (conceived fifty years before *Wealth of Nations*), for example, sought to illustrate that strong economies thrive only on lusts and vices of all kinds, rather than on self-restraint.[11] (Such a view undoubtedly works in favor of some who seek policies friendly to the production and consumption of luxuries or harmful items.) There certainly are strands of economics that are pessimistic about human nature; and these have tended to justify a value system that fosters a wide division between rich and poor, as well as the subordination of unskilled laborers under the domination of owners.

But there are many others who aim deliberately not to do this.[12] In this book I have sought to show that individualistic self-interest, while perhaps convenient for economic modeling in the ivory tower, is not the given "spirit of capitalism" for all economists everywhere. (Indeed, those who insist on such narrow, abstract disciplinary constructs may in fact make their science prey to an almost "scholastic" irrelevance on the world stage.)[13] There are many thinkers who take the focus off the wealthy captain of industry and turn their gaze toward others who have traditionally supported him—his wife, housekeeper, nanny, gardener, farmer, factory worker—in order to see where the dominant system has failed to work humanely. If the ethicist's task is, as Long says, "a charitable and generous engagement with the best rationality present in the social

---

10. One journalist recently wrote that "economics is at last a science" and praised what he saw as ten hard core principles of market economics. Sorman, "Economics Does Not Lie." He was immediately shot down by another economic blogger who felt he had correctly named the scientific principles of economics but misunderstood their import. Tucker, "You Call This Capitalism?"

11. Mandeville, *Grumbling Hive*. Mandeville argued, poetically, that the liveliness of economic exchange could not survive if a given market's participants ceased to follow their most vicious instincts in favor of virtue. Smith did not agree with Mandeville; his thought bears closer resemblance to French "physiocrats" who saw markets in more biological terms (healthy markets as healthy bodies).

12. Barker and Feiner, *Liberating Economics*, 18.

13. Nelson, "Scholasticism vs. Pietism," 3.

sciences,"[14] then those who wish to engage economics cannot dismiss it altogether based on its most compassionless forms. Those economists who cultivate what one author calls the "soulful science"[15] deserve more attention from Christian critics of capitalism.

Before moving on, it must also be said that Calvin's choice to distinguish the "earthly" from the "heavenly" sets an unfortunate precedent for later conversations in economics and ethics, particularly theological ethics. While it is a welcome development in so far as it demonstrates a hint of disciplinary humility on his part, it also makes palatable the idea that, on the one hand, there are matters in material life in which a self-consciously narrative ethics has no concern; and on the other hand, that there is such a thing as science untouched by human narratives, assumptions, or interests. In doing so, Calvin gives license to scientists to ignore ethical concerns as irrelevant to their inquiry, and may encourage theologians to leave science alone to do whatever it wants, without having to engage in any pesky ethical conversations. The heavenly/earthly dichotomy downplays the "profound materiality of Christianity, centred [sic] on its incarnational beliefs and practices,"[16] and may give theologians an excuse to shirk any duty for trying to come up with genuine solutions to real-world problems, such as global poverty, and to hide behind "heavenly" concepts like Christian charity rather than to work for "earthly" systemic justice.

In spite of these caveats about both economic science and Calvinist theology, I affirm Calvin's point that Christian ethicists would do well to give economists their due and listen carefully (rather than dismiss them out of hand as many of us are wont to do), namely because we—no less than they—suffer from imperfect and partial understandings of how the world works. Because none of us can comprehend anything on our own,

14. Long et al., *Calculated Futures*, 5.

15. Coyle, *Soulful Science*, uses this term in contrast to its usual characterization as the "dismal science." Stephen Webb writes bluntly: "Theologians [he refers especially to the Radical Orthodoxy school] who read the wrong kind of economists are not just wasting their time. They are also missing out on conversations that could be productive." Where I look to feminism and social business, he proposes a shift toward "new institutionalists" such as Douglass C. North. Webb, "New Theology, Old Economics," 12.

16. Atherton, *Transfiguring Capitalism*, 102. Atherton's book is an excellent and innovative (if not always easy to follow) example of economic thought that draws from an extremely wide range of academic inquiries, including philosophy, politics, economics, theology, and psychology.

however honorable our intentions, the diversity of our perspectives offers the greatest hope for our ongoing pursuit of economic justice for everyone, especially those who are usually left out of univocal solutions. (This diversity of ideas includes, of course, not just theology and economics, but all the sciences, social sciences, arts, and humanities known to humankind, as well as ideas that come from the margins of each of these the disciplines—and from no discipline at all.) Among these diverse voices are many who advocate for the value of freedom-based economics, resting on the assumption that individuals are capable of making rational decisions, even while acknowledging that concrete rationality and freedom are inextricable from communities and contexts.

MUST CHRISTIAN THEOLOGIANS REJECT CAPITALISM (OR MARKET ECONOMIES) OUTRIGHT?

Having sought to demonstrate to my readers (especially those who share the suspicions with which I approach economics) that neighbor-loving Christians need not reject freedom-oriented economic science altogether, I must also address whether or not economic systems we know as "capitalism" must also be abolished from human social life. Students of Christian economic ethics probably know that when capitalism comes up in left-leaning circles, it is frequently used as shorthand for a variety of social ills including greed, exploitation, profit motives, cold-hearted efficiency, scarcity, covetousness, theft, private property, and above all, individualistic self-interest.[17] Such a view is not without merit. In seeking to argue for the inherent injustices of capitalism, one need only point to things like environmental degradation, the vast and growing gap between the world's richest people and their hard-working but perpetually poor neighbors, industrial sweat shops and child labor, increased rates of depression among people of industrialized countries, or the unjustly distributed effects of Hurricane Katrina on citizens of the Gulf Coast. The proverbial glass can most certainly be seen as at least half empty.

Ethicist Jon Gunnemann explains these negative effects of market economies by arguing that "capitalism is by definition interested chiefly in external or extrinsic goods rather than in internal or intrinsic

17. Michael Moore's 2009 documentary, *Capitalism: A Love Story*, appropriately summarizes the associations many of us bring to discussions of "free enterprise" or "free markets," and raises crucial questions that free market economists must address.

goods."[18] By this he means it is a system of economic organization that is predicated upon actors who engage in exchange *solely* for the purpose of obtaining goods external to the exchange process itself. To illustrate, he uses a chess analogy (from Alasdair McIntyre); in order to teach the game to a child, a teacher might use candy as an incentive. When the child plays well she earns a piece of candy, which represents the external or extrinsic good. This may be an effective teaching strategy in the short term except for one thing: as long as candy is the goal, there is no incentive for the child not to cheat. If the candy is all that she desires, then she will do whatever she must to win—including cheating if she can get away with it. Eventually a child must learn to love chess for its intrinsic goods—the challenge, the beauty, the chance to excel; otherwise the game itself will be nothing more than a means to an end.

Gunnemann claims that capitalism (apparently unlike chess) is a game that offers no intrinsic goods. There is nothing to love about capitalism itself; it exists, by its very nature, only as a means to obtaining goods that are extrinsic to the system. Thus it cannot help but foster a community of cheaters and rent-seekers, because it has nothing intrinsic to recommend itself—no inherent beauty, no *telos* of its own. Any attempt at a counter-argument to Gunnemann's serious and perennial critique must somehow demonstrate that capitalist exchange is actually constituted by internal, not merely external, goods. We must note that it is not only critics who may point to capitalism's lack of intrinsic goods; many *proponents* of capitalism also share the conviction that its genius lies precisely in operating according to a single human trait—self-interest—which seeks only the external goods to which markets are the most efficient means. As Atherton puts it, the "selfish" form of capitalism cannot seem to help but "erode those values, virtues and associations on which it is dependent for its flourishing."[19] If selfishness is the necessary pre-condition, or at the very least the inevitable result, of the "free" markets that neoliberals promote, do not Christians have a duty to support some other model?

My research has persuaded me that a lack of intrinsic goods is not a *necessary* part of capitalism's character. I think Calvin and Smith, as well as many contemporary economists and ethicists, enable us to see capitalism or market economics as a potentially humane way of organizing economies that depends upon a freely sympathetic division of labor

18. Gunnemann, "Christian Ethics in a Capitalist Society," 51.

19. Atherton, *Transfiguring Capitalism*, 52.

and sympathetically rational free exchange. We need not be suspicious (as ethicists sometimes are) of using the term "exchange" here, because in this scenario economic exchange does not define all other sorts of exchange; rather economic exchange is one example of the many virtuous and sympathetic exchanges we encounter all the time in our families, friendships, and other social situations, all of which include—but are not reduced to—self-interest. Recall that Smith first wrote about human sympathy as it came up in everyday human interactions, and only later explored more deeply the way it worked in the marketplace. Capitalist exchange is not necessarily more corrupting, exploitive, or selfish than any of our other social, religious, or political institutions. (The fact that socialists have employed concentration camps, that a democracy employed atomic bombs, that husbands abuse wives, or that the Roman Catholic priesthood has recently been unveiled as a breeding ground for pedophilia, should not automatically rule out socialism, democracy, marriage, or Catholicism as incorrigibly corrupting—though such horrors certainly demand close scrutiny and analysis.) The "spirit of capitalism" can be idealized as *cooperation* rather than competition; it can be a win-win, not a zero-sum, game.

For one thing, the game of capitalism has rules, all of which are rooted in what Robert Nelson calls the "market paradox" of liberal economic thought: "the requisite normative foundation for the market requires a dual attitude with respect to self-interest—*strong cultural inhibitions against the expression of self-interest* . . . in many areas of society, but at the same time strong encouragement for . . . the individual pursuit of profit within the specific confines of the market."[20] In a free market, in other words, individuals may seek their own benefit, but only as limited by obedience to the rules (or laws) of sympathy and self-discipline. When people neglect to obey the rules of the game, the game breaks down. Economists themselves have terms for such bad economic behavior—terms like rent-seeking, monopoly, and theft—which are loaded with the discipline's own value judgments against excessive self-interest. Looking back to Calvin's first and second uses of the law, we recall that he believed laws were useful for both revealing and restraining human wickedness. Having rules for the game is the first line of defense against cheating; they are there to show human beings what is right and to discourage them from disobedience. This is not the ultimate goal, though; ideally, human

20. Nelson, *Economics as Religion*, 3. Emphasis added.

beings learn to love the rules so much that their very obedience to them is transformed into freedom. The truly free human being—in economic life, no less than any other area of life—is the one who spontaneously but mindfully does the right thing. Though virtue must at first be infused into a person from outside herself, through simple enforcement and then through exhortation, over time she becomes so shaped by the rules that virtue defines her essential nature. She is freely obedient and obediently free. Capitalism, like any good game, can have a kind of intrinsic beauty when played well. When it goes beyond acting as a mere means to other ends, it can become something worth doing largely because it allows people to exercise their creativity and full humanity. If the current rules of the game do not cultivate an intrinsic beauty, then—because there is no orthodox capitalism—the rules of the game can be changed to reflect more closely the norms of sympathy, in order to achieve the desired, humane effect.

It is possible that at this point in history "capitalism" may have acquired such an irrevocably negative shape that revision is impossible and the term should be retired altogether. Though I have discussed capitalism throughout this book, I would argue that the use of the plural term "markets" can be a helpful first step in allowing for more complex Christian ethical and economic narratives in the twenty-first century.[21] Even speaking of "the market" implies the presence of a monolith, an impervious and impersonal machine over which humans have no control, and within which there can be no variation. Such an image stifles creative critical engagement by unwisely privileging the most extreme voices of neoliberalism. Just as those working from the margins of theology call into question monolithic terms like "orthodoxy" or "virtue" or "the church" (which often hide a privileged norm), so must anyone with a genuine interest in freedom and human flourishing be willing to move beyond the apparently all-encompassing, apparently self-evident entity of "capitalism" (or "globalization" or "Marxism" for that matter) and allow for more particular analyses of diverse markets. Christians need to free ourselves from the illusion that there is only one market,

---

21. Part of this section has been previously published online in *The Other Journal*; see Blanchard, "Should Christians Give Markets Another Chance?" I am grateful to the editors of *The Other Journal* for allowing me to use this material here.

which hates workers, the earth, and taxes; and which loves corporations, profits, and selfish individualism.[22]

If we treat them plurally, markets, we must admit, vary in degree of goodness; they do so because they are instruments used by humans in the pursuit of a variety of goods. Some markets are designed for provisioning, some for domination or exploitation. Markets in cocaine, child pornography, or sexual slavery are evils by almost anyone's standards because they destroy human health and rest on the annihilation of human compassion. Markets in food, shelter, and clothing, on the other hand, are generally received as positive developments. Who among us, after all, wants to be required to act as farmer, chef, cleaner, builder, wood-chopper, weaver, investor, pharmacist, seamstress, gestator, and caregiver of children all at the same time? This list does not even touch on bourgeois luxuries like art, leisure, or education—the person working to provide all the necessities of her own life certainly has no time or energy left over for school, music, comedy, sculpture, rollerblading, poetry, video games, or film. It is fair to say that the person who does not exist by division of labor does not exist this side of Eden. (And it's really not fair to compare, say, folks in modern Michigan to Adam and Eve in the beginning, since the latter could run around naked and did not have to freeze food in order to eat in February. Plus there were only two of them, making exchange somewhat more straightforward; Michigan—although currently shrinking—was up to almost ten million people as of the last census.)

Pope Benedict writes, "In a climate of mutual trust, the *market* is the economic institution that permits encounter between persons, inasmuch as they are economic subjects who make use of contracts to regulate their relations as they exchange goods and services of equivalent value between them, in order to satisfy their needs and desires. . . . *Without internal forms of solidarity and mutual trust, the market cannot completely fulfil* [sic] *its proper economic function*."[23] Economic activity, in other words, is part and parcel of social activity more broadly. We

22. Rebecca Todd Peters, for example, recognizes and describes not one but four possible ways to analyze globalization, distinguishing them in order to be able to critique them more fairly, thereby opening up space for a plurality of new markets, corporations, and economic systems reflective of "the values of democratizing power, caring for the planet, and attending to the social well-being of people." Peters, *In Search of the Good Life*, 193.

23. Benedict XVI, *Caritas in Veritate*, 35. Emphasis original.

have already seen that Adam Smith knew this; he was correct to pin-point the division of labor among the most fundamental acts of human society, as well as among the kindest things humans could do for one another. Although he wrote that, "Nobody but a beggar chuses [sic] to depend chiefly upon the benevolence of his fellow-citizens,"[24] he did not dismiss benevolence altogether. Stripped of its Dickensian caricature, Smith's idea of a market is simply a relationship among people who need each other. Jane needs bread, Jamal needs wool, Jin needs bricks; they trade among themselves in a way that saves each of them a lot of effort and benefits them all equally. Moreover, this trading creates an interde-pendent community, miraculously peaceable, built on faithfulness and trust. This holds true even when currency is substituted for one half of the exchange; as economist Julie Nelson argues persuasively, money is not an external measure of value that somehow insinuates itself into human interactions, but is rather a socially created symbol of apprecia-tion which arises from them.[25] Ideally speaking, markets depend on and promote friendship, sympathy, and mutual solidarity.

Of course ideals are just that, and evil markets—like evil people—do exist. Most markets in the real world, however, tend to fall some-where in the grey area between good and evil. They are the media by which moderately well-off, educated, responsible, and well-intentioned Christians (you know who you are) acquire objects of *adiaphora* and ambivalence, such as artisanal cheese, hybrid cars, liberal arts educa-tions, haircuts, cable TV, modest homes, fashionable shoes, Italian wine, the internet, skis, air conditioning, jogging strollers, basketball tickets, or comfortable beds. These are items that most of us not only enjoy (or hope to enjoy someday) but, if we are honest with ourselves, believe we cannot live without. This makes things somewhat awkward for those of us who might wish to critique the system. If we are pastors, our careers in the church depend upon our parishioners' good will and monetary donations. If we are scholars, our work reading and writing books and training other people to read and write books depends largely upon the financial support of folks at work in markets other than higher educa-tion. If we are students, we may depend on bank loans, institutional endowments, or our parents' money to help us achieve our degrees. The

24. Smith, WN, 22.

25. Nelson, *Economics for Humans*, 69. We will return to a fuller treatment of Nelson later in this chapter.

love-hate relationship between the Christian critics of capitalism and the market systems under which we labor could be compared to a love-hate relationship between a child and his parent, or between a religious reformer and her religious tradition. The markets in which we have been raised have made us what we are; American Christians expect freedom, including freedom for all kinds of choices. Yet at the same time, our market context has also bred conceptual and practical tools by which we recognize its flaws and try to change it. We desire *real* freedom to be who we truly are as human beings, rather than consumer drones or exploitative demons.

Take, for example, the observation that all human relationships can be read as markets of sorts. There are certainly reasons for this to make a Christian cringe. "The market" based on the monstrous antihero, *homo economicus*, is a wicked model indeed. As we saw with Becker, applying the market paradigm to marriage makes it little more than a glorified form of prostitution; sex-sellers, normally assumed to be women, offer exclusive sex privileges on an open market, in exchange for money, homes, and other material gains (albeit sentimentalized with religious or romantic narratives), which are acquired from sex-buyers, usually men (who are also in it for the free childcare). Likewise, the love between parents and children is reduced to a self-interested investment plan, in which people have children and raise them in particular ways based on what they hope to get out of them in the future. Children, in turn, learn how to manipulate their parents so as to get what *they* want. In scenarios like these, self-interest trumps love as the defining characteristic of "the market"; and there is little point in arguing for other motivations because the economists have already demonstrated that these other motivations can be boiled down to self-interest as well.[26] These arguments bother us most likely because they hit so close to home. (Who among us, after all, has considered marriage without thinking about the pluses and minuses of binding ourselves legally to a particular person for life; or what parents did not weigh the very real costs and benefits of having their first or fourth child?) But rather than self-deceptively pretending that self-

26. This is not the only scientific view available to us, however. Neuroeconomists and behavioral economists are busy demonstrating that humans often choose against self-interest, for reasons that still baffle those who wish to leave ethics out of the discussion. See Basu, "Traveler's Dilemma," 90–95, and Shermer, "Prospects for Homo Economicus," 40–42.

interest plays *no* role in the way we live our lives, such arguments call us to make our cost-benefit analyses explicit and examine them out in the open, laying bare both the complex interplay of our many motives, and the implicit narratives that give rise to them. The goals of real-life economic actors are not givens; neither are their motivations, understandings, and judgments.

The symbiotic blending of wisdom and love is what capitalism—again, speaking ideally—can be about: sympathetic individuals and groups working out human relationships (of which markets are only one type) in ways that benefit all parties involved, both in the short term and the long run. As economist Peter Boettke puts it, "we put trust in strangers and bring them into the extended order of the division of labor from which we benefit. Trust and friendship are both the foundation of the market economy, and the by-product of the expansion of the market economy."[27] We know, however, that such optimism does not always reflect markets as they actually are, and markets deserve critique and require intervention when they do not live up to the ideal; it does not benefit our common humanity to be Pollyannas about this reality. People do sometimes steal from one another, cheat or lie to one another, hijack government power for their own interests, or take more than their share, all in the name of "freedom." But as we have seen, even the most anti-sentimental economist does not envision a healthy economy based on greed, lies, lawlessness, and utter disregard for human dignity.

Perhaps the greatest and gravest threat to the cooperative ideal of freedom-oriented markets is the issue of "externalities" (Friedman's "neighborhood effects")—effects on parties outside a given market transaction, for which economists traditionally give no account. These may be physical consequences, such as when a buyer and seller in Atlanta exchange money for water; this trade may benefit both parties to their satisfaction, but it does not factor in the costs to people in Alabama or Florida who wish to use the same water source and now no longer have access to it. Or such as when a contractor clear-cuts a forest in order to build new homes as cheaply as possible; the contractor and home buyer are happy, but the costs passed onto others in the forms of greenhouse gases, traffic congestion, soil erosion, species endangerment, or the proliferation of pests such as deer ticks, are ignored as irrelevant to the transaction. Market externalities can also be pecuniary (price related),

27. Boettke, review of *The Bourgeois Virtues*, 85.

as Albino Barrera thoroughly explains in his book on the coercive effects of unintended market consequences, such as the hardship caused in the developing world by American and European farm subsidies.[28] Truly just economic systems that respect the interconnectedness of humans to other humans, and humankind to the rest of creation, must learn to expect and account for unintended consequences, and must take both pre-emptive and rehabilitative action in response to these so-called externalities.

Rebecca Todd Peters rightly argues that "transformation of globalization," or, I would add, of capitalism "does not require the elimination of business, or markets, or even corporations. . . . What it does require is a metamorphosis of corporate self-identity in ways that reflect the moral norms" of justice and human flourishing.[29] Christian doctrines of nature and grace mean we have the capacity and responsibility not to buy into overly-reductive, fear-driven stereotypes about selfish capitalism, imagination-crushing socialism, or tyrannical globalization. But by the same token, the Christian doctrine of sin means we must also resist urges to romanticize the wonders of poverty or the good-old days, the godliness of corporations, or the selflessness of governments. Living in the "already but not yet" does not mean that Christians spend our time in a fantasy world where we are not implicated in the evils we see around us; it means Christians—both individuals and churches—must focus on what we can do here and now to heal the world, even amidst its brokenness.

This requires us to go beyond both tithing and prophetic jeremiad. At a most basic level, Christians must first become comfortable with the idea of hybridity when it comes to economic systems. Not only are there no *perfect* systems that make everyone happy, but there are no *pure* ones that adhere precisely to any particular ideal, either. As historian Eugene McCarraher rightly notes, a "market oriented economy . . . isn't necessarily capitalist,"[30] nor does the socialism dreaded by most Americans necessarily entail absolute equality, government control of all property, or an end to possibilities for free and fair trade. Meanwhile, human suffering from want is real, and Christians must resist the urge to offer our

---

28. Barrera, *Economic Compulsion and Christian Ethics*.

29. Peters, *In Search of the Good Life*, 198.

30. McCarraher, "Break on Through to the Other Side," 40. A self-defined Christian socialist, he elsewhere notes that "Marx dismissed equality as a bourgeois concept."

neighbors visions of spiritual beatitude to the exclusion of addressing their material needs. With this in mind, quixotic attacks on a generalized capitalism (or socialism) can give way to more fruitful critiques and interactions with *particular* markets, players, behaviors, and policies—starting with our own—especially with an eye toward the coercive externalities they may visit on our neighbors near and far.

A PLACE TO BEGIN: NEW CONVERSATION PARTNERS FOR CHRISTIAN ECONOMIC ETHICS

We recall Gunnemann's argument that capitalism has no intrinsic rewards; I have sought to persuade readers that this is not *necessarily* the case, particularly if we are able to let go of illusions about "pure" or "orthodox" capitalism and allow for the revision that may arise from cross-pollination with the best that other systems (both theological and ideological) have to offer. Critics of capitalism will cite a vast number of historical manifestations of evil for which they hold it solely responsible, and while these criticisms have obvious basis in reality, one claims too much by laying all the blame at the feet of a single idea or institution. Christian ethicists are not alone in envisioning an economic system that is rich in intrinsic rewards; we are not alone in caring about the poor, justice, freedom, agency, community, or charity. There are also economists who see capitalism as a process of human interactions that is constituted by *both* intrinsic *and* extrinsic goods—both the game and the candy. I offer the following introductions to three economists who demonstrate the potential for markets to help shape caring communities of mutual support, fostering abundance by locating self-interest within the context of interdependence, and individual freedom within the boundaries of self-limitation and neighbor love. Such abundance takes the form not only of production and distribution of material goods and services, but also of spiritual goods for individuals and communities.[31]

---

31. The economic principle of scarcity is a frequent object of critique from Christian critics of capitalism (such as Long and McCarraher), who offer "abundance" as a theological antidote. Such a topic is far too large for this book (I have addressed it briefly elsewhere, Blanchard, "Review of *God and the Evil of Scarcity*," 304–5) but is worthy of further dialogue between theologians and economists.

Deirdre McCloskey: Capitalism as Training Ground for the Virtues

An excellent example of this type of thought is the first installment of Deirdre McCloskey's magnum opus, *The Bourgeois Virtues: Ethics for an Age of Commerce*, which she directs toward two separate but related audiences that make up what she calls the "clerisy"—intellectuals on both the right and left, some of whom (including ethicists) find the term "bourgeois virtues" oxymoronic because the bourgeoisie is clearly evil; others of whom (economists) find it oxymoronic because the bourgeoisie requires no ethics in order to be bourgeois.[32] Her main argument to both sides is that capitalism not only *requires* virtuous players in order to work properly, but it even goes a step further and actually *cultivates* virtue in its participants. Such an unusual claim bears repeating: rather than encouraging the worst in human nature, McCloskey is confident that people actually learn to be more virtuous, not less, through participation in capitalism—both in its idealized form and as it really exists.

Capitalism, according to McCloskey, by which she means "merely private property and free labor without central planning, regulated by the rule of law and by an ethical consensus,"[33] is the system that has done the most to create genuine flourishing in human communities. She notes that capitalist systems have been the engines of unprecedented increases in real per capita income and decreases in the percentages of people on earth living in deep poverty.[34] It also allows for higher standards of living and longer life expectancies. But most important from her point of view are not the material gains associated with free markets: "[F]attening up the people, or providing them with inexpensive silk stockings . . . is not the only virtue of our bourgeois life. The triple revolutions of the past two centuries in politics, populations, and prosperity are connected. They have had a cause and a consequence, I claim, in ethically *better* people. I said 'better.' Capitalism has not corrupted our souls. It has

32. McCloskey, *Bourgeois Virtues*, 5–6.

33. Ibid., 14.

34. See McCloskey, "Avarice, Prudence, and the Bourgeois Virtues," 327, in which she notes that per capita income in the United States rose by more than sixteen-hundred percent between 1820–1994. She neglects, unfortunately, to account for slavery, genocide, and general exploitation of labor and resources in this period of growth. Nevertheless, I am persuaded that such exploitations are historical contingencies not *necessary* to market systems; moreover, as a woman and a mother I am particularly unable and unwilling to make any romantic claims about the virtues of rural life, life in the past, or life in non-market societies.

improved them."[35] Market systems, she thinks, can allow human beings to create individual and communal meanings, and to pursue individual and communal purposes more efficiently than feudal or centrally directed systems. Capitalist markets have encouraged the abolition of slavery, rights for women, higher education, and the flourishing of the arts.[36] To be sure, she notes (echoing Calvin), certain people and groups of people will abuse whatever freedoms they enjoy in ways that dehumanize themselves and others; but certainly the proportion of these people in free markets does not outnumber the proportion of vicious people elsewhere in time or space. Indeed, she believes the exact opposite is true; when people are sufficiently fed, they are less likely to view all of life as a life-or-death competition for scarce resources. She admits that the wealthy and powerful in market economies have certainly twisted politics to work in their favor, "But when have the rich not done that?"[37] Her broader point here is that such sin is inherent to *human nature*, rather than unique to market systems; but rather than resign herself to a sad state of affairs, she instead sees market systems as curtailing sin rather than celebrating it. This occurs both positively and negatively, with carrots and sticks; people who behave viciously in the marketplace suffer the consequences, while those who behave virtuously are rewarded.[38]

Moreover, she argues, the "bourgeois" virtues that capitalism so effectively fosters are not uniquely bourgeois; they include not only the prudence that economists celebrate in the guise of rational self-interest, but *all* the pagan and Christian virtues—including courage, temperance,

35. McCloskey, *Bourgeois Virtues*, 23. Emphasis original.

36. Ibid., 142. McCarraher is right to note that these and many other boons of capitalism, such as the eight-hour day, are also due to "worker agitation and political struggle, both opposed, often viciously," by business owners. McCarraher, "Break on Through," 40. But he acknowledges elsewhere certain goods of capitalism when he writes (to "theocons" overly obsessed with natural law), "If you really want patriarchy and traditional, 'natural' gender roles back, you've got to destroy capitalism in the name of some reactionary proprietary vision." The point I take here is that freedoms for women—which many opponents of capitalism approve—are tied, both conceptually and historically, to market freedoms. It is difficult to have one without the other. McCarraher, "Meet the New Boss, Same as the Old Boss," part 3.

37. Ibid., 493. All the more reason, she thinks, to limit the power of the governments they seek to appropriate. "The more comprehensive and effective is the state, the greater is the incentive for interests and parties to seize control of it, there being in that case more to gain." Ibid., 36.

38. Reality, of course, does not always reflect economic ideals. I beg the scoffing reader to bear with me a bit longer; I will offer a critique of McCloskey before I move on.

and justice, and even faith, hope, and love. Prudence, to be sure, matters, but there is more to a market economy than this. Temperance encourages people to exercise moderation, resist theft, and find compromises; justice honors individuals' labor and property; love cares for employees and fellow citizens; hope imagines a better future.[39] "[T]he bourgeois virtues," in other words, "are merely the seven virtues exercised in a commercial society."[40] Of her two major points in this book, this is the one she hopes to demonstrate to her left-leaning audience—members of the clerisy who worry that capitalism necessarily requires vice in order to function properly. These critics will hasten to underline the many abuses that have taken place (and continue to take place) in the name of capitalist freedom. But from the perspective of Christian ethics, if there is any possibility that markets can, given the proper context, help foster the truly good life for human beings, we would be foolish to dismiss them without serious conversation (whether or not market economics originated in church doctrine).

The other side of McCloskey's argument, though, is to convince the clerisy on her right—particularly those in her economics cohort who wish to reduce the ethical decision-making faculties of humankind to a single utility-seeking trait—that they too are missing the big picture. "The most characteristic virtues of humans," she says to this audience, "are not a rationality or a persistence that one can see plainly in ants and bacteria as well. They are hope and faith."[41] What sets human actions apart from those of their fellow creatures is that they arise from more complicated motivations; humans depend not only on momentary survival instincts, but on rhetoric, narrative, meaning, character, and an orientation toward the future—including an eschatological future. "Any monism denies the dilemmas," she writes:

> Come now, no dilemma [the economist says]; just do what maximizes utility. Or an evolutionary psychology of the we-brain-scientists-have-it-all-worked-out variety says: Face up to it, there's no dilemma; just do what your genes are telling you to do. Or a revealed theology of the we-already-know-God's-will variety says: Bless you, no dilemma; just do what God so evidently wishes. . . . Or the reason-loving-side-of-the-late-Enlightenment-project

39. Ibid., 507–8.
40. Ibid., 508.
41. Ibid., 168.

variety: Seriously, no dilemma; just follow the rule of reason, such as the categorical imperative.[42]

She concludes, "The opposite side of the Enlightenment's love of reason, as I've said, is love of freedom. That side does not think dilemmas are so easily resolved."

McCloskey's refusal to embrace any overly simplified center puts her in an awkward position, but like Calvin she recognizes both the importance and complexity of individual human freedom. Perhaps she exhibits less fear and trembling about it than most Protestant reformers; nevertheless, she recognizes that human freedom is not merely a matter of a fully formed, autonomous entity making instinctual choices from among given options. It is a complicated, ongoing process of "self-creation," but one that takes place within a context of community, identity, virtues, stories, and histories.[43] For this human being, market capitalism is not primarily a system of competition but rather of cooperation, of many people in the process of *becoming* fully human themselves and encouraging others to do so as well—a system to which all seven of the virtues are essential. ("Real economies depend on real virtues," she argues, and for this reason economic scientists "would do well to test explicitly for virtues other than Prudence. Substantively speaking, they would then merge with social psychologists, as economic historians have merged with historians."[44]) Like Smith, in whose tradition of hopefulness she situates herself, McCloskey sees market exchange as a subset of a sympathetically formed society of virtue. She insists that well-functioning markets depend upon people who are sympathetic to their neighbors (faith, hope, justice, and love), even while they are being creative in their solutions to their own needs and wants (prudence, courage, temperance). As in Calvin's vision of law and freedom, players may begin by *obeying* externally imposed rules, but in the end they are shaped by these such that they abide by them *freely*;

---

42. Ibid., 355.

43. Ibid., 357. On this very important point, McCarraher's critique of McCloskey is unfair; he implies that she is unaware that "*virtue can't be merely personal . . . virtues . . . can only be exercised properly in a community, be it a polis, a commune, or some other arrangement of human affairs that encourages the performance of those practices indispensable to flourishing.*" McCarraher, "Break on Through," 38. It seems clear to me that this awareness is at the very heart of her argument that bourgeois virtues are fostered in and by the community that practices capitalism.

44. Ibid., 128.

the virtues are not natural or inborn, but over time and with practice they can become second nature.

In this scenario—and in stark contrast to capitalism's "dismal" (however well-earned) reputation—a market governed solely by self-interest is a perversion rather than the norm. When most of us think through our own experience in markets, we know that utility is not a necessary or even a common way of narrating human relationships, even in our most "purely" economic dealings. "[L]ook around at your own workplace," she writes. "In the capitalist West now the chances are that it is not a satanic mill in which you labor in noise and dust and isolation for twelve hours a day. . . . [E]mployees go to work expecting to be treated like human beings, expecting to be even a little loved."[45] Capitalism for McCloskey (who as an economist is an economic insider, but she is also a philosopher, historian, and self-proclaimed Christian[46]) is not merely a pragmatic least-of-evils; it is actually good—having virtue built into it as both requirement and consequence. It is a thing of interconnected humanity, a game of intrinsic beauty and excellence, worth playing, at least in large part, for its own sake. When played well (that is, when it is not allowed to deteriorate into rent-seeking and monopoly), capitalism is the system by which humans can best create communities in which they and their neighbors can be truly free.

In short, McCloskey gives us reason to think that market economies might be threatening to the Christian life only when interpreted according to a strictly utilitarian model that considers the utility of an isolated person (or corporation), rather than the human community and creation as a whole. Such interpretation is favored by some on both the right and left, as we have seen, and McCloskey's greatest flaw is to glance over the dark side of capitalism as if its historical evils were petty anomalies.[47] Certainly most middle-class folks are not monsters, but

---

45. Ibid., 137.

46. See McCloskey, "Christian Economics?" 477. Regarding her insider/outsider status, she writes to her economics colleagues, "hear, oh, *Economici*, that someone like me, who was persuaded of precisely the position you espouse, and is not a total dope, has changed her mind. Let that play on yours." McCloskey, *Bourgeois Virtues*, 344.

47. In his review of McCloskey, McCarraher uses her own text against her to argue that capitalism is at fault for every evil in the West, apart from those evils caused by Marxists ("Other than that, Mrs. Lincoln, how was the theater?" McCarraher, "Break on Through," 40). While McCloskey herself may invite such critique by treating capitalism as a monolith, it is unhelpful to force hard and fast choices between two imaginaries—

we must not ignore the fact that middle-class people (not just the rich) have often failed to avail themselves of all of the virtues capitalism has to offer.[48] (Lynchings, for example—of African-Americans, homosexuals, or gypsies—have historically been the purview of the salt of the earth; genocides likewise require broad-based participation from average citizens and not merely the actions of a few elites.) Or in her celebration of how wonderful some workplaces now are for many people, she ignores the reality that—in spite of two centuries of capitalist imperialism—a number of folks in the United States and elsewhere still do work in "satanic mills" (or their modern equivalents) for twelve or more hours a day. And though she is highly sanguine about the power of markets to punish the vicious and reward the virtuous, every day the media slaps us in the face with evidence to the contrary, particularly since the market crash of 2008. History, in other words, offers much ammunition for those who wish to shoot holes in capitalism.

Moreover, McCloskey's use of "the virtues" does not replicate, in any orthodox terms, the thinking about virtues usually celebrated in Christian moral theology. Her argument that earth-bound capitalism can contribute to the formation of all seven classical and Christian virtues goes against Thomas Aquinas's claim that, while the four cardinal virtues (prudence, justice, temperance, and fortitude) can indeed be deduced and implemented through earthly means, the three theological virtues (faith, hope, and charity) can be obtained only by grace.[49] "Man's happiness is twofold," he writes; "One is proportionate to human nature, a happiness, to wit, which man can obtain by means of his natural principles. The other is a happiness surpassing man's nature, and which man can obtain by the power of God alone, by a kind of participation of the Godhead [through Jesus Christ]. . . . such happiness surpasses the capacity of human nature."[50] Thus, though McCloskey certainly does not imply that humans are born with faith, hope, and charity fully formed

socialism and capitalism, which are hybrids in reality—supported by selective evidence chosen from life on earth. My goal is to extract the proverbial baby (sympathetic freedom) from the dirty bathwater (history of exploitation) for the sake of current and future economies.

48. Ibid., 79. She actually claims that the middle-class "have not been monsters," but as she also notes that education is crucial to the cultivation of virtues—markets alone will not achieve it—she has the resources to critique her own excesses.

49. Thomas Aquinas, *Summa*, I–II, Q. 61–62.

50. Ibid., I–II, Q. 62, art. 1.

in their natures—nor does she exclude the possibility that it is God who uses markets to shape these higher virtues in humankind—she does meld Thomas's two kinds of happiness in a way that will make some Christian readers uncomfortable.

Nevertheless, what I take away from McCloskey, and what I think she offers to future conversations about Christian economic ethics, is the idea that Christians need not take utilitarian theories or evidence of human self-centeredness as God's gospel truth about economics. We are free to revise capitalism by re-imagining it; or perhaps we can retire "capitalism" in favor of "markets" (and a science of markets) that behave according to a variety of virtuous norms, not just one, nor even only four. McCloskey (along with Calvin and Smith) would likely agree with Benedict's statement on the importance of *all* the virtues in the economy:

> To desire the *common good* and strive towards it *is a requirement of justice and charity*. To take a stand for the common good is on the one hand to be solicitous for, and on the other hand to avail oneself of, that complex of institutions that give structure to the life of society, juridically, civilly, politically and culturally, making it the *pólis*, or "city." The more we strive to secure a common good corresponding to the real needs of our neighbours, the more effectively we love them.[51]

Homo sympatheticus (Christian or not) does more than make simple choices between A and B, individual pleasure and individual pain. Truly human markets are constituted by humans-in-community, many of whom genuinely do care about their neighbors (starting with the nearest ones, but stretching outward from there) and do, as a rule, seek to behave in ways that benefit people other than themselves alone.

Christians are also free to make distinctions among markets, to discern which ones foster genuine human freedom (or at least do no harm) and which ones hinder it. A market can indeed be built on a mix of pride, gratitude, and neighbor love, such as the philanthropic sector (a very large market in this supposedly selfish country of ours, which cannot be cynically reduced to the hobby of robber barons or lazy beggars).[52] A market

---

51. Benedict XVI, *Caritas in Veritate*, 7.

52. According to the Urban Institute's web site, "the nonprofit sector accounts for 5.2 percent of gross domestic product (GDP) and 8.3 percent of wages and salaries paid in the United States. While these figures shed light on the size and scope of the sector, a complete picture cannot be obtained without considering two critical components of the sector, voluntarism and charitable giving. In 2005, individuals, corporations, and

can be based on a mix of courage, love, and fear, such as the markets for suicide bombers, soldiers, or private elementary schools. A market can be based on perverted appetites and an utter lack of human sympathy, such as prostitution or sales of harmful substances to self-destructively addicted people. A market can reflect a mix of love, hope, and desperation, such as markets in organs or fertility technologies. McCloskey is surely correct that though prudence is undoubtedly a factor in all of these markets, none of them need be boiled down to rational self-interest alone; they certainly should not all be painted with the same brush. Christian ethicists interested in a humane, just, loving, and freedom-fostering global economy do not have to embrace McCloskey's argument uncritically in order to engage her attempt to foreground the virtues that are *already* present (if sometimes nascent) in market systems.

Julie Nelson: Markets as Vital Organs

Another economist who argues persuasively for the inherently humane qualities of markets is Julie Nelson. In her recent book (as brief as McCloskey's is long), *Economics for Humans*, she takes to task the dominant economic metaphor of the market system as an impersonal "machine" that exists only for the efficient production of extrinsic goods: "This machine operates in an automatic fashion, following inexorable and amoral 'laws.' While the machine organizes provisioning for our bodies, it is itself soulless and inhuman. . . . Since machines are incapable of morality, thinking about economies as machines puts commerce firmly outside the ethical realm."[53] She, like McCloskey, notes that this unhealthy way of looking at economies can be found coming from many different sectors—both the pro-market and anti-market clerisy, both economists and critics of economics, as well as among those who would like to see certain "ethical" areas of life kept separate from "economic" motivations and calculations. In questioning this mechanistic model of economies, she is also calling into question any perspective that would draw a clean line between "economic" and other spheres of human life.

---

foundations gave $260 billion in charitable contributions to nonprofits and 29 percent of Americans volunteered through a formal organization." While not all of this can be chalked up to virtue, it would be equally unfair to insist that it is all about self-interest. Urban Institute, "Nonprofit Sector in Brief," 1.

53. Nelson, *Economics for Humans*, 1–2.

Such a view, she argues (in spite of her economics PhD), "is a *belief*, not a fact"; and moreover, it is a belief with concrete harmful effects.[54]

As someone who (again like McCloskey) is "the 'wrong' gender" for economics, Nelson has found herself free to be an "unusual economist," free to depart from ossified disciplinary paradigms.[55] She began with a disagreement about the way economics views people, especially men, as self-interested and rational (while women, if they are on the radar at all, are self-sacrificing and/or emotional). She noticed as well the concomitant systematic marginalization and denigration in economic circles of "characteristics and realms of work traditionally associated with women," which finally led her to cast off the mechanical metaphor she inherited.[56] Metaphors, she argues (surprisingly for a scientist), are no minor part of the sciences.[57] Drawing from linguistics and philosophy, she is cognizant that, "metaphor is not merely a fancy addition to language. Instead it is the fundamental way in which we understand our world and communicate our understanding from one person to another."[58] They shape the understandings, not only of average folks, but even of natural or "hard" scientists—who used to view all of creation as a living being, then viewed it as a machine, and now tend to view it as a "whirlpool of energy" or a system of "musical notes."[59] Nelson, whose criticism is informed by theories of both science and economics, seeks a metaphor that would allow economists to see complexity and specificity (and, we might add, hybridity) instead of being bound by an "iron cage" of over-simplification or orthodoxy.[60]

Nelson thinks it is more accurate, and more fruitful, to view the economy as something organic and alive, which is constituted by interlocking human relationships, and which also serves to cultivate humane goods. In order to help revise capitalist systems according to this vision,

54. Ibid., 4. Emphasis original.

55. Ibid., 41.

56. Ibid., 43. It is noteworthy that Julie Nelson (here and on 49) takes a less sympathetic view of Adam Smith than McCloskey, in that she marks him as the beginning of economics as a separative science, rather than as the end of economics as a part of moral philosophy.

57. Perhaps not surprisingly, McCloskey too has written widely about the "rhetoric of economics."

58. Nelson, *Economics for Humans*, 45.

59. Ibid., 46.

60. Ibid., 51.

she promotes the metaphor of a market as "beating heart"—an entity that is not separate from its inputs and outputs but is integrally connected to them, and requires care in order to maintain its own good health and the health of all those organs upon which it is mutually dependent.[61] A heart is like a machine, in that it has regularities and structures, but it is also personal in that it is "a living, vital organ . . . essential for the life of an individual body."[62] Moreover, a beating heart needs different things at different times—sometimes it needs water, other times oxygen, exercise, rest, medicine, and even surgical intervention. Economies, like bodily organs or living beings, require flexibility and close attention to context in order to maintain their good health. "When money and goods do not circulate," for example, "but rather build up in unhealthy concentrations, an economy can be said to be in danger of congestive 'heart' failure."[63] Nelson's shift allows markets and economies to be measured according to how healthy they are in *human* terms; economists must be attentive to real life, instead of assuming that "the market" is always and everywhere the same, in 1776 as in 2007, in Chile as in post-Cold War Russia.

Somewhat jarringly, she also notes (in virtual concert with McCloskey) that the heart (the market, remember!) is the "center of love," as well as of integrity, conscience, and courage.[64] Such a vision changes many of our pre-conceptions about markets and the interconnections of economic persons who constitute them. Conceptualizing the market as a beating heart trickles down to smaller elements of the economy as well; for example, it changes the idea that a corporation is by definition a profit-seeking machine, "free" from government intervention but en-slaved by the imperative to maximize shareholders' earnings. This, she says, is not an idea that comes from economists' observations of *actual* corporations, but is rather part of "the mythical ideal of a smoothly functioning, perfectly competitive economy. It is popular exactly to the extent that the mechanistic, clockwork image of the economy is taken for granted."[65] (Readers will not be surprised to learn that she names the Chicago school as being particularly blameworthy in this regard.[66])

61. Ibid., 57.
62. Ibid., 58.
63. Ibid.
64. Ibid., 59.
65. Ibid., 93.
66. Ibid., 100.

Nelson's new metaphor opens up possibilities for corporations to be re-imagined as vital organs, connected to other vital organs, with potentially worthy purposes, free to pursue genuine goods and not just profits, which thrive in the long term only by living harmoniously with their social, economic, and environmental surroundings.

In another example of how metaphors can change economics, she investigates the care industry, including child and elder care. The machine metaphor, she says, has long been connected with a Victorian "love-or-money" paradigm; that is, people can be motivated by one or the other, but never both at once.[67] Love is generally associated with women and the home and money with men and the public sphere, a division which has traditionally pushed women into low-paying "caring" professions, and men into high-paying "selfish" positions. She argues that seeing the market as a beating heart undermines the idea that nannies, teachers, and other care workers earn low pay as a natural consequence of the nature of their love-based work, which must remain untainted by greed-based motivations. They are expected to choose these jobs out of virtue, without any allowance for the importance of money. "Economic behavior," she argues however, "is not just about getting money," and a desire to earn money is not always selfish.[68] Care workers need to be well paid not because they are greedy, but because truly caring workers, so beneficial to society, deserve to benefit themselves by doing what they are good at. People need money to support themselves and their families; people also understand money as a measure of social appreciation and low pay as a lack of appreciation. (Who among us, having suffered during an economic downturn, cannot relate?) Any argument that people in the caring professions do not deserve good pay merely perpetuates outdated metaphors for economic life, which tend to favor those who continue to model themselves on old models.

Most basically, Nelson's decision to view the economy as a beating heart questions the dominant anthropology that underlies traditional economics. If the economy is a machine, it stands to reason that it is made up of mini-machines (or, worse, bits of machine) who are programmed like robots to chase after extrinsic goods. But if the economy is viewed as a living organ, it allows for a re-imagination of economic

67. Ibid., 65–66. Such an overly simple paradigm is exploited not only by capitalists, but also by critics.

68. Ibid., 73.

players as interdependent social creatures who operate on a multitude of complex motivations, and whose economic interactions—far more than just means to other ends—are part and parcel of the whole picture of human life. According to this narrative, each human being has a basic need to do good work; that work arises and evolves through a lifetime of interactions with her neighbors, and she needs to have that work acknowledged and appreciated by her neighbors along the way (to say nothing of the need to live free from anxiety about how to pay for basics like food, shelter, and health care). Nelson's is an economic vision that leaves plenty of room for rational sympathy and sympathetic rationality, in which individual self-interest is understood as a necessary human instinct that can be good when it does not exist in isolation from other human traits and motivations, from self-limitation and neighbor love. "If people perceive themselves to be in a society of decent folks who are generally willing to be honest and carry their share of the load," she thinks, "they will also be generally honest and willing to carry their share of the load."[69]

Such a vision of human economic activity—in which interconnected, living things participate freely in an organic system that benefits them all—seems highly preferable to the mechanistic vision, particularly because such visions have the tendency to become "self-fulfilling prophecies."[70] A selfishness-based economic model (or policy or science) is likely to breed selfishness among economic players by making it the *only* rule by which people can benefit materially. (Some studies have concluded, for example, that economics majors are more selfish or less altruistic than their classmates in other majors; and the longer they have been indoctrinated into the self-interest model, the more self-interested they are. Others argue that economists were more self-interested to begin with, which is why they went into economics in the first place.)[71]

69. Ibid., 74. This perception, of course, is not always viable in so-called capitalist markets, particularly when corporations and the state collude to disenfranchise the people. The solution is not to disavow markets or governments *per se*, but rather to revise, reform, and transform them into more virtuous systems constituted by self-limiting, sympathetic entities.

70. Ibid., 75.

71. Frank, "The Theory that Self-Interest is the Sole Motivator is Self-Fulfilling." Obviously there are others who dispute both of these interpretations; economics training doesn't make people self-interested, any more than ethics classes make them ethical. See Lanteri, "(Why) do selfish people self-select in economics?"

Economic rhetoric that emphasizes freedom together with sympathy, interdependence, and mutual benefit is more likely to foster economic players who do not see greed as the given basis for markets. The world is not what it was two hundred or even twenty years ago, and in twenty years it can be different again if we acknowledge that new economic times call for new economic metaphors.

Muhammad Yunus: Social Business and the End of Poverty

To understand the contribution my third interlocutor, Muhammad Yunus, can bring to this discussion, it is worth contextualizing the conversation once again in terms of Christian ethics. I submit that a shift toward more fruitful, even useful, Christian economic thought will occur through finding alternative conversation partners. While it is easy for folks in theology-and-economics circles to float in the realm of theory, appeals (even this one) to Calvin and Smith, Aquinas and Milbank tend to perpetuate a deadlocked debate that never gets to the level of particular, "on the ground" economic solutions.[72] Dwelling in theory alone perpetuates the idea that we can speak fruitfully about economics by addressing concepts alone (freedom, rationality, self-interest), without addressing specific issues of race, gender, sexuality, ethnicity, and nationality, or historical and political particulars such as wages, environmental costs, tariffs, or corporate governance. Moreover, the appeal of theoretical analysis tends to be limited to a scholarly audience, middle-class or even upwardly-mobile. It is not a waste of time to speak to American middle-class Christians; we do, after all, have more buying power than a majority of people in the world, thus making our cultural patterns of thought and behavior extremely relevant to the lives of people in places whose names we do not even know. But I am also mindful that there are voices shockingly unrepresented in much Christian ethical discourse, including my own. As Miguel de la Torre writes, "if the ultimate goal of ethics is to create a Christian response that brings change to existing oppressive structures, then no one group contains the critical mass

---

72. One example of concrete Christian economic thought is Albino Barrera, who (being trained in both economics and theology) applies sophisticated theological principles directly to concrete economic issues, such as American agricultural protectionism. See especially Barrera, *Economic Compulsion and Christian Ethics*, and also Barrera, *God and the Evil of Scarcity*.

required to bring about the desired just society."[73] Middle-class American Christian theologians, whether on the ideological right or left, cannot alone come up with structures that will do justice to everyone. Freedom for us must be freedom for all, and in order for that to happen, our freedom must obey norms of sympathy that are forged out of a more broadly-based, one might say ecumenical, conversation.[74]

In addition, Christian ethics needs to bring more non-Christian voices into our conversations about economics. "A liberative Christian social ethic," writes Traci West, "is desperately needed by most U.S. Christians in order for them to equitably participate in building a shared communal (public) ethic with non-Christians and to find a way to force a rupture between prevailing cultural arrangements of power that reproduce oppressive conditions, like poverty, and communal tolerance for permanently maintaining such conditions."[75] History (of the United States and elsewhere) teaches that Christians—in spite of our ancient and venerable sacraments, traditions, and scriptures—have not always been on the side of true justice. Christians with power and wealth tend to favor ethics that will maintain their power and wealth, and we have been remarkably adept at interpreting the gospel in ways that justify our own status. In our attempts to live ethically in our local and global economies, with particular attention to extending justice toward those on the margins of our societies, we need to look away from the "usual suspects" for wisdom.

To that end, I would like to highlight the stunning example of one final economist, who is also an active business person and Nobel Peace Prize winner. Muhammad Yunus, the "banker to the poor," is a Bangladeshi economist with a degree from Vanderbilt, who became passionate about eliminating poverty in the 1970s following a famine in which hundreds of thousands of Bangladeshis died.[76] In response to the hopelessness he saw all around him, Yunus (a believer in the positive

73. De La Torre, *Doing Christian Ethics from the Margins*, 19.

74. "All of this implies placing issues of distribution, equality, ethics, the environment, the nature of individual happiness, collective well-being, and progressive social change at the center of our agenda. The urgent task for economists and social scientists is to translate these broad objectives into theoretical models and specific policies and actions." Benería, "Economic Rationality and Globalization," 128.

75. West, *Disruptive Christian Ethics*, xviii.

76. Yunus, *World Without Poverty*, 44–46. Biographical information from the Yunus Centre website.

potential of free enterprise) began offering tiny loans to poor people—who otherwise would have had no access to capital—in order for them to start their own businesses and sustain the lives of their families. Pope Benedict expresses well the truth that Yunus discovered:

> Hunger is not so much dependent on lack of material things as on *shortage of social resources, the most important of which are institutional*. What is missing, in other words, is a network of economic institutions capable of guaranteeing regular access to sufficient food and water for nutritional needs, and also capable of addressing the primary needs and necessities ensuing from genuine food crises, whether due to natural causes or political irresponsibility, nationally and internationally. The problem of food insecurity needs to be addressed within a long-term perspective, eliminating the *structural* causes that give rise to it and promoting the agricultural development of poorer countries.[77]

Such can also be said of poverty; people (unless they take voluntary vows)[78] need capital in order not to be victims, to become interdependent rather than dependent and insecure. What developed over the next four decades was Grameen Bank, a social entity that has made over eight billion dollars in loans—mostly to women—since its inception, and ninety-five percent of which is now owned by the poor themselves.[79] Grameen Bank has also been instrumental in the development of dozens of other "social businesses" (a term I will explain below) that are currently improving the lives of people who live on one dollar or less per day—not through charity, but through entrepreneurial and unabashedly interdependent models of production and distribution.

Yunus's ability to make such tremendous inroads toward the elimination of world poverty came not only from sheer brain power and energy, but also largely from his ability to think (like McCloskey and Nelson) beyond the doctrine of self-interest. He was not himself poor, but he freely used what Smith might have called his "sympathetic imagination" to put himself in the places of those Bangladeshis who were dying, and

---

77. Benedict XVI, *Caritas in Veritate*, 27. Emphasis added.

78. While vows of poverty are not the focus of this book, it is important to note that religious communities that cultivate and support mendicants have their own problematic externalities. Thai Buddhist monks, for example, are heavily supported by the prostitution of women and girls, often their own family members. See Attie & Goldwater Productions, *What Harm Is It To Be a Woman?*

79. Yunus Centre website.

watching their children die, at the same time that others around the world were enjoying unprecedented surpluses of wealth and material goods. At the same time, as an economist he also believed in the engine of self-interest, a natural and good instinct in human beings, and he felt certain that the poor would not remain poor if only there were more opportunities for agency and self-betterment of which they could avail themselves. In other words, he argues, poor people are human just like everyone else, and they are no less entrepreneurial than their wealthier counterparts.[80] "If the poor are to get the chance to lift themselves out of poverty, it's up to us to remove the institutional barriers we've created around them. We must remove the absurd rules and laws we have made that treat the poor as nonentities."[81] He saw that current governmental and financial structures were simply not working for the poor, nor was international aid, so he used his creativity and economic know-how to invent something new.

And yet his invention was not entirely new, but is perhaps better described as a hybrid between existing models of charity and profit-making, socialism and capitalism—something that works with individual self-interest, yet within a larger communal context of sympathy and neighbor love. One example of how Grameen Bank has successfully linked self-interest and the common good together is the deliberate way in which it has sought to build community, along with a shared social agenda, among those who borrow money. Somewhat akin to what Christians might call "accountability groups," Grameen Bank ties borrowers together in groups of five as friends. "No one who borrows from Grameen Bank stands alone," he writes; "When one of the five friends wants to take out a loan, she needs approval from the remaining four."[82] These friends (again, mostly women, none of whom may be closely related) provide a close social network that helps each member think through her business plans. These small groups, in turn, meet monthly with ten to twelve other small groups in their village; and there are now approximately 130,000 village centers in Bangladesh. Moreover, in addition to just talking about money, these Grameen Bank members commit to "Sixteen Decisions" for lifting themselves and their families out

---

80. "Once the poor are allowed to unleash their energy and creativity, poverty will disappear very quickly." Yunus, *World Without Poverty*, 54.

81. Ibid., 49.

82. Ibid., 57.

of poverty, such as keeping tidy houses, growing their own vegetables, limiting their fertility, refusing to receive or offer dowries for their sons and daughters, resisting injustice, and participating in social activities.[83] Here is living proof that business and banking need not exist in a theoretical vacuum, nor must the virtues of home life and work life, or spiritual and material life, interfere with each other. (Would that all Christian churches included such theological-economic partnerships!)

If ending poverty for real human beings through their own entrepreneurial efforts is possible, why is it so uncommon? Yunus raises the question, posed so often by Christian ethicists and others who care about the poor and marginalized in the global economy: "What is wrong? In a world where the ideology of free enterprise has no real challenger, why have free markets failed so many people? . . . *The reason is simple. Unfettered markets in their current form are not meant to solve social problems and instead may actually exacerbate poverty, disease, pollution, corruption, crime, and inequality.*"[84] The reason for this, he argues, is that the unfettered markets loved by technicians are still based on the selfish, mechanistic models that Julie Nelson also deplores, or on the monistic, prudence-only model that McCloskey warns against. Capitalism as we know it is "a half-developed structure," he writes, based on an incomplete anthropology:

> [It] takes a narrow view of human nature, assuming that people are one-dimensional beings concerned only with the pursuit of maximum profit. The concept of the free market, as generally understood, is based on this one-dimensional human being. Mainstream free-market theory postulates that you are contributing to the society and the world in the best possible manner if you just concentrate on getting the most for yourself.[85]

In addition, he notes, economic theory still sees *homo economicus* as a male head of household, and has yet to fully account for concepts like "woman" or "child."[86] Yunus, like Nelson and McCloskey, is an economist who proves that not all economists (even those who favor markets) have drunk the proverbial Kool-Aid of self-interest and rational maximization.

83. Ibid., 59.
84. Ibid., 5. Emphasis added.
85. Ibid., 18.
86. Ibid., 54.

It is important to note that Yunus is not against the concept of running a business for profit. He continues to believe there is room for such entities in a market economy, because the world is made up of all kinds of people. But he also believes there is room for philanthropy, for government, and for "another kind of business—one that recognizes the multi-dimensional nature of human beings."[87] What he calls a "social business" is one that has as its objective, not merely the earning of profits, but of achieving certain social goals. Its goal may be to eliminate poverty through micro-loans to women and through ownership by the poor, such as Grameen Bank's. Or it may be to provide low-cost goods to people in need, such as yogurt for under-nourished children.[88] Social businesses are not charities, in that they do not live or die with the unpredictable flows of altruistic good will (spurred on, for example, by sensational hurricanes, earthquakes, or other media frenzies). Instead, they get investors up front and eventually pay those investors back; once the business becomes self-sustaining, any remaining profits are reinvested in the business itself to help support and expand its mission. Social businesses can compete with one another for customers, just as traditional businesses do; but this competition helps to foster the social missions for which they are founded, rather than profiting a few executives or shareholders with inordinate shares.

Yunus understands that, from the point of view of economic fundamentalists, such a business model "has no place in their existing theology of capitalism," but he believes that capitalism is capable of development and change and can accommodate alternatives to standard options; more importantly, he believes capitalism *must* change and make room for more kinds of business, because too many people are suffering under current practices.[89] Anyone who insists that traditional models are the only solution to poverty, and that the poor must simply wait for goods to trickle down to them, is simply not thinking freely or imaginatively enough. "When we look back at human history," he says, "it is clear that we get what we want—or what we fail to refuse. If we are *not* achieving something, it is because we have not put our minds to it. We are accepting psychological limitations that prevent us from doing what we claim

87. Ibid., 21.
88. Ibid., xv.
89. Ibid., 21.

we want."[90] Like Nelson's self-fulfilling prophecy, Yunus warns that if we take poverty for granted as a natural and inevitable part of life and of global market economics ("the poor will always be with you" being a familiar Christian temptation[91]), we will surely get it.

Yunus is not the only person clamoring for alternative business models in the twenty-first century economy. Journalist William Greider, for example, sees external shareholders as the main reason that so many businesses benefit a few wealthy people rather than their customers, employees, or more broadly, the societies in which they operate. (Pope Benedict agrees: "Without doubt, one of the greatest risks for businesses is that they are almost exclusively answerable to their investors, thereby limiting their social value."[92]) Greider urges more businesses to adopt a partnership or cooperative model, fragments of which already exist all over the capitalist marketplace, such as law firms, universities, or medical practices, in which workers own the fruits of their labor instead of having the profits they produce traded away to others.[93] He cites the Baltimore temp agency, Solidarity, as a prime example of the positive benefits (efficiency, pride, and profits) that come with a greater sense of ownership among employees.[94] Because human beings know when they are being exploited, when someone else is reaping the benefits of what they have sown, they are less productive and less satisfied than when their work reflects directly upon them. Greider, like Yunus, is not against capitalism altogether, but he sees it as high time for critique; "it's now okay to think and talk critically about captialism's own shortcomings. At this point in history, it may even be the patriotic thing to do."[95] Capitalism with a soul, from Greider's point of view, radically questions the tyranny of "more":

> Character and values can guide people toward wiser choices, but neither individuals nor the society can easily escape the present system because the principles of "more" are everywhere. "More"

90. Ibid., 232.

91. John 12:18, Mark 14:7.

92. Benedict XVI, *Caritas in Veritate*, 40.

93. Greider, *Soul of Capitalism*, 75. Interestingly, he sees college professors, particularly those with tenure, as a good example of self-governance or "owning one's own work."

94. Ibid., 69–74.

95. Ibid., 26.

is embedded in the behavior of every business enterprise and the principles of marketing, in the self-interested decisions of every investor and consumer. . . . Faith in "more" as a blunt instrument for achieving the greater good for the greatest number is what legitimizes the confinements and social distress, from families to communities. It does require real character to step back and question what others regard as natural law.[96]

Giving greater attention to who human beings truly are demands looking beyond the simple, material measures of "more," and can result in both individual businesses and broader economic systems that can foster genuine human sympathy, imagination, virtue, and freedom.

An important point that Greider, Yunus, Nelson, and McCloskey have all raised is that good people and good businesses *do already exist*. This is not merely a banal point that not all people living in capitalist systems have to be evil, but that people within globalized capitalism subvert its supposedly orthodox paradigms all the time. There are, of course, still too many examples of system-wide bad behavior (that is to say, not merely obvious "corruption" as in the case of Enron, but less obvious bad behavior that is part of a company's *modus operandi*, such as deliberately externalizing environmental and human costs[97]), but there are also many others who are exercising their creativity to put their human sympathies, and of course their desires to better their own and their families' lives, into action. Yunus sums up the potential that comes from acknowledging the *genuine human beings* who exist in the marketplace:

[T]he success of Grameen Bank has grown from our willingness to recognize and honor motivations and incentives that transcend the purely economic. Human beings are not just workers, consumers, or even entrepreneurs. They are also parents, children, friends, neighbors, and citizens. They worry about their families, care about the communities where they live, and think a lot about their reputations and relationships with others. For traditional bankers, these human concerns don't exist. But they are at the heart of what makes up Grameen Bank.[98]

96. Ibid., 15.

97. See, for examples, Hill, "Toxic Ten"; Bernhardt et al., "Broken Laws, Unprotected Workers"; and Urbina and Cooper, "Deaths at West Virginia Mines Raise Issues About Safety."

98. Yunus, *World Without Poverty*, 60.

Such thoughtful attention to real human beings in economic systems does not have to wait for Christian ethicists to think it up. Real change in the global economy might include, but does not require, a revolution to overthrow the entire market system. While both "top-down" policy solutions and "bottom-up" improvements and innovations in individual and cultural virtues are indeed needed for real transformation, insistence that everything must change at once (or that corporations *as such* are incorrigible, or that governments must change completely before individuals, churches, or businesses can change even a little) usually succeeds in nothing but breeding hopelessness and resignation in the face of the overwhelming problems humankind faces today. This brief look at the work of Deirdre McCloskey, Julie Nelson, and especially Muhammad Yunus has been designed to persuade Christian ethicists and other people interested in a just, humane economy that such a thing is possible, and that we can participate in it right now—beginning with new sight—regardless of the economic situation in which we find ourselves.[99] *The not yet is already here.* It is happening every day for those with eyes to see and ears to hear, and like a mustard seed it contains great potential.

PROTESTANT ETHICS, SPIRITS OF CAPITALISM, AND OTHER HYBRIDS

I began this book with John Calvin because I believe he is problematically linked—by people on the right *and* left of economic debate—with the kind of free-market capitalism that has defined two centuries of life in the United States, and which seems to have exploded in our communal face in 2008. Calvin did indeed celebrate individual (and congregational) freedom, including in the sphere of life that is typically thought of as "economic," but his understanding of freedom bears little to no resemblance to the rhetoric we so often hear from the libertarian wing of public debate. His vision of freedom was not simply to be free from taxation (though *some* taxes may indeed impinge upon freedom of conscience), free from governmental mandates (though some of these may do the same), or free from all moral constraints not explicitly spelled

99. Dorothy Sayers argues that people must turn from "the nation-wide and world-wide acceptance of a false scale of values about work, money, and leisure" in order to "think first and foremost about the true needs of man [sic] and the right handling of material things." In other words, new economic thinking must be linked to new economic virtues. Sayers, "Vocation in Work," 412.

out in the laws that govern us.[100] On the contrary, economic freedom for Calvin meant freedom to pursue the tasks to which God calls them;[101] freedom from excessive self-love and other sinful tendencies; freedom from guilt over poverty or riches; freedom to see oneself as part of a community, in which one exists to benefit one's neighbors near and far; freedom, even, to steward and enjoy the wide variety of wondrous material goods that God has provided in creation.

In the end, my use of Calvin as the primary theological voice in this book has located me closer than I had originally intended to the economic mainstream. I have come away from it seeing individual freedom as an important aid to both individuals and communities in their material provisioning (and, more basically, I see material well-being as a prerequisite to virtue or ultimate beatitude, for all but the holiest among us). But where I depart from modern economics is in reiterating Calvin's insistence that self-interest is not the primary norm for freedom, and is not a quality that most of us need to cultivate.[102] Although it comes most naturally to us, it should not be given free rein (and it bears reemphasizing that even economists do not believe that *unbridled* self-interest will create healthy markets); it is normative only in so far as it can be approved of by one's neighbors. While some economists argue that self-interest is "beneficial" for providing the most utility for the greatest number of people, I agree with Calvin that it is never beneficial for individuals to think only of themselves. True benefit comes from knowing who one truly is, which is wrapped up with who God is, who

100. Benedict warns, "*The principle of subsidiarity* [the favorite concept of those on the economic "right"] *must remain closely linked to the principle of solidarity* [the favorite of those on the "left"] *and vice versa*, since the former without the latter gives way to social privatism, while the latter without the former gives way to paternalist social assistance that is demeaning to those in need." Benedict XVI, *Caritas in Veritate*, 58. Emphasis original.

101. Benedict shares an interest in freedom in vocation as well: "A vocation is a call that requires a free and responsible answer. *Integral human development presupposes the responsible freedom* of the individual and of peoples: no structure can guarantee this development over and above human responsibility . . . Only when it is free can development be integrally human; only in a climate of responsible freedom can it grow in a satisfactory manner." Ibid., 17. Emphasis original.

102. It is worth mentioning that feminist theology has sometimes said just the opposite—that women do indeed need to cultivate self-interest, because they are too often socialized to accept self-sacrifice (for Christians, the cross) as their lot in life. In fact it is powerful men (like Calvin) who need to learn self-sacrifice, while women need to un-learn it. A fuller exposition is beyond the scope of the current work.

one's neighbors are, and loving those neighbors as oneself. In relationships with others, Calvin argues that anything less than the "violent" love that people lavish upon themselves is insufficient (II.viii.54). Such an idea seems virtually impossible to most of us, bogged down as we are in self-love, but this is the difficult command that the gospel bestows upon us. Small groups (whether instituted by churches or Grameen Bank) can be baby steps toward creating cultures that realize our interdependence with one another.

Even more shocking about this difficult command is its insistence that neighbor love is not limited only to family and friends, but to one's enemies and, as Calvin puts it (although he does acknowledge that closer bonds serve to create greater responsibilities), "even [to] the most remote person" (II.viii.55). Everyone, in Christian terms—including the lazy free-rider, the undocumented worker, and the sworn enemy—"should be contemplated in God, not in themselves" (II.viii.55-56). Such a radically un-American mode of being, though expressed in sixteenth-century terms, is a goal to which Christians in all times and all places may aspire. "The lifestyle of inner asceticism," writes Esser of Calvin's approach, "of 'having as if one had not' . . .has lost nothing of its model character for modern technological nations outdoing one another in selfish bickering, doctrines of growth, and the throwaway mentality."[103]

This, I am arguing, is the real Protestant ethic: to love God by freely loving one's neighbor, not merely in prayer, not merely through charitable giving, but through *every moment of our embodied lives*—worshipping and resting, laboring and consuming, producing and distributing, saving and spending, voting and volunteering, with family and with strangers, with co-workers and with beggars. This is a tall order, to be sure, but not an impossible dream. Christ has already done it, and made it possible for us as well by setting us free from our self-imposed hopelessness. Calvin believes that a proper appeal to eternal happiness, which has always been humans' true end (II.x.2), will have concrete effects on earthly life. The first step toward claiming this God-given freedom is to expand our economic consciousness through education (or, as Adam Smith might say, to allow our understandings to be shaped by sympathy so that our emotions may follow). The Dalai Lama puts it this way:

> just telling someone, "Oh, it's very important to be compassionate; you must have more love" isn't enough. A simple prescrip-

103. Esser, "Contemporary Relevance of Calvin's Social Ethics," 377.

tion like that alone isn't going to work. But one effective means of teaching someone how to be more warm and compassionate is to begin by *using reasoning* to educate the individual about the value and practical benefits of compassion, and also *having them reflect* on how they feel when someone is kind to them and so on. In a sense *this primes them* so there will be more of an effect as they proceed in their efforts to be more compassionate.[104]

Changing how we think, in other words, is a first step to changing how we behave, and together these create and foster virtues in us over time. We begin to see, for example, that the luxury items we buy are as much a reflection of our neighbor love as our tithes. Freedom in *adiaphora* does not exempt us from being mindful of the hungry and destitute as we whip out our credit cards. Nor are we exempt from being mindful about the garbage our church or company or school puts into community landfills every day; or about the fact that, as we take out a loan for a home, our neighbors are unable to scrounge up even a one-month security deposit for a new rental; or about the maternity leave we enjoy, while the women who clean our offices get no paid time off at all. Such mindfulness may lead eventually to differences in the policies we promote, in our purchasing behaviors, or in the choices we make about how and where we work. Not all at once, perhaps, but slowly and surely. In all of these areas of our lives, freely-given neighbor love remains our overriding vocation. This is not a simple undertaking, of course, but religious traditions have rarely offered an easy path.

We learn to love our neighbors because, as the Christian narrative tells us, all persons were created in God's image and reaffirmed as good by the incarnate Christ. They are equal to us in dignity and freedom. As we become more mindful of our neighbors in the global economy, things like national identity become less important than the flourishing of *all* one's siblings. The exhortation to neighbor love calls us to consider how our actions affect not only our families or the folks across the street, but also the folks on the other side of the tracks, the other side of the Rio Grande, and the other side of the ocean. The idea that, for example, Americans should avoid buying goods made by Chinese citizens is as untenable as the idea that Chinese citizens exist to provide cheap labor for American corporations. Seeing faraway people as neighbors is a way to begin seeing our own happiness as interdependent with theirs, helps

---

104. Dalai Lama, *Art of Happiness*, 88. Emphasis added.

us to re-think what we "need," or what counts as "external" to the multiple market exchanges that involve us personally and directly every day. When there is no "Chinese" or "American" (except perhaps provisionally for the sake of order—a qualification worthy of its own book), Christians have to allow one another greater freedom, according to the standards by which we want freedom for ourselves. Freedom-oriented Calvinist economics cannot plead "human nature" when markets put (for example) undocumented workers in jobs where they risk life and limb, with no legal recourse for employers' abuses.[105] It demands instead that employers treat workers (no less than shareholders) the way they would wish to be treated. In an ideal world this occurs freely, but it may also be enforced through government where virtue has not yet prevailed.

The monolithic "spirit of capitalism" needs to give way to multiple spirits of capitalism or market economics. Those of us dissatisfied with the one-size-fits-all approach of Chicago-style neoliberalism have the ability to revise market systems by embodying other norms, both locally and globally. Like feminist economists, we can de-center the conversation and "conceive of the economy as culturally instituted habits for material provisioning and accumulation" in order that economics can "remain open to evaluation and change."[106] A de-centered marketplace based on a more robust understanding of freedom will rest, of course, on reclaiming an economic anthropology that goes deeper than prudence, extends beyond the individual, and allows for growth and change. In Benedict's words, *"God is the guarantor of man's [sic] true development, inasmuch as, having created him in his image, he also establishes the transcendent dignity of men and women and feeds their innate yearning to 'be more.' Man is not a lost atom in a random universe: he is God's creature, whom God chose to endow with an immortal soul and whom*

---

105. The free-market argument goes this way: They are "free" so they wouldn't work there if they didn't think the benefit of their earnings was greater than the potential risks to an arm or a hand. This argument ignores the fact that such workers have limited options and are thus coerced by circumstances: i.e., to work or to starve (rather than to work there or work somewhere better, or to work there or go to Harvard). True freedom is not determined by its options, but by how well it allows a person to flourish in a fully human way. See "The Most Dangerous Job" in Schlosser, *Fast Food Nation*, 169–90. On similar questions of economic free agency, see also the Oscar-nominated documentary *Which Way Home* (2009), which follows Latin American children trying to migrate to the U.S.

106. Barker and Kuiper, "Sketching the Contours," 15.

he has always loved."[107] While Adam Smith (and even Frank Knight), Deirdre McCloskey, Julie Nelson, and Muhammad Yunus do not speak in such explicitly theological terms of human nature, all of them share the conviction that human nature cannot be summed up in the basic urge to survive that they share with animals, insects, and viruses. At the same time, these thinkers also recognize the natural human impulse to better oneself, often through the betterment of the material conditions of one's life. The instinct of self-interest and the desire to benefit one's neighbors exist in tension, to be sure, but they do both exist, and together they make up the impulse to "be more" that can be the fruitful building block of economic justice and freedom.

THE PARADOXES OF ECONOMIC FREEDOM AND FREEDOM-ORIENTED ECONOMICS

Human freedom is paradoxical—it is freedom to obey, and freedom to serve. As we learned through Calvin's narrative, freedom is a gift from God, received by humans once at creation and received *again*, eternally, through the redeeming work of Christ. Human beings are "imperfect," as Friedman says, but they are not doomed to remain so. On the contrary, perfection is possible—indeed, is already a reality—through participation in Christ. The redeemed human is in a constant process of being transformed into the image of God that is her true nature. Freedom for this person is not a self-interested free-for-all, a license to sin or exploit, but is instead a newfound ability to love in the way we were created to love. It is a rediscovered capacity to serve our neighbors with gladness, because we see in them the same image of God that we see in ourselves. Their joy is our joy; their suffering is our suffering.

Adam Smith's narrative echoed this understanding of humankind. Without one another, humans cannot know happiness. Freedom for Smith's human is freedom to participate in a community of shared approval and disapproval, in which self-love is limited by the rule of mutual benefit. What was lost in the Chicago school of economics was this understanding of paradoxical freedom shaped by sympathy. In these economists' hurry to rid themselves of responsibility for moral truths in order to be more "scientific," their freedom became one-dimensional (self-interested choice) and was eventually abandoned altogether in

---

107. Benedict XVI, *Caritas in Veritate*, 29. Emphasis original.

favor of sheer power. Such a result was inevitable once economics lost its moorings in moral philosophy (and even moral philosophers have been known to make mistakes.) In Benedict's words, "Without truth, without trust and love for what is true, there is no social conscience and responsibility, and social action ends up serving private interests and the logic of power, resulting in social fragmentation, especially in a global-ized society at difficult times like the present."[108]

Because there are multiple ways to think about freedom, there are also multiple ways to think about economic freedom, and even free-market capitalism. Whether we re-imagine economies as schoolhouses of virtue, healthy beating hearts, or markets of social business and part-nerships, we see the importance of maintaining a varied and paradoxical approach to the traditional economic themes of freedom and rational self-interest. The economics of Smith, McCloskey, and Nelson make it clear that freedom—even for *homo economicus*—is paradoxical; it is obedient freedom, or free obedience to learned, shared norms. Moreover rational self-interest—again, even for *homo economicus*—is paradoxical as well; it is sympathetic self-interest, or rational sympathy.

In my experience of economic debates—including academic, popu-lar, and personal—there is too often a stark dichotomy set up between freedom and un-freedom, choice and no choice. There is little sense that our understandings of freedom or choice may need analysis or tweak-ing; little sense that there may be a messy gray area between divergent perspectives in which some agreement may be found. Either you are a capitalist or a socialist, we are told; either you are for liberation or you are for exploitation; either you want government-funded welfare or you hate the poor; either you want people to take responsibility for themselves or you are an enabler of laziness and vice. There is no monopoly on ethical dualism in this arena. People on both the left and the right, Christians and others, wish to present economic questions as if they have one flaw-less model that will work for everyone, everywhere, at all times. People of wisdom and good will are seemingly not allowed to disagree over eco-nomics, any more than they are allowed to disagree over abortion.

I would like to encourage a certain degree of equanimity and "epistemic modesty"[109] among Christians (both economists and ethi-cists) when it comes to deeply complicated issues of money, markets,

---

108. Benedict XVI, *Caritas in Veritate*, 5.

109. Brennan and Waterman, "Christian Theology and Economics," 87.

and globalization. Economists and ethicists need to listen to one another, without fearful alarmism or dismissive caricature. No single person, regardless of political status or academic degrees, can know everything about the global economy, so before we issue irrevocable statements and harsh judgments we should step back and hear—really hear—what others are saying. There need to be lively and serious debates about specific policy questions on topics like the regulation of banks, the rationing of health care, the outsourcing of jobs, the effects of corporate pollution, or the value of public education. There needs also to be careful interrogation of the underlying ideas about humans and freedom that underlie our own and others' economic positions. Fruitful conversation will arise only out of the mutual respect that comes from acknowledging our shared humanity, with all its flaws and glories.

There is no such thing as a truly free market; all freedom is obedience to something. A Protestant ethic (or ethics) is neither essentially capitalist nor anti-capitalist; it is pro-freedom, in so far as freedom enables individuals and communities to love their neighbors as themselves. Likewise, the revised spirit (or spirits) of capitalism—of the sort we've seen in Smith and these later economic thinkers—is also pro-freedom, but only in so far as that freedom is shaped by rational sympathy and sympathetic self-interest. To form a more humane and virtuous system of markets, it is necessary to shape the players within it. And to form more humane players, one must shape the rules of the system according to mutual sympathy. Christian ethicists must be willing to allow for a certain amount of liberty, even if it presents risk; every parent knows this to be the case. At the same time, we must also be willing to give up certain freedoms and allow Christian theologies and just laws to critique, restrain, and teach us how to be more loving toward our neighbors. While there is no specific economic law for all people at all times, there will always need to be humane laws that cultivate in us an appreciation for that "great precept of nature": "to love ourselves only as we love our neighbour, or what comes to the same thing, as our neighbour is capable of loving us."[110]

110. Smith, TMS, 25.

CONCLUSION

Economic Freedom as Sympathetically Self-Interested Service

A s I wrote in the introduction to this book, this look at the economic teachings of a few intellectual heavy-hitters from history has been motivated by a desire, not to reconstruct the past, but to help Christians in the twenty-first century think more clearly about the beliefs about human beings that underlie their own economic ideas. In chapters 1 and 2, I began with Calvin as a way of demonstrating that emphasizing "freedom" in economic matters is indeed part of a longstanding Christian tradition, but that for Christians this emphasis is only one piece of a larger, ongoing narrative about the creation, fall, and redemption of human beings. The Christian narrative presents all human beings as siblings under one divine parent, and therefore equals, all equally (un) deserving of the material gifts that God offers in the created world.[1] As siblings, God calls humans to love one another (and one another's children) in equal measure as they love themselves, and to do to others as they would have done to them. In Christ, God sets humans free from sin and its consequences; they are no longer bound by the law, but the twin virtues of *neighbor love*

1. Pope Benedict writes of Christianity, "The Christian revelation of the unity of the human race presupposes a *metaphysical interpretation of the 'humanum' in which relationality is an essential element*." This, he argues, makes it a more helpful religious underpinning for the global economy than some other religious traditions that draw faith-based distinctions among people or peoples. Benedict XVI, *Caritas in Veritatae*, 55.

and *self-limitation* remain as ever-present boundaries of the God-given freedom they enjoy.

We heard echoes of this Christian vision of interconnectedness in Adam Smith's economic theory in chapter 3, though he (for the most part) tried to leave God out of it. He believed that humans in community naturally and spontaneously *cooperate*, dividing labor among themselves, thereby not only making their own lives easier, but also making themselves dependent upon one another (or perhaps more precisely, allowing them to *acknowledge* the interdependence that is always already there).[2] His fundamental belief in the human capacity for sympathy caused Smith to think that such things as government-issued tariffs, price controls, subsidies, and the like, were unnecessary to prevent exploitation or dog-eat-dog chaos; in the right ethical context, he thought, economic freedom would be to the greatest advantage of everyone involved, directly and indirectly. The Smithian vision of sympathetic capitalism stands in stark contrast to the descriptions many of us have come to take for granted about greed or exploitation; but as Weber put it:

> The impulse to acquisition, pursuit of gain, of money, of the greatest possible amount of money, has in itself nothing to do with capitalism. This impulse exists and has existed among waiters, physicians, coachmen, artists, prostitutes, dishonest officials, soldiers, nobles, crusaders, gamblers, and beggars. One may say that it has been common to all sorts and conditions of men at all times and in all countries of the earth, wherever the objective possibility of it is or has been given. It should be taught in the kindergarten of cultural history that this naïve idea of capitalism must be given up once and for all. Unlimited greed for gain is not in the least identical with capitalism, and still less its spirit.[3]

The spirit of capitalism (or of the economic science that has arisen to foster it) is not necessarily resignation to the idea that profit-based economics is the best we can do; ideally, it can become a particular method for allowing *peaceful* interpersonal relations with regard to material goods. A "capitalistic economic action," Weber goes on, is "one which rests on the expectation of profit by the utilization of opportunities for exchange, that is on (formally) peaceful chances of profit."[4] It is an al-

---

2. Smith, WN, 12–13.

3. Weber, *Protestant Ethic*, 17.

4. Ibid.

ternative to both theft and outright gift-giving, a decent, orderly, and non-coercive form of reciprocity or mutually beneficial exchange between two parties, which involves a shared calculation of goods in terms of their money value. It is not primarily dependent upon self-interest but on *rationality*, which in Lüthy's words, "overcome[s] all the forms of resistance offered by the pre-rational elements of human nature: magic and tradition, instinct and spontaneity."[5] Greed is not the active ingredient here, but rather deliberate, rational *restraint* of the kind of greed that Smith believed ran rampant in pre-Reformation Europe.

Smith was able to think beyond naked self-interest because, unlike some of his intellectual descendants, he did not seek to take *homo economicus* out of its historical, social, and environmental context. Smith's economic actor was always and everywhere an individual-in-society, part of a human community shaped by interlocking, reason-based (rather than emotional) sympathies that were no less active in the marketplace than in the home. Ideally speaking, Smith's capitalist economic interactions are contextualized by what might be called "a world of shared meanings and mutual knowledgeability."[6] The popular understanding of *homo economicus* as a human being motivated solely by his own material gain is not the necessary—nor even the rightful—basis of capitalist markets or economic science. The *ideal* economic agent must act in her own self-interest, *but not too much*; and although this vision sometimes goes underground in favor of a more streamlined rational actor, the market paradox is still present as an assumption. The protagonist of economics is not a monster after all; she rather approaches her neighbors with a sympathetic understanding of their material needs.

But from our perspective in the early twenty-first century, we may see Weber and Smith as willfully blind, or at best naïve. We look daily upon exploitation of sweatshop workers, factory-farmed animals, or irreplaceable rain forests, not to mention the basest appetites of consumers, and we may conclude that capitalism is merely the rationalist curtain behind which greed and the desire to dominate are at the controls. This is due in large part to the way economics developed in the twentieth century. Although economic thinkers drawing from Calvin or Smith could affirm that "a strong market economy depends on a strong social capital, such as values, relationships and institutions, including civil

5. Lüthy, *From Calvin to Rousseau*, 18–19.

6. Gunnemann, "Capitalism and Commutative Justice," 104.

society and religion,"[7] we have seen with the Chicago school in chapters 4 and 5, from Knight to Becker, a willful denial of the necessity of viewing economic behavior in such an explicitly "ethical" context. Instead they have systematically and self-consciously sought to eliminate the "non-neutral" from their economics, choosing (for the most part) not to discuss the meanings of human nature or freedom, even though these are integral factors in their analyses. Neoliberalism's lowest common denominator, the power to choose, is assumed to be free of the ethical baggage that prevented economics from becoming truly scientific in earlier generations. This does not *necessarily* belie an evil plot to take over the world for the rich and the powerful (though certain historical data may point us in that direction). Where some economists become opponents of a Christian vision of human flourishing is in their unwillingness to engage non-economists in serious dialogue (rather than a lecture) about the best way to manage the real-world economy—an unwillingness due largely to a lack of consciousness about their own historical and social locations, ethical assumptions, and political agendas.[8]

Christians in the twenty-first century must continue to affirm, in spite of scientific pronouncements to the contrary, that an economy based on such Christian virtues as love, justice, and prudence is not a mere pipe-dream. In the words of Pope Benedict XVI, who echoes Calvin in his recent encyclical on economic development, *Caritas in Veritate*, the spark of charity remains an essential part of human nature, despite the fall. "All people feel the interior impulse to love authentically," writes Benedict; "love and truth never abandon them completely, because these are the vocation planted by God in the heart and mind of every human person," both in terms of personal, intimate relationships and also "macro-relationships," such as the global economy.[9] Human beings are not greedy to the core; they have sympathetic imaginations that, if properly formed (and reformed and transformed), enable them to behave with compassion.

7. Atherton, *Transfiguring Capitalism*, 281.

8. A recent online article underlines the point that the willful *exclusion of particularity and context* is the main problem with contemporary neoliberal economic thought. "[T]he best rap on libertarians isn't that they're racist, or selfish. . . . It's that they're thoroughly out of touch with reality. It's a worldview that prospers only so long as nobody tries it," writes Gabriel Winant, "Lesson of Rand Paul."

9. Benedict XVI, *Caritas in Veritate*, 1–2.

Chapter 6 grew out of my conviction that Christian theologians are not the only ones who believe in the possibility of more humane economies, that are based on more hope-filled readings of humankind. Christians seeking a more humane global economy can look to economics as well. If one believes that human beings are oriented toward that which they believe to be good, even if they are sometimes mistaken, then it is also safe to believe in the good intentions of most economists. No less fervently than theologians, many economists believe they can change the world (or at least the portion they can see) for the better, specifically by setting people free. Thus far they can and should be seen as allies to Christians and others who seek true human freedom, especially for the weakest members in society. If we turn our gaze away from fundamentalists who insist upon the most simplistic and reductionist views of humankind and freedom, we will find that there are many others who share Christians' belief that, "Striving to meet the deepest moral needs of the person also has important and beneficial repercussions at the level of economics. *The economy needs ethics in order to function correctly*—not any ethics whatsoever, but an ethics which is people-centred."[10]

Eugene McCarraher has characterized the first decade of the twenty-first century as one of "erosion or atrophy of the conviction that something beyond capitalism is possible."[11] This may be a fair description of the way most people who spend their time talking and writing about the economy present themselves. Some lovers of classical, liberal capitalism seem to think that its models are perfection itself; the protection of private property can fix anything and everything, while hindrances to individual liberty can be blamed for every manifestation of evil. On the other side of the table, haters of capitalism decry property as theft, corporations as liars and killers, and scarcity and freedom as carefully manufactured illusions. These folks usually dream of revolution, or at least of changing governmental structures (sometimes explicitly toward socialism) to act as correctives to corporate culture; but others—unable to see how any *pure* economic system could ever *really* arise in the world as we know it—simply give up or settle for whatever system they've got as the least among evils. Purists on both sides often make creative thinking and cooperation so difficult that the paralysis of hopelessness sets in.

---

10. Ibid., 45. Emphasis original.

11. McCarraher, "Meet the New Boss," part 1 of 3.

("Ah, to be among the true believers, breathing only the clean air of sanc-
timony. Nothing is ever done, no lives improved, no laws passed.")[12]

An insistence on purity, however, discounts the countless people
in the world (not all of them pundits, preachers, or scholars) who are
already imagining and realizing a world beyond capitalism, every day
of their lives. This not only on some heavenly, metaphysical level—they
are making it real moment by moment, right where they are. I count
the borrower-owner-friends of Grameen Bank among them, but I am
convinced those subverting "bad capitalism" may also be found among
artists, farmers, middle managers, nonprofit workers, teachers, lawyers,
homemakers, filmmakers, hat makers, manufacturers, union workers,
engineers, CEOs, and even legislators. They may live under a nominally
capitalist regime (albeit one with large public subsidies for all kinds of
corporations), they may even lapse into destructive or exploitive patterns some of the time, but little by little they are working with their
neighbors to foster justice in their homes and workplaces, tempering
their own self-interest with sympathy for their neighbors' interests.
Every day people commit "works of mercy."[13] Every day they are forging
micro-cultures of mutuality, equality, and service. Every day people are
"living—often with great difficulty—in harmony with reality."[14]

The role of the Christian churches with regard to the economic
order is much the same as it was in first-century Judea. Christians—
through our varied practices of preaching and sacraments, scripture
reading, meditation, and works of love and justice—are un-learning the
half-truths we have imbibed from the world about ourselves and our
neighbors, un-learning the vices that have become our habits. Having
been steeped in the Word, we gradually cease to view ourselves as competitors for scarce resources and begin to view our neighbors as potential partners, helpers, and friends in our efforts to claim our common
birthright as children of God. Having understood the role of human sin
in the world's oppressive and exploitive systems of power, we proclaim
the very real possibility of their transformation. Having been refreshed
with the body of Christ, we get up off the communion rail (or out of the
pew, as the case may be) and bear witness to the "kin-dom" of God with

12. Timothy Egan, "The Purists," par. 8.

13. Bell, "What is Wrong with Capitalism?" par. 17.

14. McCarraher, "Meet the New Boss," part 2 of 3.

virtuous acts, small and large, from the congregation to the household to the global economy.

This is our hope, anyway. There is no "sociologically real" perfect church in the world as we know it,[15] any more than there can be a perfect market or a perfect form of governance. Different churches may come closer to perfection than others; while some strive to let Christian theology define them, plenty of Christians also have our false beliefs and vices reaffirmed for us in church (if indeed we are even awake). But while we await our ultimate perfection there are preliminary measures we can take, baby steps toward economic love and justice. We may write to our elected representatives or to corporations about justice for migrant workers; listen to and cry out on behalf of the victims of human trafficking; treat our co-workers or employees with the respect due people bearing the image of God; meditate on our own work as an opportunity to be co-creators with God; alert the public to issues of systemic wrongdoing; forego products from manufacturers that unjustly externalize their costs onto the earth and its inhabitants; insist that the custodian of our church is paid a living wage; or simply plant a tree.[16] With God's help, such humble acts may lead us into bolder ones. Like "the church," "the market" is people; neither is a static entity, neither exists alone, and both are capable of change. Our economic task as Christians—regardless of the system we find ourselves living under—is to create and support *just* exchange, while crying out against and divesting from *unjust* exchange.

This takes effort and patience. If we hope to effect positive change, we must first educate and re-train ourselves. In order to bring our behaviors in line with justice, we need to know about economic theory and policy, understanding their assumptions and tendencies in order to inform them with Christian faith(s) and practice(s). If its reigning model tends to encourage domination of some by others, a theory most likely has a fatal flaw.[17] But we must also learn about history, paying attention

---

15. Ibid., part 3 of 3. McCarraher's comment is that the school of Radical Orthodoxy offers a church that is "sociologically unreal; it certainly doesn't correspond to any church I know."

16. A recent book designed for congregational discussion groups offers some concrete ways for people to start acting upon their desires to live justly and love mercy, both individually, in communities, and in the public sphere. "Kin-dom" is a term, coined by A. M. Isasi-Díaz, which the editors use in place of the more hierarchical "kingdom." Brubaker et al., *Justice in a Global Economy*, 3.

17. Barker and Feiner note that feminist economics aims deliberately not to justify

to the past as well as what is going on around us, educating ourselves in empirical evidence about economic practices and their effects. (Is outsourcing necessary, and if so, does it have to be traumatic and brutal or can it be done in a way that is beneficial to workers and communities both at home and abroad? Does raising the minimum wage actually hurt the poor, as economists like to argue, or does history prove the model incorrect?)[18] Economic theory and history are intertwined; Christian critics who ignore one or both will find themselves stuck in the Sunday school room wishing for justice, while corporate interests maintain apparent free rein in the marketplace.

Capitalism is not necessarily the Christian's enemy, not only because there is more than one theory of markets (some more humane than others) but also because none of these theories is embodied in any pure way. Certain laws and policies approximate more or less closely the ideal of perfect competition and free markets favored by growth-driven economists, or the model of justice favored by Christian tradition, but this does not change the fact that capitalism is, like any other tradition, open to critique, reinterpretation, and reimagination. As William Baumol et al., write:

> [C]apitalism is not a monolithic form of economic organization but . . . it takes many forms, which differ substantially in terms of their implications for economic growth and elimination of poverty. . . . The implicit assumption underlying the idea of a homogeneous capitalism, the notion that all capitalist economies are fundamentally the same, reflects something of the mentality common during the cold war when two superpowers, representing two great ideologies, were struggling for the hearts and minds of the peoples of the world.[19]

the value system behind the status quo of domination and subordination, frequently upheld by traditional economics, thus opening a door for theologians who wish to engage in economic conversations. Barker and Feiner, *Liberating Economics*, 18.

18. Economist Jay Corrigan concedes that historical evidence has not shown most employers to be particularly sensitive to wage hikes, but goes on to argue that wage hikes (paid for only by consumers and employers, received by all wage workers including wealthy teenage part-timers) are, both practically and theoretically, a less effective way of improving the lot of the poor than the earned income tax credit (paid for by all taxpayers, received by those working adults in need of wage supplements). Corrigan, "Burning Question," 41.

19. Baumol et al., *Good Capitalism, Bad Capitalism,* vii.

We owe it, especially to those suffering in our globalized economy, to focus on and enhance the *best* that markets have to offer, while also decrying and refusing to participate in the worst.

From a Christian point of view, the best is that which lets us love our neighbors as ourselves. As a Christian, I share others' doubts as to whether the kin-dom of God can accommodate the traditional baggage of "capitalism" and its presumed antagonism. Indeed, as Kathryn Tanner notes, the selfish, dog-eat-dog image of capitalism seems to be Christianity's exact opposite.[20] But I do not believe God's redeemed creation precludes the presence of markets based on the division of labor, forward-thinking behavior, mutual and sympathetic self-interest, or human cooperation. Community-building markets already exist in our homes, towns, churches, workplaces, and nations, where people with various gifts and capacities find ways to make exchanges (sometimes using money, sometimes not) that create mutual benefit. With increasing education and consciousness, markets could begin to alleviate or eliminate the negative externalities to which they give rise. With added imagination they might even *benefit* the earth and its inhabitants. Because markets are made up of humans-in-community rather than machines, the goodness of a market system depends *entirely* on the theories and practices of its participants. In so far as a human individual can be freed from sin and transformed into the image of God, so can markets, which are made up of human beings and in which humans are joined into multiple, overlapping bodies—churches as well as families, corporations, and nation-states. The economic freedom that Christians enjoy is this: constantly to fashion and participate in exchanges built on love of God and neighbor, which benefit *all* human beings rather than exploiting or ignoring the weakest ones, and which do justice to the *whole* human being rather than squeezing us into the constricting suit of *homo economicus*.

20. Tanner argues that capitalism today provides many of the world's presumptions and practices; thus Christian theology in the twenty-first century will contest capitalism, offering noncompetitive forms of exchange in the place of competition, grace in the place of just deserts, and plenitude in the place of scarcity. Tanner, *Economy of Grace*, 1. If market systems are re-imagined, however, as systems of cooperation rather than competition, then theologians might have to look elsewhere to figure out what Christianity is *not*.

BIBLIOGRAPHY

Althaus-Reid, Marcella. *The Queer God: Sexuality and Liberation Theology*. New York: Routledge, 2003.

Ashraf, Nava, et al. "Adam Smith, Behavioral Economist." *Journal of Economic Perspectives* 19:3 (2005) 131–45.

Asso, Pier Francesco, and Luca Fiorito. "Waging War against Mechanical Man: Frank H. Knight's Critique of Behavioristic Psychology." *Economics Working Paper* 340 (2001) 1–33.

Atherton, John. *Transfiguring Capitalism: An Enquiry into Religion and Social Change*. London: SCM, 2008.

Attie & Goldwater Productions, directors. *What Harm Is It To Be A Woman?* (DVD) Milwaukee: The Religious Consultation on Population, Reproductive Health and Ethics, 2007.

Backhouse, Roger E. *The Ordinary Business of Life*. Princeton, NJ: Princeton University Press, 2002.

Balke, W. "Calvin's Concept of Freedom." In *Studies in Reformed Theology: Freedom*, edited by A. van Egmond and D. van Keulen, 25–54. Baarn, NL: G. F. Callenbach, 1996.

Barker, Drucilla K., and Susan F. Feiner. *Liberating Economics: Feminist Perspectives on Families, Work, and Globalization*. Ann Arbor: University of Michigan Press, 2004.

Barker, Drucilla K., and Edith Kuiper. *Toward a Feminist Philosophy of Economics*. New York: Routledge, 2003.

Barrera, Albino. *Economic Compulsion and Christian Ethics*. New York: Cambridge University Press, 2005.

———. *God and the Evil of Scarcity: Moral Foundations of Economic Agency*. Notre Dame, IN: University of Notre Dame Press, 2005.

Barth, Karl. *Church Dogmatics* III.4: *The Doctrine of Creation*. Edinburgh: T. & T. Clark, 1961.

Basu, Kaushik. "The Traveler's Dilemma." *Scientific American* (June 2007) 90–95.

Battles, Ford Lewis. "Against Luxury and License in Geneva." *Interpretation* 19 (1965) 182–202.

Baumol, William J., et al. *Good Capitalism, Bad Capitalism, and the Economics of Growth and Prosperity*. New Haven, CT: Yale University Press, 2007.

Blank, Rebecca M., and William McGurn. *Is the Market Moral?: A Dialogue on Religion, Economics, and Justice*. Washington, DC: Brookings Institution, 2004.

Becker, Gary S. *Accounting for Tastes*. Cambridge: Harvard University Press, 1996.

———. *Autobiography*. From *Les Prix Nobel. The Nobel Prizes 1992*, edited by Tore Frängsmyr. Stockholm: Nobel Foundation, 1993. Online: http://nobelprize.org/economics/laureates/1992/becker-autobio.html.

———. *The Economic Approach to Human Behavior*. Chicago: University of Chicago Press, 1976.

———. "The Economic Way of Looking at Behavior : The Nobel Lecture." *Essays in Public Policy* 69. Stanford: Hoover Institution on War, Revolution, and Peace, 1996.

———. *The Essence of Becker*. Stanford: Hoover Institution, 1995.

Becker, Gary S., and Guity Nashat Becker. *The Economics of Life: From Baseball to Affirmative Action to Immigration, How Real-World Issues Affect Our Everyday Life*. New York: McGraw-Hill, 1997.

Becker, Gary S., and Kevin M. Murphy. *Social Economics: Market Behavior in a Social Environment*. Cambridge: Belknap, 2000.

Benería, Lourdes. "Economic Rationality and Globalization: A Feminist Perspective." In *Feminist Economics Today: Beyond Economic Man*, edited by Marianne A. Ferber and Julie A. Nelson, 115–33. Chicago: University of Chicago Press, 2003.

Bentham, Jeremy. *An Introduction to the Principles of Morals and Legislation*. 1823 ed. Oxford: Clarendon, 1879.

Bell, Daniel. "What is Wrong with Capitalism? The Problem with the Problem with Capitalism." *The Other Journal* 5 (2005). No pages. Online: http://www.theotherjournal.com/article.php?id=55.

Benedict XVI. Encyclical Letter: *Caritas in Veritate*. June 29, 2009. Online: http://www.vatican.va/holy_father/benedict_xvi/encyclicals/documents/hf_ben-xvi_enc_20090629_caritas-in-veritate_en.html.

Bernhardt, Annette, et al. *Broken Laws, Unprotected Workers: Violations of Employment and Labor Laws in America's Cities*. Los Angeles: Center for Urban Economic Development, National Employment Law Project, and UCLA Institute for Research on Labor and Employment, 2009.

Berry, Stephen R. "Jean Calvin and the Development of Printing in Geneva, 1535–1575." PhD diss., Duke University, 2002.

Bieler, André. *La Pensée Economique Et Sociale De Calvin*. Vol. XIII, *Publications De La Faculté Des Sciences Economiques Et Sociales De L'Université De Genève*. Geneva: Librairie de L'Université Georg, 1961.

Blanchard, Kathryn D. "The Gift of Contraception: Calvin, Barth, and a Lost Protestant Conversation." *Journal of the Society of Christian Ethics* 27 (2007) 225–50.

———. "Not Our Own: Christians and the Paradox of Economic Freedom." PhD diss., Duke University, 2006.

———. "Review of *God and the Evil of Scarcity*." *Journal of the Society of Christian Ethics* 27 (2007) 303–5.

———. "Should Christians Give Markets Another Chance?" *The Other Journal* 9 (2007). No pages. Online: http://www.theotherjournal.com/article.php?id=244.

Blaug, Mark. "Kuhn versus Lakatos, or Paradigms versus Research Programmes in the History of Economics." In *Economic History and the History of Economics*, 233–64. New York: Columbia University Press, 1986.

Boettke, Peter. "Deirdre McCloskey's *The Bourgeois Virtues: Ethics for an Age of Commerce.*" *Economic Affairs* 27:1 (2007) 83–85.

Brennan, Anthony, and A. M. C. Waterman. "Christian Theology and Economics: Convergence and Clashes." In *Christian Theology and Market Economics*, edited by Ian R. Harper and Samuel Gregg. Northampton, MA: Edward Elgar, 2008, 77–93.

Brubaker, Pamela K., et al. *Justice in a Global Economy: Strategies for Home, Community, and World.* Louisville: Westminster John Knox, 2005.

Bush, George W. "Proclamation 7714: Marriage Protection Week, 2003." *Weekly Compilation of Presidential Documents* 39:41 (October 13, 2003) 1327–28.

Butler, Judith. *Undoing Gender.* New York: Routledge, 2004.

Calvin, John. *Commentaries on the First Book of Moses Called Genesis.* Translated by John King. Grand Rapids: Eerdmans, 1948.

———. *Commentary on the Book of Psalms* V. Translated by James Anderson. Grand Rapids: Eerdmans, 1949.

———. "De Usuris (Letter to Sachinus, 1545)." In *John Calvin: The Man and His Ethics,* by Georgia Harkness, 206. New York: Holt, 1931.

———. "De Usuris Responsum (1579)." In *Economic Tracts IV: Usury Laws,* 32–36. New York: Society for Political Education, 1881.

———. *Institutes of the Christian Religion.* 2 vols. Translated by Ford Lewis Battles. Edited by John T. McNeill. Philadelphia: Westminster, 1960.

Cammisa, Rebecca, director. *Which Way Home.* HBO Documentaries/Mr. Mudd, 2010.

Charusheela, S., and Eiman Zein-Elabdin. "Feminism, Postcolonial Thought, and Economics." In *Feminist Economics Today: Beyond Economic Man*, edited by Marianne A. Ferber and Julie A. Nelson, 175–92. Chicago: University of Chicago Press, 2003.

Clement of Alexandria, "Who Is the Rich Man That Shall Be Saved?" No pages. Online: http://www.ccel.org/ccel/schaff/anf02.vi.v.html.

Corrigan, Jay. "Burning Question: Will It Help or Hurt to Increase the Minimum Wage?" *Kenyon College Alumni Bulletin* 29:4 (2007). No pages. Online: http://bulletin.kenyon.edu/x2397.xml.

Coyle, Diane. *The Soulful Science: What Economists Really Do and Why It Matters.* Princeton, NJ: Princeton University Press, 2007.

Dalai Lama. *The Art of Happiness: A Handbook for Living.* New York: Riverhead, 1998.

De La Torre, Miguel A. *Doing Christian Ethics from the Margins.* Maryknoll, NY: Orbis, 2004.

Douglass, Jane Dempsey. "Christian Freedom in Calvin's Theology: The Foundation and Significance of Christian Freedom." *Princeton Seminary Bulletin* 4:2 (1983) 69–83.

Egan, Timothy. "The Purists." *New York Times* (March 17, 2010). Online: http://opinionator.blogs.nytimes.com/2010/03/17/the-purists/?ref=opinion&8ty&emc=ty.

Emmett, Ross B. "De Gustibus *Est* Disputandum: Frank H. Knight's Reply to George Stigler and Gary Becker's 'De Gustibus Non Est Disputandum.'" Michigan State University Working Papers Series (2005).

Epstein, Abby, and Ricki Lake. *The Business of Being Born.* DVD. New Line Home Video, 2007.

Esser, Hans-Helmut. "The Contemporary Relevance of Calvin's Social Ethics." Translated by Lisa Dahill. In *Toward the Future of Reformed Theology*, edited by D. Willis et al., 366–85. Grand Rapids: Eerdmans, 1999.

Evensky, Jerry. *Adam Smith's Moral Philosophy.* New York: Cambridge University Press, 2005.

Flanagan, Caitlin. "Why Marriage Matters." *Time Magazine* (July 13, 2009) 45–49.

Forell, George. *Faith Active in Love*. New York: American, 1954.

Frank, Robert. "The Theory That Self-Interest Is the Sole Motivator Is Self-Fulfilling." *New York Times* (February 17, 2005). Online: http://www.robert-h-frank.com/PDFs/ES.2.17.05.pdf.

Frank, Thomas. *What's the Matter with Kansas?: How Conservatives Won the Heart of America*. New York: Henry Holt, 2004.

Franzese, Alexis T. "An Exploration of Authenticity." PhD diss., Duke University, 2006.

Freeman· Katherine B. "The Images of Human Nature in Economics." *Rivista Internazionale di Scienze Economiche e Commerciali* 40 (1993) 625–39.

Friedman, Milton. *Capitalism and Freedom*. Chicago: University of Chicago Press, 1982. First published 1962.

Friedman, Milton, and Rose Friedman. *Free to Choose: A Personal Statement*. New York: Harcourt Brace, 1980.

Fullbrook, Edward. "A Brief History of the Post-Autistic Economics Movement." No pages. Online: http://www.paecon.net/PAEhistory02.htm.

Gilbreath, W. J. S. "Martin Luther and John Calvin on Property." *Evangelical Review of Theology* 11 (1987) 218–28.

Greer, Germaine. *Sex and Destiny*. London: Secker & Warburg, 1984.

Greve, Lionel. *Freedom and Discipline in the Theology of John Calvin, William Perkins, and John Wesley: An Examination of the Origin and Nature of Pietism*. Ann Arbor, MI: University Microfilms, 1977.

Gunnemann, Jon P. "Capitalism and Commutative Justice." *Annual of the Society of Christian Ethics* 5 (1985) 101–22.

———. "Christian Ethics in a Capitalist Society." *Word & World* 5 (1985) 49–59.

Gustafson, James M. *Ethics from a Theocentric Perspective*. Vol. 1, *Theology and Ethics*. Chicago: University of Chicago Press, 1981.

Gutierrez, Gustavo. *A Theology of Liberation*. Maryknoll, NY: Orbis, 1988.

Haas, Guenther H. *The Concept of Equity in Calvin's Ethics*. Waterloo, Ontario: Wilfrid Laurier University Press, 1997.

Haddon, Mark. *The Curious Incident of the Dog in the Night-time*. New York: Vintage, 2004.

Hallett, Adrian. "The Theology of John Calvin: The Christian's Conflict with the Flesh." *Churchman* 105 (1991) 197–245.

———. "The Theology of John Calvin: The Christian's Conflict with the World" *Churchman*: 105 (1991) 102–38.

Harkness, Georgia. *John Calvin: The Man and His Ethics*. New York: Henry Holt, 1931.

Harper, Ian R., and Samuel Gregg, editors. *Christian Theology and Market Economics*. Northampton, MA: Edward Elgar, 2008.

Henderson, James W., and John Pisciotta, editors. *Faithful Economics: The Moral Worlds of a Neutral Science*. Waco, TX: Baylor University Press, 2006.

Heslam, Peter S. "The Role of Business in the Fight against Poverty." In *Christian Theology and Market Economics*, edited by Ian R. Harper and Samuel Gregg, 164–80. Northampton, MA: Edward Elgar, 2008.

Hesselink, John. "John Calvin on the Law and Christian Freedom." *Ex Auditu* 11 (1995) 77–89.

Heyne, Paul T. *The World of Economics*. Christian Encounters. St. Louis: Concordia, 1965.

Hill, Lisa. "The Hidden Theology of Adam Smith." In *Economics and Religion*, edited by Paul Oslington, 292–320. Northampton, MA: Edward Elgar, 2003.

Hurt, Harry III. "The Toxic Ten." *Conde Nast Porfolio* (March 2008). No pages. Online: http://www.portfolio.com/news-markets/national-news/portfolio/2008/02/19/10-Worst-Corporate-Polluters.

Iannaccone, Laurence. "Why Strict Churches Are Strong." *American Journal of Sociology* 99 (1994) 1180–1211.

Keesecker, William F. "The Law in John Calvin's Ethics." In *Calvin and Christian Ethics*, edited by Peter de Klerk, 14–49. Grand Rapids: Calvin Studies Society, 1987.

Klein, Naomi. *The Shock Doctrine: The Rise of Disaster Capitalism.* New York: Picador, 2007.

Knight, Frank H. "Ethics and the Economic Interpretation." In *The Ethics of Competition and Other Essays*, edited by Milton Friedman et al., 19–40. New York: Harper, 1935.

———. "Ethics and Economic Reform." In *Freedom and Reform: Essays in Economics and Social Philosophy*, edited by Hubert Bonner et al., 45–128. New York: Harper, 1947.

———. "The Ethics of Competition." In *The Ethics of Competition and Other Essays*, edited by Milton Friedman et al., 41–75. New York: Harper, 1935.

———. "Freedom as Fact and Criterion." In *Freedom and Reform: Essays in Economics and Social Philosophy*, edited by Hubert Bonner et al., 1–18. New York: Harper, 1947.

———. "The Limitations of Scientific Method on Economics." In *The Ethics of Competition and Other Essays*, edited by Milton Friedman et al., 105–47. New York: Harper, 1935.

———. "Marginal Utility Economics." In *The Ethics of Competition and Other Essays*, edited by Milton Friedman et al., 148–160. New York: Harper, 1935.

Langholm, Odd. "Martin Luther's Doctrine on Trade and Price in its Literary Context." *History of Political Economy* 41 (2009) 89–107.

Lanteri, Alessandro. "(Why) Do Selfish People Self-select in Economics?" *Erasmus Journal for Philosophy and Economics* 1 (2008) 1–23. Online: http://ejpe.org/pdf/1-1-art-1.pdf.

Lawson, Tony. *Reorienting Economics.* Economics as Social Theory. New York: Routledge, 2003.

Leith, John H. *Introduction to the Reformed Tradition.* Atlanta: John Knox, 1981

Lewis, James W. "Christianity and Capitalism: A Critique of Selected Roman Catholic and Protestant Accounts of Economic Ethics." PhD diss., Duke University, 1994.

Long, D. Stephen. *Divine Economy: Theology and the Market.* Radical Orthodoxy. New York: Routledge, 2000.

Long, D. Stephen, and Nancy Ruth Fox with Tripp York. *Calculated Futures: Theology, Ethics, and Economics.* Waco, TX: Baylor University Press, 2007.

Luther, Martin. "Disputation on the Power and Efficacy of Indulgences (1517)." In *Works of Martin Luther*, 6 vols., vol. 2. Philadelphia: Muhlenberg, 1915.

———. "An Open Letter to the Christian Nobility of the German Nation Concerning the Reform of the Christian Estate (1520)." In *Works of Martin Luther*, 6 vols., vol. 2. Philadelphia: Muhlenberg, 1915.

Lüthy, Herbert. *From Calvin to Rousseau; tradition and modernity in socio-political thought from the Reformation to the French Revolution.* New York: Basic, 1970.

Lux, Kenneth. *Adam Smith's Mistake: How a Moral Philosopher Invented Economics and Ended Morality.* Boston: Shambhala, 1990.

Mandeville, Bernard. *Fable of the Bees: or, Private Vices, Publick Benefits.* Oxford: Clarendon, 1714.

———. *The Grumbling Hive: Or, Knaves Turn'd Honest (1704).* Edited by Jack Lynch. No pages. Online: http://andromeda.rutgers.edu/~jlynch/Texts/hive.html.

Mann, Michael. *1491: New Revelations of the Americas Before Columbus*. New York: Knopf, 2005.

Martin, Dale B. *Sex and the Single Savior: Gender and Sexuality in Biblical Interpretation*. Louisville: Westminster John Knox, 2006.

McCarraher, Eugene. "Break on Through to the Other Side: Review of *The Bourgeois Virtues: Ethics for an Age of Commerce*." *Books & Culture* 13.6 (2007) 37–41.

———. "Meet the New Boss, Same as the Old Boss: An Interview with Eugene McCarraher." *The Other Journal* 17 (2010). Online: http://www.theotherjournal.com/article .php?id=924.

McCloskey, Deirdre N. "Avarice, Prudence, and the Bourgeois Virtues." In *Having: Property and Possession in Religious and Social Life*, edited by William Schweiker and Charles T. Mathewes, 312–36. Grand Rapids: Eerdmans, 2004.

———. *The Bourgeois Virtues: Ethics for an Age of Commerce*. Chicago: University of Chicago Press, 2006.

———. "Other Things Equal: Christian Economics?" *Eastern Economics Journal* 25 (1999) 477–80.

McGrath, Alister E. *A Life of John Calvin*. Cambridge, MA: Blackwell, 1990.

McKee, Elsie Anne. *John Calvin*. The Classics of Western Spirituality. New York: Paulist, 2001.

McNeil, Donald G., Jr. "When Human Rights Extend to Nonhumans." *New York Times* (July 13, 2008) 3.

Meeks, M. Douglas. *God the Economist: The Doctrine of God and Political Economy*. Minneapolis: Fortress, 1989.

Menzies, Gordon. "Economics as Identity." In *Christian Theology and Market Economics*, edited by Ian R. Harper and Samuel Gregg, 94–109. Northampton, MA: Edward Elgar, 2008.

Milbank, John. *Theology and Social Theory: Beyond Secular Reason*. Malden, MA: Blackwell, 1990.

Moore, Michael, director. *Capitalism: A Love Story*. DVD. Starz/Anchor Bay, 2010.

Neill, Thomas P. *Makers of the Modern Mind*. Milwaukee: Bruce, 1949.

Nelson, Julie A. *Economics for Humans*. Chicago: University of Chicago Press, 2006.

Nelson, Robert H. *Economics as Religion: From Samuelson to Chicago and Beyond*. University Park: Pennsylvania State University Press, 2001.

———. "Scholasticism vs. Pietism: The Battle for the Soul of Economics." *EconJournal Watch* 1 (2004) 473–97.

———. "What Is Economic Theology?" No pages. Online: http://www.metanexus.net/ magazine/tabid/68/id/8525/Default.aspx.

Novak, Michael. "The Economic System: The Evangelical Basis of a Social Market Economy." *The Review of Politics* 43 (1981) 355–80.

Pelikan, Jaroslav, and Helmut T. Lehmann, editors. *Luther's Works*. 55 vols. Philadelphia and St. Louis: Fortress and Concordia, 1955–1986.

PERC (Property & Environment Research Center) Web site. Online: http://www.perc.org/.

Peters, Rebecca Todd. *In Search of the Good Life: The Ethics of Globalization*. New York: Continuum, 2004.

Polanyi, Karl. *The Great Transformation: The Political and Economic Origins of Our Times*. New York: Farrar, Straus & Giroux, 1975.

Rector, Robert E., and Melissa G. Pardue. *Understanding the President's Healthy Marriage Initiative*. Washington, DC: Heritage Foundation, 2003. Online: http://www.heritage .org/Research/Reports/2004/03/Understanding-the-Presidents-Healthy-Marriage-Initiative.

Reder, Melvin W. "Chicago Economics: Permanence and Change." *Journal of Economic Literature* 20 (1982) 1–38.

Riedemann, Peter. *Account of Our Religion, Doctrine and Faith.* Rifton, NY: Plough, 1970.

Rosario, Ruben. "Calvin or Calvinism: Reclaiming Reformed Theology for the Latin American Context." *Apuntes* 23:4 (2003) 124–55.

Rutherford, Malcolm. *Chicago Economics and Institutionalism (Draft #4).* Online: http://web.uvic.ca/~rutherfo/Chicago4.pdf.

Sauer, James B. *Faithful Ethics According to John Calvin: The Teachability of the Heart.* Toronto Studies in Theology 74. Lewiston, NY: Edwin Mellen, 1997.

Sayers, Dorothy. "Vocation in Work." In *Callings: Twenty Centuries of Christian Wisdom on Vocation,* edited by William C. Placher, 405–12. Grand Rapids: Eerdmans, 2005.

Schlosser, Eric. *Fast Food Nation.* New York: Houghton Mifflin, 2001.

Schwarz, Barry, Hazel Rose Markus, and Alana Conner Snibbe. "Is Freedom Just Another Word for Many Things to Buy?" *New York Times Magazine* (February 26, 2006) 14–15.

Shermer, Michael. "The Prospects for Homo Economicus." *Scientific American* (July 2007) 40–42.

Shils, Edward. *Remembering the University of Chicago: Teachers, Scientists, and Scholars.* Chicago: University of Chicago Press, 1991.

Shulman, Steven. "Metaphors of Discrimination: A Comparison of Gunnar Myrdal and Gary Becker." *Review of Social Economy* 50 (1992) 432–52.

Siegel, Hannah. "Christians Rip Glenn Beck Over 'Social Justice' Slam." *ABC News* (March 12, 2010). No pages. Online: http://abcnews.go.com/WN/glenn-beck-social-justice-christians-rage-back-nazism/story?id=10085008.

Smith, Adam. *An Inquiry into the Nature and Causes of the Wealth of Nations.* New York: Oxford University Press, 1998.

———. *The Theory of Moral Sentiments.* Indianapolis: Liberty Fund, 1982.

Sorman, Guy. "Economics Does Not Lie." *City Journal* 18:3 (2008). No pages. Online: http://www.city-journal.org/2008/18_3_economics.html.

Stevenson, William R. *Sovereign Grace: The Place and Significance of Christian Freedom in Calvin's Political Thought.* New York: Oxford University Press, 1999.

Stigler, George J. "Economics or Ethics?" Tanner Lectures on Human Values. Cambridge, MA: Harvard University, 1980. Online: http://www.tannerlectures.utah.edu/lectures/documents/stigler81.pdf.

Stigler, George J., and Gary S. Becker. "De Gustibus Non Est Disputandum." *The American Economic Review* 67:2 (1977) 76–90.

Stiglitz, Joseph E. "The Ethical Economist." Review of *The Moral Consequences of Economic Growth,* by Benjamin Friedman. *Foreign Affairs* (November/December 2005). No pages. Online: http://www.foreignaffairs.com/articles/61208/joseph-e-stiglitz/the-ethical-economist.

Surya Das, Lama. *Awakening the Buddha Within.* New York: Broadway, 1997.

Tanner, Kathryn. *Economy of Grace.* Minneapolis: Fortress, 2005.

Tawney, R. H. *Religion and the Rise of Capitalism.* London: John Murray, 1926.

Thomas, Aquinas. *Summa Theologica.* 5 vols. New York: Benziger, 1948.

Thomas, George. *Christian Ethics and Moral Philosophy.* New York: Scribners, 1955.

Tiemstra, John P. "Financial Globalization and Crony Capitalism." *Crosscurrents* 56 (2006) 26–33.

Tucker, Jeffrey. "You Call This Capitalism?" Ludwig von Mises Institute Economics Blog (July 27, 2008). Online: http://blog.mises.org/archives/008339.asp.

Urban Institute. "The Nonprofit Sector in Brief: Facts and Figures from the *Nonprofit Almanac* 2007." Washington, DC: Urban Institute, 2006. Online: http://www.urban.org/UploadedPDF/311373_nonprofit_sector.pdf.

Urbina, Ian, and Michael Cooper. "Deaths at West Virginia Mines Raise Issues About Safety." *New York Times* (April 6, 2010). Online: http://www.nytimes.com/2010/04/07/us/07westvirginia.html?pagewanted=1&th&emc=th.

Valdés, Juan Gabriel. *Pinochet's Economists: The Chicago School in Chile*. Historical Perspectives on Modern Economics. New York: Cambridge University Press, 1995.

Valeri, Mark. "Religion, Discipline, and the Economy in Calvin's Geneva." *Sixteenth Century Journal* 28 (1997) 123–42.

Veblen, Thorstein. *Theory of the Leisure Class*. New York: MacMillan, 1912. First published 1899.

Verhey, Allen. "Calvin and the 'Stewardship of Love.'" In *Ten Commandments for Jews, Christians, and Others*, edited by Roger Van Harn, 157–74. Grand Rapids: Eerdmans, 2007.

Waterman, A. M. C. "The Beginning of 'Boundaries': The Sudden Separation of Economics from Christian Theology." In *Economics and Interdisciplinary Exchange*, edited by Guido Erreygers, 41–63. New York: Routledge, 2001.

———. "Economics as Theology: Adam Smith's Wealth of Nations." In *Economics and Religion*, edited by Paul Oslington, 321–35. Northampton, MA: Edward Elgar, 2003.

Webb, Stephen H. "New Theology, Old Economics." *First Things* 172 (2007) 11–13.

Weber, Max. *The Protestant Ethic and The "Spirit" Of Capitalism and Other Writings*. Translated by Peter Baehr and Gordon C. Wells. New York: Penguin, 2002.

West, Traci C. *Disruptive Christian Ethics: When Racism and Women's Lives Matter*. Louisville: Westminster John Knox, 2006.

———. "The Policing of Poor Black Women's Sexual Reproduction." In *God Forbid: Religion and Sex in American Public Life*, edited by Kathleen M. Sands, 135–54. New York: Oxford University Press, 2000.

Weintraub, E. Roy. *How Economics Became a Mathematical Science*. Science and Cultural Theory. Durham, NC: Duke University Press, 2002.

Wendel, François. *Calvin: The Origins and Development of His Religious Thought*. Translated by Philip Mairet. New York: Harper & Row, 1950.

Winant, Gabriel. "The Lesson of Rand Paul: Libertarianism is Juvenile." *Salon* (May 21, 2010). Online: http://www.salon.com/news/politics/war_room/2010/05/21/libertarianism_who_ needs_it/index.html?source=newsletter.

Wolterstorff, Nicholas. *Until Justice and Peace Embrace*. Grand Rapids: Eerdmans, 1983.

Wuthnow, Robert, and Tracy L. Scott. "Protestants and Economic Behavior." In *New Directions in American Religious History*, edited by Harry S. Stout and D. G. Hart, 260–95. New York: Oxford University Press, 1997.

Yunus, Muhammad. *Creating a World Without Poverty: Social Business and the Future of Capitalism*. New York: PublicAffairs, 2007.

Yunus Center Web site. Online: http://www.muhammadyunus.org/.

INDEX